Writers and their Background

S. T. COLERIDGE

S. T. Coleridge by W. Allston, 1814

Writers and their Background

S. T. COLERIDGE

EDITED BY R. L. BRETT

LONDON · G. BELL & SONS · 1971

© G. BELL & SONS LTD. 1971
PUBLISHED BY G. BELL & SONS LTD,
YORK HOUSE, 6 PORTUGAL STREET, LONDON, WC2

PRINTED IN GREAT BRITAIN BY
W & J MACKAY & CO LTD, CHATHAM

ISBN 0 7135 1900 2

Contents

ILLUSTRATIONS

The Contributors

THE REV. J. A. APPLEYARD, S.J.
Boston College, U.S.A.

DR JOHN BEER
*Fellow of Peterhouse and University Lecturer in English,
University of Cambridge*

PROFESSOR R. L. BRETT
Professor of English, University of Hull

PROFESSOR JOHN COLMER
Professor of English, University of Adelaide, Australia

PROFESSOR DOROTHY EMMET
*sometime Sir Samuel Hall Professor of Philosophy,
University of Manchester*

PROFESSOR R. H. FOGLE
Professor of English, University of North Carolina, U.S.A.

PROFESSOR A. R. JONES
Professor of English, University College of North Wales, Bangor

PROFESSOR GEORGE WHALLEY
Professor of English, Queen's University, Kingston, Ontario, Canada

PROFESSOR BASIL WILLEY
*sometime King Edward VII Professor of English Literature,
University of Cambridge*

General Editor's Preface

THE STUDY of literature is not a 'pure' discipline since works of literature are affected by the climate of opinion in which they are produced. Writers, like other men, are concerned with the politics, the philosophy, the religion, the arts, and the general thought of their own times. Some literary figures, indeed, have made their own distinguished contributions to these areas of human interest, while the achievement of others can be fully appreciated only by a knowledge of them.

The present volume is the first in a series which has been planned with the purpose of presenting major authors in their intellectual, social, and artistic contexts, and with the conviction that this will make their work more easily understood and enjoyed. Each volume will contain a chapter which provides a reader's guide to the writings of the author concerned, a Bibliography, and Chronological Tables setting out the main dates of the author's life and publications alongside the chief events of contemporary importance.

R. L. BRETT

Editor's Preface

IT IS fitting that the first volume in this series should be devoted to Coleridge for he, perhaps more than any other great English writer, demonstrates the value of the approach which characterizes the series. Coleridge himself demands, as Professor Whalley rightly observes in the chapter he has contributed to this volume, the epithet 'myriad-minded'; a term Coleridge applied to Shakespeare, but one which so aptly describes the range of his own writings and powerful intellect. The extent of this range has only come to be recognised fully in our own day and is such that any scholar or critic must feel daunted at trying to chart the currents and depths of so universal a genius. It is an endeavour that calls for joint enterprise and I feel privileged that such a distinguished team of Coleridge scholars should have been ready to join me in writing this book.

I am grateful to all my collaborators, but I owe an especial debt to Professor George Whalley who, as well as contributing his own excellent chapter to the book, has been responsible for preparing the Bibliography. Professor Whalley wishes to acknowledge his indebtedness to the introduction and bibliography published in Professor Kathleen Coburn's *Coleridge: A Collection of Critical Essays*, Spectrum Books, 1967. A similar acknowledgement is due to Miss Barbara Rooke's edition of *The Friend*, vol. 4 of the *Collected Works of S. T. Coleridge*, 1969, which I consulted in drawing up the Chronological Tables. In both instances there remain differences of content and presentation, but our respective tasks have been made easier by the work of these two scholars.

Mr Richard Barber, of G. Bell & Sons Limited, deserves my warm gratitude, not only for technical advice on the production of the book, but for his lively interest and encouragement from its inception. I should like also to thank Mrs Kathryn Horne for the care she has taken in compiling the Index.

R. L. BRETT

The main events of Coleridge's life	*The main events of literary and intellectual importance in Coleridge's lifetime**	*The main events of historical importance in Coleridge's lifetime*
1772 Coleridge born (21 Oct.) at Ottery St Mary		George III king
1774	Southey born	
1775	Lamb born	American War of Independence
1776	A. Smith's *Wealth of Nations* Gibbon's *Decline and Fall*	
1778	Hazlitt born Rousseau and Voltaire die	
1781 Death of Coleridge's father	Kant's *Kritik der reinen Vernunft* Schiller's *Die Räuber*	
1782 School at Christ's Hospital (until 1791)	Priestley's *Corruptions of Christianity* Rousseau's *Confessions*	
1789	Bentham's *An Introduction to the Principles of Morals* Blake's *Songs of Innocence* Bowles's *Sonnets*	Beginning of French Revolution
1790	Burke's *Reflections on the Revolution in France*	
1791 Coleridge at Cambridge (—end of 1794)	Paine's *Rights of Man*, Pt. I, (Pt. II 1792)	Anti-Jacobin riots in Birmingham
1792	Shelley born	Pitt's attack on slave trade
1793 Coleridge enlists in the Dragoons (Dec. —April 1794) & returns to Cambridge	Wordsworth's *Descriptive Sketches & An Evening Walk* Godwin's *Political Justice*	Execution of Louis XVI War with France Reign of Terror in France
1794 Coleridge meets Southey & is engaged to Sara Fricker. Publishes (w. Southey) *The Fall of Robespierre* Coleridge meets Godwin	Paine's *Age of Reason* Paley's *Evidences of Christianity* Godwin's *Caleb Williams*	Robespierre executed, end of The Terror Tooke and Thelwall charged w. treason but acquitted

* Books are entered under date of first publication

xii

1795	Coleridge first meets Wordsworth Coleridge marries Sara Fricker (4 Oct.) Coleridge gives lectures in Bristol, pubd. as *Conciones ad Populum* and the *Plot Discovered*	Wordsworth & his sister at Racedown (26 Sept.) Schelling's *Vom Ich als Prinzip der Philosophie* Keats born	Treason & Convention Acts passed
1796	Coleridge's *Poems on Various Subjects* pubd.; *The Watchman* (1 March —13 May) Hartley Coleridge born (19 Sept.) Coleridge moves to Nether Stowey (31 Dec.)	Robert Burns dies	Invasion of England threatened
1797	Wordsworth at Nether Stowey (Mar.) Coleridge visits Wordsworths at Racedown (June) Writes *Lime-Tree Bower*. *Poems* 2nd ed. *The Ancient Mariner* (begun Nov., completed Mar. 1798)	The Wordsworths move to Alfoxden (16 July) Burke dies	Battle of Cape St. Vincent France & Austria sign peace treaty
1798	Writes First Part of *Christabel, Frost at Midnight, France: an Ode, Fears in Solitude*, and (?) *Kubla Khan* Wedgwoods give Coleridge annuity of £150 Coleridge goes to Germany w. Wordsworths (Sept.) *Lyrical Ballads* pubd.		Battle of the Nile Malta captured by French
1799	Coleridge returns to England (July) First meets Sara Hutchinson Writes political leaders for *Morning Post* (Nov.—autumn 1802)	The Wordsworths stay at Sockburn (May) & move to Grasmere (Dec.) Schiller's *Wallenstein* & *Die Piccolomini* Schleiermacher's *Reden über die Religion*	Napoleon First Consul

1800	Coleridge moves family to Keswick (July) Writes Second Part of *Christabel; Lyrical Ballads*, 2nd edn. (pubd. Jan. 1801) Coleridge's trans. of *Wallenstein* pubd.	Schelling's *System des transcendentalen Idealismus*	Malta captured by English
1801	Coleridge's health breaks down; spends the winter in London	Scott's *Ballads* Southey's *Thalaba*	Pitt resigns; Addington Prime Minister
1802	Coleridge's *Dejection* pubd.; spends the winter in London Sara Coleridge born	Wordsworth's *Immortality* Ode begun Wordsworth m. Mary Hutchinson (4 Oct.) Cobbett's *Weekly Political Register* founded *Edinburgh Review* founded Chateaubriand's *Génie du Christianisme* Paley's *Natural Theology*	Treaty of Amiens French army invades Switzerland
1803	Coleridge visits Poole at Stowey & Lamb in London Coleridge tours Scotland w. Wordsworth & Dorothy *Poems*, 3rd ed.	Chatterton's *Works* (ed. Southey & Cottle)	The war against France renewed
1804	Coleridge in Malta & Sicily Private Secretary to Alex. Ball, High Commissioner at Malta	Wordsworth completes *The Prelude*, I–V, before Coleridge leaves for Malta Blake's *Jerusalem*	Buonaparte proclaimed Emperor Spain declares war on Britain Pitt Prime Minister
1805	Coleridge appointed Acting Public Secretary in Malta (Jan.–Sept.) visits Sicily, Naples and Rome (Sept.–Dec.)	Scott's *Lay of the Last Minstrel*	Battle of Trafalgar
1806	Coleridge in Italy (Jan.–June) Coleridge returns to England (17 Aug.) and decides to separate from his wife	Hegel's *Phänomenologie des Geistes*	Pitt dies (Jan.) 'Ministry of all the Talents' Fox dies (Sept.) Grenville Prime Minister

1807	Coleridge writes *To W. Wordsworth* Coleridge in Bristol (where he meets De Quincey), Nether Stowey & London	Wordsworth's 1807 *Poems* Fichte's *Reden an die deutsche Nation*	Abolition of Slave Trade
1808	Coleridge stays w. the Wordsworths at Allan Bank Lectures on literature at Royal Institution, London	Scott's *Marmion* Lamb's *Specimens of English Dramatic Poets* Goethe's *Faust*, Pt. I	Peninsular War begins
1809	*The Friend* (1 June 1809 –15 Mar. 1810)	A. W. Schlegel's *Vorlesungen über dramatische Kunst und Litteratur* Wordsworth's *Convention of Cintra* Byron's *English Bards & Scotch Reviewers* Tennyson born	Napoleon captures Vienna
1810	Coleridge at Keswick (May to Oct.), then moves to London after quarrel with Wordsworth	Scott's *Lady of the Lake* Southey's *Curse of Kehama* Wordsworth's *Guide to the Lakes*	First Reform Bill
1811	Lectures on Shakespeare (1811–12)	J. Austen's *Sense and Sensibility* Shelley's *Necessity of Atheism*	Prince of Wales made Regent Luddite uprisings (until 1815)
1812	Last visit to the Lakes Coleridge reconciled to Wordsworth (May) *The Friend*, 2nd ed.	Byron's *Childe Harold* (I–II)	U.S. declares war on Britain
1813	*Remorse* at re-opening of Drury Lane Lectures in Bristol (1813–14)	Byron's *The Giaour* Shelley's *Queen Mab* J. Austen's *Pride and Prejudice* Southey's *Life of Nelson*	Austria declares war on Napoleon Wellington victorious in Peninsular War
1814	*Remorse* performed in Bristol Coleridge in care of Dr Daniel for opium addiction & depression	Wordsworth's *The Excursion* Scott's *Waverley* Southey's *Roderick* J. Austen's *Mansfield Park*	Invasion of France by Allies Napoleon's abdication Congress of Vienna

1815	Coleridge at Calne *Remorse* performed at Calne	Wordsworth's *Poems* Wordsworth's *White Doe of Rylstone*	Napoleon escapes Elba Battle of Waterloo Restoration of Louis XVIII
1816	Settles at Highgate w. Dr Gillman *Christabel, Kubla Khan, The Pains of Sleep* & *The Statesman's Manual* pubd.	Byron's *Childe Harold* (Canto III) J. Austen's *Emma*	
1817	*Biographia Literaria, Zapolya, Sibylline Leaves* pubd.	Byron's *Manfred* Keats's *Poems* Peacock's *Headlong Hall* Ricardo's *Principles of Political Economy* J. Austen dies	
1818	*The Friend* revised & enlarged Gives three courses of lectures (on poetry and philosophy) Writes two pamphlets in support of Peel's Bill against child-labour *Treatise on Method* pubd. in *Encyclopædia Metropolitana*	Schopenhauer's *Die Welt als Wille und Vorstellung* Peacock's *Nightmare Abbey* Shelley's *Revolt of Islam* Keats's *Endymion* Hazlitt's *Lectures on the English Poets* Byron's *Childe Harold* (Canto IV) Lamb's *Collected Works*	Parliamentary motion for universal suffrage defeated
1819		Wordsworth's *Peter Bell* J. H. Reynolds's *Peter Bell* Shelley's *Peter Bell the Third* written Shelley's *The Cenci* Byron's *Don Juan* (Cantos I & II)	Queen Victoria born Peterloo massacre First Factory Act First appearance of 'Radical Reformers'
1820		Shelley's *Prometheus Unbound* Keats's *Odes* Wordsworth's *Sonnets on the River Duddon*	Accession of George IV
1821		Byron's *Cain* De Quincey's *Confessions of an Opium Eater* Shelley's *Adonais* Keats dies	Napoleon dies

1822	Coleridge's 'Thursday-evening class' begins	Wordsworth's *Ecclesiastical Sonnets* Lamb's *Essays of Elia* Byron's *Vision of Judgment* Shelley dies	Death of Castlereagh
1824	Coleridge elected FRSL, granted an annuity of £100	Byron dies	Repeal of Combination Laws
1825	*Aids to Reflection* pubd.	Hazlitt's *Spirit of the Age*	Catholic Relief Bill defeated by House of Lords
1827		Keble's *Christian Year* Tennyson's *Poems by Two Brothers* Blake dies	Canning Prime Minister (dies in Aug.)
1828	Continental tour with Wordsworth (June to August) *Poetical Works* pubd.		Wellington Prime Minister
1829	*Poetical Works* 2nd ed. *On the Constitution of Church and State* pubd.		Catholic Emancipation Act
1830		Lyell's *Principles of Geology* Tennyson's *Poems, chiefly Lyrical* Comte's *Cours de Philosophie Positive*	Accession of William IV Grey Prime Minister
1831	Last meeting with Wordsworth	J. S. Mill's *The Spirit of the Age* in the *Examiner* Jan.–May	British Association founded
1832		Scott dies	Reform Bill passed
1833		*Tracts for the Times*, ed. Newman (1833–41) Carlyle's *Sartor Resartus*	Factory Act ('Children's Charter') Abolition of Slavery in British colonies Keble's sermon on 'National Apostasy' opens Oxford Movement
1834	*Poetical Works*, 3rd edn. Coleridge dies at Highgate (25 July)	Lamb dies	New Poor Law

1: On Reading Coleridge

GEORGE WHALLEY

NOSING THROUGH William Cave's *Scriptorum ecclesiasticorum historia literaria* for heaven knows what purpose, in December 1801, Coleridge came upon the word μυριόνους and immediately thought of the man he was later to call 'the greatest genius, that perhaps human nature has yet produced, our *myriad-minded* Shakspear'.[1] The epithet 'myriad-minded' goes well with Coleridge too, not simply for the depth and range of his learning, impressive though that certainly is, but rather for the power, daring, and integrity of a mind that throughout the years of his life strove to find unity in multeity. The record, in its bare bones, is not trifling—

> Author of *The Ancient Mariner* and other unforgettable poems. Great literary critic, psychologist, philosopher, theologian, lecturer, journalist, constructive critic of church and state, his works comprise some twenty volumes and seventy notebooks.[2]

To read Coleridge's work carefully, to enter into the activity of a mind so vivid, patient, and perceptive, brings the exhilaration (as Coleridge himself would have wished) of heightened awareness. For his many-faceted work is unified by a most searching mind, and is nourished by a personal sanity and rich memory that few thinkers of comparable force have enjoyed.

[1] *Biog. Lit.*, II, 13. The discovery of the word in Cave is recorded in *Notebooks*, I, 1070 & n. For other references to Shakespeare as 'myriad-minded', see *e.g. Sh. Crit.*, I, 89; II, 250.
[2] Kathleen Coburn, introduction to *Coleridge: A collection of critical essays* (Englewood Cliffs 1967) [hereafter *Twentieth Century Views*], 2.

We think of him dominantly and always as a poet; when he is philosophizing he brings a poet's way of mind to questions that, being in the discursive mode, we do not think of as within the compass of poetry and which yet, in a positivist age, are not within the compass of philosophy either. With a memory (as he said) 'tenacious & systematizing', his mind is also by instinct comprehensive and synthesizing. 'What are my motives but my impelling thoughts—' he writes in the margins of Tetens' *Philosophische Versuche*; 'and what is a Thought but another word for "I thinking"?' Sometimes, it is true, his thoughts would 'crowd each other to death'. Yet 'The term, Philosophy,' he says, 'defines itself as an affectionate seeking after the truth; but Truth is the correlative of Being.'[1] So his work does not reward us primarily with the formulated conclusions that we are perhaps too inclined to expect of philosophy and theory; rather, his work—though by no means devoid of substantial and well-thought-out theory—stands rather for that more nourishing and hazardous order that is 'tentative and exploratory', and is no less positive or philosophical for that. For he was determined, as he noted at midnight on 5 April 1805, to 'write as truly as I can from *Experience* actual individual *Experience*—not from Book-knowlege'.[2] Books threw an intense light across his poetry and his thinking, but 'experience' was paramount: like Keats, he must prove everything upon the pulses. What Coleridge meant by 'experience' was not simply what happened *to* him—in the Quantocks, at Gallow Hill and Keswick, in the Mediterranean and London—but what happened *in* him, as man, as poet, as thinker, as aspiring religious being; and a prominent element in his experience was the experience of making poetry and the continuous effort to see clearly and to unravel '*the Goings-on* within'.[3] Certain arguments that had placed him 'on firm land' in his early thinking, he says in the first number of *The Friend*, 'were not suggested to me by Books, but forced on me by reflection on my own Being, and Observation

---

[1] *Biog. Lit.*, I, 94. The phrase 'tenacious & systematizing' is from CL, I, 71, of 4 Mar., 1794. The Tetens note is also printed in *Inquiring Spirit*, 30; for the thought-crowding, see *Notebooks*, III, 3342.
[2] *Notebooks*, II, 2526, but the same note, as it goes on, shows that he did not despise the riches to be found in books.
[3] *Aids to Reflection*, 259n. The phrase occurs earlier: *Notebooks*, I, 979.

of those about me, especially of little Children'.[1] Questions about being and knowing were in his mind inevitably linked to questions about our inner goings-on; his statement that 'metaphysics and psychology have long been my hobby-horse' accounts for the strength and fertility of his critical philosophy: 'I labored at a solid foundation, on which permanently to ground my opinions, in the component faculties of the human mind itself, and their comparative dignity and importance.'[2] His capacity for minute observation, whether it is to terminate in a poem like *Frost at Midnight* or in a suite of philosophical recognitions, is dynamic, formative, heuristic.

> In looking at objects of Nature while I am thinking, as at yonder moon dim-glimmering thro' the dewy window-pane, I seem rather to be seeking, as it were *asking*, a symbolical language for something within me that already and forever exists, than observing anything new. Even when that latter is the case, yet still I have always an obscure feeling as if that new phaenomenon were the dim Awaking of a forgotten or hidden Truth of my inner Nature / It is still interesting as a Word, a Symbol! It is Λoγos, the Creator! <and the Evolver!>[3]

[1] *Friend*, II, 8.

[2] *Biog. Lit.*, I, 62, 14. See also *Inquiring Spirit*, 14–15: 'The more one reads Coleridge the more impressed one becomes with what can only be called a psychological approach to all human problems. Whether it be punctuation, or political sovereignty, a criticism of *Richard II*, the position of the mediaeval Church, or the baby talk of children, the state of Ireland or the work of the alchemists, he sees it as a piece of human experience, understandable in relation to the whole human organism, individual or social, so far as that organism can be comprehended as a whole. Politics are not a matter of events, facts, theories, and the isolated external circumstances only. No more is what passes for logic. Nor chemistry. Emotion comes in, motives, unknown ones as well as those that are acknowledged. Unknown especially to the participants.' See also *Biog. Lit.*, II, 120: Wordsworth's Immortality Ode 'was intended for such readers only as had been accustomed to watch the flux and reflux of their inmost nature, to venture at times into the twilight realms of consciousness, and to feel a deep interest in modes of inmost being. . . .'

[3] *Notebooks*, II, 2546: 14 Apr., 1805. See also the remarkable note of

His attention, directed both inward and outward, is characteristically impetuous and (as he said of some of Wordsworth's poetry) 'of a sinewy strength'.

> Sometimes when I earnestly look at a beautiful Object or Land-scape, it seems as if I were on the the *brink* of a Fruition still denied—as if Vision were an *appetite*: even as a man would feel, who having put forth all his muscular strength in an act of pro-silience, is at that very moment *held back*—he leaps & yet moves not from his place. . . .[1]

Many years later he could tell the young Thomas Allsop how

> A naturally, at once searching and communicative disposition, the necessity of reconciling the restlessness of an ever-working Fancy with an intense craving after a resting-place for my Thoughts in some *principle* that was derived from experience, but of which all other knowledge should be but so many repetitions under various limitations, even as circles, squares, triangles, etc., etc., are but so many positions of space.[2]

And within a few weeks of his death

> I am by the law of my nature a reasoner. A person who should suppose I meant by that word, an arguer, would not only not understand me, but would understand the contrary of my mean-ing. I can take no interest whatever in hearing or saying anything merely as a fact—merely as having happened. It must refer to something within me before I can regard it with any curiosity or care. My mind is always energic—I don't mean energetic; I require in everything what, for lack of another word, I may call *propriety*—that is, a reason why the thing *is* at all, and why it is *there* or *then* rather than elsewhere or at another time.[3]

---

[2] Nov., 1803 (*Notebooks*, I, 1635)—'The Voice of the Greta, and the Cock-crowing'—written immediately after a long marginal note about Hartley's baptism in a copy of Anderson's *British Poets*. Five days earlier he had asked himself 'What is it, that I employ my Metaphysics on?' (*Notebooks*, I, 1623)

[1] *Notebooks*, III, 3767: Apr.–June, 1810.

[2] Printed in *Inquiring Spirit*, 33–4, from T. Allsop, *Letters, Conversations and Recollections of Coleridge*, 1836, II, 134–7.

[3] *Table Talk*, 1 Mar., 1834.

Concerned from his early years with 'Facts of mind'; convinced, as Aristotle was, that 'In Wonder all Philosophy began: in Wonder it ends: and Admiration fills up the interspace'; he developed a most sensitive psychological *tact* (a favourite word of his). A sense of tactile immediacy lies equally at the roots of his poetry, his philosophy, his criticism, his religion.[1] His sketch of Plato's mind, in the *Philosophical Lectures* of 1818-19, is drawn with an imaginative force that, like his account of Hamlet, more than half suggests a self-portrait.

Plato began in meditation, thought deeply within himself of the goings-on of his own mind and of the powers that there were in that mind, conceived to himself how this could be, and if it were, what must be the necessary results and agencies of it, and then looked abroad to ask if this were a dream, or whether it were indeed a revelation from within, and a waking reality. He employed his observation as the interpreter of his meditation, equally free from the fanatic who abandons himself to the wild workings of the magic cauldron of his own brain mistaking every form of delirium for reality, and from the cold sensualist who looks at death as the alone real, or life of the world, by not considering that the very object was seen to him only by the seeing powers, and what a little further consideration would have led him to deduce, that that which could make him see it must be an agent, and a power like his own, whilst that which was merely seen, which was purely passive, could have no other existence than what arose out of an active power that had produced it.[2]

[1] For 'Facts of mind', see CL, I, 260. The statement about philosophy and wonder is in *Aids to Reflection*, 228-9. On 'tact' and 'tactile', see especially CL, II, 810, of 13 July, 1802: 'a great Poet must be, implicité if not explicité, a profound Metaphysician. He may not have it in logical coherence, in his Brain and Tongue; but he must have it by *Tact* / for all sounds, and forms of human nature he must have the *ear* of a wild Arab listening in the silent Desart, the eye of a North American Indian tracing the footsteps of an Enemy upon the Leaves that strew the Forest—; the *Touch* of a Blind Man feeling the face of a darling Child—/.' See also *Philosophical Lectures*, 115, and for many examples, *Notebooks*, II *passim*.

[2] *Philosophical Lectures*, 186. Kathleen Coburn draws attention to this passage in *Inquiring Spirit*, 18.

To come upon vision, to see clearly and to know deeply, were for him not enough: he must *make known* what he had come to know. His educative instinct—propaedeutic rather than paedagogic—is a strong impulse to affirm the nature and power of the human spirit. Denied all the easy means of access to an attentive public, he yet wished to make the journey towards truth 'as much easier' to others as it had been difficult for him; he wished 'to convey not instruction merely, but fundamental instruction; not so much to shew my Reader this or that fact, as to kindle his own torch for him, and leave it to himself to chuse the particular objects, which he might wish to examine by its light'.[1] He wished to establish

> Education of the Intellect, by awakening the Method of self-development, . . . not any specific information that can be conveyed into it from without . . . not storing the passive Mind with the various sorts of knowledge most in request, as if the Human Soul were a mere repository or banqueting-room, but to place it in such relations of circumstance as should gradually excite its vegetating and germinating powers to produce new fruits of Thought, new Conceptions, and Imaginations, and Ideas.[2]

If we are to follow him, we should be prepared to venture on 'strange seas of thought'—stranger seas perhaps than Wordsworth can have imagined when he thought of Roubiliac's 'marble index' of Newton's mind. For one commanding element in Coleridge's experience was his experience of making poetry, and above all the experience of making *The Ancient Mariner*; whereby almost at the very beginning he had drawn out of his moral nature a profound and imaginative sense of himself as an individual creature under the eye of heaven—a vision elusive, even terrifying, yet germinal, urgent, and prophetic. From his own notebooks and letters, and from the many things reported of him by Lamb and Southey, by William and Dorothy Wordsworth, by

[1] *Friend*, I, 16.
[2] From the Treatise on Method: used as epigraph to the Education section of *Inquiring Spirit*, 71. For the urgency of Coleridge's educative impulse, see *Notebooks*, III, 4082,— 'Why do I make a book?' and the epigraph from Goethe's *Propyläen* placed at the beginning of *Biog. Lit.*

Humphry Davy, Hazlitt, De Quincey, and Henry Crabb Robinson—from all these, and much more, we are able to move into his presence, often day by day and hour by hour; and can come to know him as a person complex yet with a childlike mind; affectionate, gregarious, and solitary; eloquent in self-revelation and at times self-pitying; hypochondriacal, and not least exuberant in self-mockery; glorious and ashamed, haunted, stricken, dismayed, triumphant; buoyant on the whole, a wonderful friend, radically fearless and most generous. To follow him so, not only on the Mariner's voyage which is also the voyage of his inner life, but also through all 'the secret confessional of [his] Thought',[1] a reader needs to be patient at times, sometimes forgiving, and more than a little Coleridgean. There will in any case be glories and astonishments, and quiet homecomings of discovery enough.

II

Any person beginning to read Coleridge needs at least two pieces of avuncular warning. One is to do with his reputation, or rather, with the dismissive lay estimate that neither the increasing authority of modern scholars nor the ever-accumulating mass of faithful commentary has yet managed wholly to reverse or rectify. The other is to do with the nature and constitution of Coleridge's writing and the form we have it in at present.

During the last thirty years of his life, Coleridge was abused, often and publicly, for being a poet *manqué*. As a young man (the argument goes) he had shown exceptional promise and accomplishment as a poet, but somewhere along the line (some have suggested *Dejection* as the watershed) he lost the thread—through neglect of his talents, through indolence, perversity, or lack of courage—and drifted into 'the holy jungle of transcendental metaphysics' propped up by the dogmatic crutch of orthodox Trinitarian theology.[2] That he became

[1] *Aids to Reflection*, 79.
[2] For Coleridge's early reputation as a poet, see *Sh. Crit.*, II, 32: 'I was called a poet almost before I knew I could write poetry'. The quoted phrase is from the essay 'On the *Prometheus* of Aeschylus', *Literary Remains*, II, 349.

addicted to opium seems to have been quite widely known in his day, even though laudanum was then as commonplace as aspirin is to us; that Coleridge took drugs was almost the only fact that most laymen knew about him, long before drug-taking had been sanctified by a bemused idolatry of *la jeunesse dorée*. His successive prose works, and even the *Christabel* volume, were roughly handled by reviewers, not least by his one-time admirer and friend William Hazlitt. Except for *Aids to Reflection* (1825) and *Church and State* (1830), his works sold so slowly that he was inclined to speak of them as 'printed rather than published' and would repeat Milton's phrase about 'winding-sheets for pilchards'. During his lifetime, his reputation as a prose writer was for gratuitous obscurity of the German sort, for whimsical archaism and oddity, for a heavy and opulent style quite unlike the snappy 'rationalist' manner fashionable in his day, for indirection and lack of concentrated force, for an unfocused brilliance that did little to illuminate pedantic speculations which were of little relevance to the modern temper.[1] One anonymous reviewer, during Coleridge's lifetime, did not hesitate to accuse him of neglecting his wife and children; and Coleridge had been dead only two months when De Quincey published the first of a series of articles drawing attention to 'a singular infirmity besetting Coleridge's mind': an alleged habit of literary plagiarism. To those who made no effort to read his writings carefully, his work seemed an abortive

---

[1] J. R. de J. Jackson's *Coleridge: The Critical Heritage* (London & New York 1970) allows us—as only the most industrious have been able to before—to see exactly what was said about Coleridge by reviewers and critics in his own lifetime. Coleridge summarises the position brilliantly in *Biog. Lit.*, I, 149: 'My prose writings have been charged with a disproportionate demand on the attention; with an excess of refinement in the mode of arriving at truths; with beating the ground for that which might have been run down by the eye; with the length and laborious construction of my periods; in short with obscurity and the love of paradox. But my severest critics have not pretended to have found in my compositions triviality, or traces of a mind that shrunk from the toil of thinking.' His distaste for 'the unnatural, false, affected Style of the moderns, that makes sense and simplicity *oddness*' (*Notebooks*, III, 4334) could be expanded into a separate essay on prose style.

curiosity (like *Kubla Khan*), ruinous, redeemed only by one great poem that had had no progeny.

A view much like this had lively currency through the second half of the nineteenth century: it gathered weight from Irving Babbitt's dismissal of all things 'romantic', was firmly (and a little patronisingly) expressed by T. S. Eliot as a young man, and is still categorically implied in F. R. Leavis's angry proposition that it is a scandal that Coleridge's work should be considered worthy of serious examination in a university.[1] A few incidental passages in the *Biographia*, it was reluctantly conceded, were of more than common interest—the bit about the origin of *Lyrical Ballads* and the much-disputed distinction between Fancy and Imagination. Otherwise all that mattered was *The Ancient Mariner* and half a hundred pages of 'pure gold' scattered elsewhere.[2] Prominent in this pervasive parody are two items: Thomas Carlyle's eloquent and malicious portrait of Coleridge at Highgate in the *Life of John Sterling*; and the closing sentence of E. K. Chambers's industrious but obtuse biography written more than a century later: 'So Coleridge passed, leaving a handful of golden poems, an emptiness in the heart of a few friends, and a will-o'-the-wisp light for bemused thinkers.'[3]

[1] For a brief history of the growth of Coleridge's reputation, see the introduction to *Twentieth Century Views*.

[2] Nevertheless Lamb, De Quincey, and Henry Nelson Coleridge seem to have been the only ones on record during Coleridge's lifetime who regarded *The Ancient Mariner* as a poem of major importance.

[3] Carlyle's *Life of Sterling* was not published until 1851, but the detailed sketch for a portrait of Coleridge is found—in even more cruel and contemptuous form—in a letter of 24 June, 1824 to his brother, with an addendum on 22 Jan., 1825: these are printed in J. D. Campbell's *Narrative* (1894), 260-1, and by Chambers (1938), 321. In 1829, however, Carlyle had had some good words for Coleridge in an essay on Novalis in the *Foreign Review*. Compared with Novalis's *Schriften*, he said, Coleridge's works might be 'but a slight business'. But that was no reason why they should be 'triumphantly condemned by the whole reviewing world, as clearly unintelligible, and among readers they have still but an unseen circulation; like living brooks, hidden for the present under mountains of froth and theatrical snow-paper, and which only at a distant day, when these mountains shall have decomposed themselves into gas and earthy residuum, may roll forth

As Francis Jeffrey said (anonymously) of Wordsworth's *Excursion*: 'This will never do!' The relation between poet and philosopher in Coleridge is a question of prime and central importance, not easy of blunt solution. The question of alleged plagiarism—a hare that has given plenty of vigorous exercise to greyhound historians of ideas—is matter not only for minute study of the intellectual and documentary evidence but also for sensitive psychological investigation.[1] We may still say with Coleridge that 'The axioms of the unthinking are to the philosopher the deepest problems as being the nearest to the mysterious root and partaking at once of its darkness and its pregnancy.'[2] But a counter-current had set in, during Coleridge's lifetime and shortly after: in two remarkable (but little-known) essays of Henry Nelson Coleridge (1821 and 1834)[3]; in the tribute of a gifted young contemporary, F. D. Maurice (in the second edition of *The Kingdom of Christ*, 1842); in John Stuart Mill's essay of 1840 which—from a more limited and less sympathetic angle of vision than Maurice's—found Coleridge (with Bentham) one of the two great seminal minds of the age;[4] in the

---

in their true limpid shape to gladden the general eye with what beauty and everlasting freshness does reside in them. It is admitted too on all hands, that Mr. Coleridge is a man of "genius", that is a man having more intellectual insight than other men; and strangely enough, it is taken for granted, at the same time, that he had less intellectual insight than any other. For why else are his doctrines to be thrown out of doors without examination as false and worthless, simply because they are obscure?' Printed in J. D. Campbell's *Narrative*, 1894, 269.

[1] Sara Coleridge examined the question of Coleridge's 'plagiarism' in detail and with great dignity in her Introduction to *Biog. Lit.* (1847). Thomas McFarland, in *Coleridge and the Pantheist Tradition*, Oxford, 1969, I, 'The Problem of Coleridge's Plagiarisms', examines the whole controversy in detail and reaches conclusions that are subtle enough to be convincing.

[2] *Statesman's Manual*, 56. *Cf. Lay Sermon* (*ibid* 265): '. . . half truths, the most dangerous of errors . . .'

[3] Reprinted in Jackson 461–70 and 620–51. HNC was 23 years old in 1821; the first entry in his collection of Coleridge's *Table Talk* is for 29 Dec., 1822.

[4] Reprinted in Mill's *Dissertations and Discussions* (1859), and restored

careful editing of his work by members of his family beginning immediately after his death; and even during his lifetime in the sudden interest
in his work in New England that led to the only collective edition of his
work we have. None of those things was decisive, however. We now
know that Coleridge's influence was profound and pervasive, though
largely anonymous and subterranean. A more accurate and subtle
understanding has had to wait upon the editing of major works and large
quantities of manuscripts. The dismissive and contemptuous view, once
fashionable, is no longer seriously tenable—not since the publication of
J. L. Lowes's *The Road to Xanadu* (1927, 1930), I. A. Richards's *Coleridge on Imagination* (1934), Kathleen Coburn's *Inquiring Spirit* (1951),
and Humphry House's Clark Lectures of 1951-2; and William Walsh's
Coleridge: the Work and the Relevance (1967) is only the most catholic of
a number of detailed studies that have been fertilised by the text of the
Collected Letters and by the text and notes of the *Notebooks*. What has
been crystallizing as a 'new' appreciation of Coleridge is well represented by the other essays in this volume. Many-sided and short of
definitiveness, it is not a doctrinal position to which conformity is
either invited or expected. Whatever it is, it is informed by the presence
of Coleridge himself as a person, as imaginative intelligence; informed
too by the ambience of his poetic-philosophical way of mind, and by his
personal need to struggle as he did in his thinking, striving to make his
work, if not shapely, certainly life-giving.

His published work being what it is, the demands on a reader or
expositor are often severe. The difficulty is intrinsic, as he himself said
about the difficulty in grasping 'the transcendent or genetic philosophy':

> One and perhaps the greatest obstacle . . . arises in the tendency
> to look abroad, *out* of the thing in question, in order by means of
> some *other* thing analogous to understand the former. But this is
> impossible—for the thing in question *is* the act we are describ-
> ing—Cohesion, for instance—and by this all coherents & all
> particular forms of cohesion are to be rendered intelligible, not it
> by them.[1]

to circulation in an edition by F. R. Leavis in *Mill on Bentham and
Coleridge*, 1950, with specific paedagogic intent.
[1] *Notebooks*, III, 4225.

So the first question, about Coleridge's reputation and how to find a just starting-point that might secure for us 'that willing suspension of disbelief for the moment, which constitutes poetic faith'[1], has already led to the second question, about the state and availability of Coleridge's work. Part of the difficulty here is the sheer quantity and minuteness of the material, even if we exclude (as we cannot) the variety and scope of ancillary and related material. Coleridge often accused himself of constitutional indolence; the charge is not easy to support. The *Collected Coleridge* edition will comprise sixteen titles in about 22 volumes; the *Collected Letters* will make six thick volumes, the *Notebooks* another five large volumes of text and five of commentary. Even by 1815 Coleridge might well say: 'By what I *have* effected, am I to be judged by my fellow men; what I *could* have done, is a question for my own conscience.'[2] And part of the difficulty arises from the variable quality of the published texts themselves, which run all the way from deliberately cavalier work like Joseph Cottle's to the refined and scrupulous editions that are now beginning to appear; and in between, still and for some time to come, the texts we have to use most, often textually imperfect, weak or uneven in annotation and critical apparatus, and poorly indexed, if indexed at all.

The Canon

For bibliographical purposes Coleridge's writing can be considered in two divisions: poetry and prose. Within each of these divisions we can recognise canonical works (published in book form by Coleridge in his lifetime) and sub-canonical works (published after his death, and varying from virtually complete works in manuscript to groups of fragmentary materials later rationalised by editors).

    POEMS: Coleridge published three early volumes of verse: *Poems on Various Subjects* (1796), *Poems* 'Second Edition' (1797), and *Poems* 'Third Edition' (1803). *Poems* 1797 includes much of the 1796 *Poems* but

---

[1] *Biog. Lit.*, II, 6. One can only deplore the habit of quoting the first five words in isolation, thereby substituting some sort of gratuitous make-believe or day-dreaming for a complex act of faith secured and shaped largely by the work under view.

[2] *Biog. Lit.*, I, 151.

has several additions (including some poems by Charles Lamb and Charles Lloyd) and is substantially a new book: *Poems* 1803 leaves out the Lamb and Lloyd poems and includes most of the 1797 poems, but the selection and arrangement were supervised by Lamb in Coleridge's absence. 'Fears in Solitude', 'France: an Ode', and 'Frost at Midnight' were published together in a 24-page pamphlet in 1798: and in that same year *The Ancient Mariner* and three other poems were included anonymously in *Lyrical Ballads*. (*The Ancient Mariner*, extensively revised for the 1800 edition, remained in *Lyrical Ballads*, with the author's name unacknowledged, until the 1805 edition was superseded by *Poems in Two Volumes* (1807).) Except for the verse translation of Schiller's *Wallenstein* (1800) and the three editions of his verse drama *Remorse* (1813), Coleridge published no poems in book form until the *Christabel, Kubla Khan, and Pains of Sleep* volume of 1816, which, despite savage reviews, ran to three editions in that year. Before *Christabel* was published, Coleridge had prepared in 1815 the materials for his collective edition, published in 1817 as *Sibylline Leaves*. The poems in the *Christabel* volume were not included, but here *The Ancient Mariner* first appeared under its author's name, enriched with an important marginal gloss; and the critical introduction projected for *Sibylline Leaves* turned into *Biographia Literaria*. After that he made no collection *con amore*. *Poetical Works* in three volumes followed in 1828, including *Remorse,* the *Wallenstein* translation, and *Zapolya* (separately published in 1817), as well as the contents of the *Christabel* volume; it was handsomely printed by William Pickering with the new Aldine device of a dolphin enfolding an anchor. This edition, hastily prepared in trying circumstances, was printed in only 500 copies. Another edition, only slightly revised, followed in 1829. When the 1834 edition was being prepared Coleridge was dying and the editorial work was largely, if not wholly, done by his nephew-son-in-law Henry Nelson Coleridge. The *Poetical Works* in their successive editions became more and more cumulative; yet, if the 1834 edition included a number of juvenilia and occasional verses that Coleridge had earlier rejected, it also included a number of interesting 'late' poems beyond those collected in 1828.[1]

[1] A bibliographical description of these volumes with detailed account of their contents is given in Appendix K to *The Poetical Works*, ed. J. D.

After Coleridge's death, Henry Nelson, Sara, and Derwent Coleridge clarified and extended the canon of poems, particularly in the editions of 1844 and 1852; and R. H. Shepherd made further additions in his anonymous four volume *Poetical and Dramatic Works* of 1877. The work of that generation culminates in two editions prepared by close friends and drawn from the rich cumulus of family manuscripts and records: James Dykes Campbell's *The Poetical Works* (Macmillan 1893 &c) based on the 1829 text, and Ernest Hartley Coleridge's *The Complete Poetical Works* (2 vol. Oxford 1912) based on the 1834 text. Campbell's edition, of which his *S. T. Coleridge: A Narrative of the Events of his Life* (1894) is the splendid by-product, is the more companionable of the two, with its two-column layout, interesting appendixes, and intelligent but unobtrusive notes. E. H. C.'s edition, with its stronger textual and bibliographical bias, is for the time being the essential scholar's edition, though from the critical point of view it needs to be supplemented with Campbell's notes.[1] In both editions the poems are arranged chronologically, a method that Coleridge himself approved but never used. The fact that both editors devote separate sections to epigrams, poetic fragments, first drafts, adaptations, and the like points to the extremely intricate problems that face any attempt to collect all Coleridge's poetical work into a single arrangement.[2] Even E. H. C.'s work has been overtaken by standards of technical scholarship and a view of Coleridge that he could not have foreseen; yet these two editions, each in its own way, remain models of care, skill, and devotion; and fortunately both continue to be kept in print.

P R O S E: Coleridge was an even more unlucky author with his prose

---

Campbell, 1893; and in greater detail, with additional record (incomplete) of poems published in periodicals, in *The Complete Poetical Works*, ed. E. H. Coleridge, 1912, II, 1135–88. T. J. Wise's *Bibliography of Coleridge*, 1913, lists the contents of volumes up to *Sibylline Leaves* but not of the *Poetical Works* 1828, 1829, 1834.

[1] The Oxford Standard Authors version is a photographic reprint of the two-volume edition omitting the dramatic works and the bibliographical matter—indeed, most of vol. II.

[2] Some of the editorial problems of the poems are discussed in 'Coleridge's poetical canon', *Review of English Literature*, 7, 1966.

works than with his poems: only *Aids to Reflection* (1825) and *Church and State* (1830) received a second edition in his lifetime. Five ephemeral pamphlets issued in 1795 were not reissued; nor was his first periodical *The Watchman* (10 numbers, 1796).[1] His first major prose work, *The Friend*, was issued in 28 numbers from June 1809 to March 1810, was reissued in volume form with supplementary matter in 1812, and again in three volumes in 1818, so revised and expanded as to be virtually a new work.[2] In April 1816 Coleridge had taken up residence with the Gillmans in Highgate and celebrated his new circumstances with an impressive series of publications. In 1816 *The Statesman's Manual* (the first *Lay Sermon*) was published shortly after the *Christabel* volume; in 1817, *Biographia Literaria* (with *Sibylline Leaves*, both of which had been practically complete by the end of 1815), and the second *Lay Sermon* ('Blessed are ye that sow beside all waters'); in 1818 the general introduction to the *Encyclopaedia Metropolitana*, 'On Method' (which was turned into the Essays on Method in the 1818 *Friend* after Coleridge had withdrawn from the encyclopaedia project), and two pamphlets in support of Sir Robert Peel's bill against the mistreatment of factory children. After that, Coleridge concentrated upon trying to complete the 'Opus Maximum' and only two prose works were to follow: *Aids to Reflection* (London 1825, New York 1829, London 1831) and *On the Constitution of the Church and State* (1830, two editions).[3]

[1] The Bristol pamphlets are included, with three hitherto unpublished lectures, in *Lectures 1795: On Politics and Religion*, ed. Lewis Patton & Peter Mann (CC 1) 1970. *The Watchman*, ed. Lewis Patton (CC 2) was also published in 1970. Parts of all these were included in Sara Coleridge's 3-volume edition of *Essays on his own Times*, 1850.

[2] In *Biog. Lit.*, I, 110, it was *The Friend* that Coleridge said had been 'printed rather than published'. *The Friend*, ed. Barbara Rooke (2 vol., 1969) was the first *Collected Coleridge* title to be published; it gives the 1818 text in Vol. I, the 1809–10 text with variants for 1812 in Vol. II, and is copiously indexed.

[3] The Royal Society of Literature essay 'On the *Prometheus* of Aeschylus', delivered in May 1825, was published in the *Transactions* of the Society in 1834; only offprints were separately issued. See 'The publication of Coleridge's *Prometheus* essay', *Notes and Queries*, Feb. 1969, 52–5.

To sketch out the history of the Coleridge prose canon is no difficult matter; but the tidiness of the account gives little hint of the nature of the work itself or of the skill that was needed on the part of editors (and is still needed) to present these works as 'living educts' of his imagination and of his whole way of mind.[1] If every piece of Coleridge's writing had been composed with the secure self-confidence that brought *The Ancient Mariner* into existence, and if every piece of his prose had been written in fortunate circumstances with the sure prospect of a sympathetic reading, his collected works might well have the orderly self-containedness of Goethe's *oeuvre*, or at least the sequential self-definition of Eliot's or Valéry's or Yeats's essays, or of Hazlitt's writings or even Carlyle's. Many factors militated against the security of his single prose works: *The Friend*, written *ex improviso* in its first version and carefully revised seven years later, is probably, despite its somewhat miscellaneous character, the least unsatisfactory; the *Biographia* was written quickly (though from materials long meditated) under conditions of extreme personal difficulty; *Aids to Reflection*, like the *Biographia*, changed and grew under his hand while he was writing it. A second edition would have allowed him to revise, as he did with *Church and State*, and reconsider, as he did with *The Friend*. When he sent corrected copies of *Sibylline Leaves* and the *Biographia* to Tom Poole he said: 'so wildly have they been printed, that a corrected Copy is of some value to those, to whom the works themselves are of any.'[2] Nevertheless Coleridge was an inveterate reviser and corrector of his own writing; he annotated several copies of the 1818 *Friend*, H.N.C. and Sara worked from an annotated copy of the *Biographia* (now lost), and marked or annotated copies of practically all his works have survived. The early editors made good use of Coleridge's notes and corrections; and many more of these remain to be brought into focus in the *Collected Coleridge*. But we shall never have Coleridge's final considered view on any of his books. Less than a month before he died, Coleridge said:

[1] Coleridge uses this phrase twice in the *Lay Sermon* (31, 110)—the first time in one of his most important statements on poetic symbols.
[2] CL, IV, 754. No annotated copy of the *Biographia* is known to have survived.

> The metaphysical disquisition at the end of the first volume of the *Biographia Literaria* is unformed and immature; it contains the fragments of the truth, but it is not fully thought out. It is wonderful to myself to think how infinitely more profound my views now are, and yet how much clearer they are withal. The circle is completing; the idea is coming round to, and to be, the common sense.[1]

But he never rewrote that section and it is clear that he did not tell H.N.C. what his revision would have been.

When Mill wrote his essays on Bentham and Coleridge in 1840 he had before him a substantial part of Bowring's collective edition of Bentham's writing. He had no corresponding edition of Coleridge; if he had, one can imagine that he could have given a rather less stereotyped account of Coleridge than he did. In fact, Mill would not have had long to wait. Immediately after Coleridge's death, members of his family made it their duty not only to restore all the major works to circulation in the best editions they could construct, but also to complete and methodize writings that they recognised would enhance the still-ambiguous reputation of their distinguished forebear. Their desire to make the best showing they could for Coleridge is understandable: it led them to rewording and excisions that we now find inadvisable, and to the silent fusion of disparate materials that we now consider injudicious. But their work was affectionate, careful, and intelligent; informed by motives beyond literary piety or archaeological obsession, their work preserves a living connexion with the man himself.[2]

---

[1] *Table Talk*, 28 June, 1834.
[2] Sara states her position in her *Biog. Lit.*: 'I have heard it said that the lives and characters of men ought never to be handled by near relations and friends, whose pride and partial affection are sure to corrupt their testimony. . . . The testimony of friends is needed, if only to balance that of adversaries: and indeed what better grounds for judging of a man's character, upon the whole, can the world have, than the impression it has made on those who have come the nearest to him, and known him the longest and the best? I, for my part, have not striven to conceal any of my natural partialities, or to separate my love of my Father from my moral and intellectual sympathy with his mode of thought. . . . Of this I am sure, that no one ever studied my

In his will Coleridge named Joseph Henry Green, his philosophical collaborator, as his literary executor. At the time of his death it was agreed that Henry Nelson Coleridge, who had married Coleridge's daughter Sara in 1829, should be responsible for editing and reissuing the published work and for preparing fragmentary and uncollected material, particularly of the literary sort, at his discretion; Green would look after the philosophical manuscripts.[1] H.N.C. was no stranger to Coleridge or his ways of working or his manuscripts: since 1822 he had been collecting from his uncle's conversation the material that was to be published by John Murray in two volumes in 1835 (*Specimens of the Table Talk of the late S. T. Coleridge*), a favourite with Coleridge readers ever since its first appearance; and he had been largely responsible for collecting and editing the *Poetical Works* of 1834, and had written for the *Quarterly Review* the most perceptive account of Coleridge's poetry ever written by a contemporary.[2] So members of

---

Father's writings earnestly and so as to imbibe the author's spirit, who did not learn to care still more for Truth than for him, whatever interest in him such a study may have inspired.' *Biog. Lit.*, 1847, I, clxxxii–clxxxiv.

[1] J. H. Green spent the last 28 years of his life trying to piece Coleridge's philosophy together. He gave Hunterian Orations on the subject in 1840 and 1847, but his book—*Spiritual Philosophy, founded on the teaching of the late S. T. Coleridge*—was published posthumously in 2 volumes in 1865. Dykes Campbell says that 'In his Hunterian Orations . . . Green probably accomplished more in the setting forth of Coleridge's philosophical views than in the *Spiritual Philosophy*. But of these high matters I have no right to speak.' (*Narrative*, 280) I am not aware that the *Spiritual Philosophy* has commended itself to Coleridgeans. J. H. Muirhead's *Coleridge as Philosopher*, 1930, Miss Coburn writes, 'was one of those books of which the failure is almost more instructive than success. The reason was that Coleridge could not be reshaped by the mould of late nineteenth-century British idealism into which Muirhead, with zest and affection, tried to pour him.' (*Twentieth Century Views*, 4)

[2] Reprinted in Jackson, 620–51. Nominally published in August as a review of the *Poetical Works*, 1834, the manuscript, and probably also the proofs, will have been shown to Coleridge before he died on 25 July.

Coleridge's family became the first careful editors of his work: his nephew Henry Nelson Coleridge (born the year *Lyrical Ballads* was first published) and his wife Sara, who was Coleridge's only daughter; then his youngest son Derwent, two years younger than Sara; and after Derwent had died, Coleridge's grandson Ernest Hartley.

With remarkable industry H.N.C. and Sara published a number of volumes in rapid succession, all of them except the *Table Talk* under William Pickering's imprint: after *Table Talk** (2 vol, John Murray, 1835), *Literary Remains** appeared (Vol I and II in 1836, III in 1838, IV in 1839); then *On the Constitution of Church and State* with *The Statesman's Manual* and *Lay Sermon* (1839), *Confessions of an Inquiring Spirit** (1840), *Poetical Works* (1842), *Aids to Reflection* (1843), and *The Friend* (1844). H.N.C. had died in 1842 when the new edition of *The Friend* was complete and work on *Biographia Literaria* well under way. Sara continued the work, publishing the *Biographia*, with H.N.C.'s valuable 'Biographical Supplement' and her own scholarly and dignified introduction, in 1847. S. B. Watson's edition of the *Theory of Life** (from manuscript) was published independently in 1848. In 1849 Sara published *Notes and Lectures Upon Shakespeare and some other Old Poets and Dramatists**, extracted from *Literary Remains* II with some additions: this was to prove an important book for Coleridge's reputation as literary critic and for the development of Shakespeare criticism altogether. *Essays on his own Times**, a three-volume selection of Coleridge's contributions to newspapers and periodicals, followed in 1850, the last of the series to be published by Pickering. Thereafter the new editions were taken by Edward Moxon, the beauty of whose printing almost tempts us to forget that he destroyed all but some sixty volumes of Charles Lamb's 'ragged regiment'. Sara and her brother Derwent prepared a new edition of the poems and dramatic works, but Sara had died before the *Poetical Works* was published in 1852. Derwent continued with a new edition of the two *Lay Sermons* (1852) and the *Dramatic Works* (1852); then *Notes on English Divines** (2 vol, 1853) extracted mostly from *Literary Remains* III and IV, and *Notes Theological, Political, and Miscellaneous** (1853), from *Literary Remains* with some interesting additions—the last two intended, with *Notes and*

* A sub-canonical work—see p. 12 above.

Lectures upon Shakespeare, to form a comprehensive and methodical arrangement of the marginalia; and finally, *Aids to Reflection* (1854).

Here the history of Coleridge's American reputation may be considered: it was to bring several American scholars and writers to visit him in Highgate in the last years of his life. *Remorse* was published in New York in the year of its first London appearance (1813); perhaps the poems had wider early currency than the first American edition of *Sibylline Leaves* in 1827 would suggest. Before Coleridge's death, understandably, a steady and increasing demand for the poems had been established. The response to the prose is more unexpected: it seems to have been more vigorous in the United States than in England. *Biographia Literaria* had its first New York edition in 1817 (the year of first publication) and other editions followed in 1834 and 1843, and a reprint of the H.N.C. and Sara edition in 1848. *Table Talk* and the *Theory of Life* had American editions also in the year of first publication, in New York 1835 and Philadelphia 1848; and *Confessions of an Inquiring Spirit* (1840) appeared in a Boston edition in 1841. In 1846 a one-volume *Works of Coleridge in Prose and Verse* (546 pages) was published by an anonymous editor in Philadelphia and sold so well that it was reissued at about three-yearly intervals for some time. The most significant event, however, was the publication of *Aids to Reflection* in Burlington in 1829 with a long 'Preliminary Essay' by the Rev. James Marsh. James Marsh, born in 1794, was President of the University of Vermont from 1826 to 1833, and then, until his death in 1842, professor of philosophy. He was responsible for the edition of the *Aids*; *The Friend* followed in 1831 and the *Statesman's Manual* in 1832, both with a Burlington imprint. A student of Marsh's, William Shedd, born in 1820 and graduated at the University of Vermont in 1839, became professor of English literature after Marsh's death (1845-52) and persisted in the enthusiasm for Coleridge that Marsh had stimulated. After leaving the University of Vermont for a theological career that later placed him on the staff of the Union Theological Seminary from 1862 until his death in 1893, he published in seven volumes with a New York imprint *The Complete Works of Samuel Taylor Coleridge* (1853). Significantly there is a long (and rather cloudy) introductory essay on Coleridge's 'Philosophical and Theological Opinions'; the emphasis of *Literary Remains* is reversed—the first volume is devoted to *Aids to Reflection* and *The States-man's Manual*, the poems are relegated to the last volume. This collection is more complete than is commonly supposed: it comprises all the canonical and sub-canonical works in their latest London editions—including *Literary Remains, Table Talk*, the *Theory of Life*, and a little new material. It is the only collective edition so far published. Reissued with titlepages dated 1854, 1858, 1860, 1863, 1868, 1871, 1875 (all presumably the first printing), it was reprinted in 1884 with a 'Complete Index' by Arthur Gilman. Beyond Shedd's edition there are reprints in the Bohn library, usually plain texts in a small format not disagreeable to read; and Thomas Ashe did some useful and original work in the Bohn editions of *Table Talk* (1884), and of the *Miscellanies, Aesthetic and Literary* including the *Theory of Life* (1885). But few scholars of Coleridge have been able to manage without Shedd.

In 1895, twelve years after Derwent Coleridge's death, Ernest Hartley Coleridge published two volumes of *Letters of Samuel Taylor Coleridge**, and an important small volume—beautifully designed and printed—of extracts from the manuscript notebooks under the title *Anima Poetae**. His edition of the *Complete Poetical Works* (1912) brings the family editing to a close. Not only did they edit diligently; they treasured up manuscripts, books, and transcripts; and these, most of them now preserved in permanent collections, make it possible for us to verify their work and to venture beyond it.

In the editorial work of this century, manuscripts have been, as they were for E.H.C., of paramount importance. The poems have always been kept in print in various forms, and editions and reprints of *The Ancient Mariner* are almost beyond numbering. The prose had had no such currency. The Nonesuch selection edited by Stephen Potter in 1933 marked and stimulated a growing interest in the prose as well as in a range of poems beyond the 'big three'. R. J. White's selection of *The Political Thought of Coleridge* (1938) and his telescoped but intelligently edited versions of the two *Lay Sermons* in his *Political Tracts of Wordsworth, Coleridge, and Shelley* (1953) drew attention to Coleridge's contemporaneity as a social and political thinker, and H. St J. Hart made a new edition of *Confessions of an Inquiring Spirit* in 1956.

* A sub-canonical work—see p. 12 above.

Biographia Literaria, caught between the monisms of the New Criticism and a new Aristotelianism that saw itself as 'anti-romantic', received no serious editorial attention after Shawcross's edition (1907) and was accorded (with a few notable exceptions) only polite lip-service until about ten years ago. Alice D. Snyder's edition of the essay *On Method* (1934) places almost as much emphasis on manuscript fragments as did her earlier book *Coleridge on Logic and Learning* (1929); collectanea rather than editions, these represent a tentative foray into the jungle of Coleridge's philosophical manuscripts. T. M. Raysor's two volumes of *Coleridge's Shakespearean Criticism* (1930, revised 1960) clarify and extend Sara's work largely through the use of manuscript sources—an important improvement in content and arrangement even if the presentation is below the technical standards now considered necessary. His volume of *Coleridge's Miscellaneous Criticism* (1936), mostly marginalia but selected with a strong anti-theological bias, draws upon originals as far as possible, includes new materials, and goes well beyond *Literary Remains* and *Notes Theological, Political, and Miscellaneous* in accuracy. R. Florence Brinkley's *Coleridge on the Seventeenth Century* (1955), restricted somewhat by the artificial limits of its theme and by the exclusion of Shakespeare, brings together an ambitious quantity of material (with varying degrees of authority) from marginalia, note-books, miscellaneous manuscripts, and printed sources in order to establish for Coleridge's philosophical and aesthetic thinking a broader reference than Kant and Schelling.

All these in various ways show the extreme difficulty of piecing together Coleridge's manuscripts in any particular area as a direct statement of his thinking: there are always severe problems of chronology and the problem of defining an area is almost invincible. The greatest success has been achieved where (as in the case of the Shakespeare materials) precise topical definition is possible, and where (as with the letters and notebooks) the manuscripts define themselves as a distinct group. The only substantial addition to the prose canon in this century is Kathleen Coburn's edition of the 1818–19 *Philosophical Lectures** (1949), ingeniously reconstructed from a shorthand transcript with the interpolation of material from contemporary notebooks and published

* A sub-canonical work—see p. 12 above.

writings: and the notes to this edition include a valuable selection of unpublished marginalia, particularly on Tennemann and Kant. Earl Leslie Griggs's two volumes of *Unpublished Letters* (1932) was the forerunner to the comprehensive edition of *Collected Letters* that started appearing in 1956; the difference between the two editions is the difference in the quality of manuscript sources used. With the publication of the first pair of volumes of the *Notebooks* in 1957, edited by Kathleen Coburn, 'Coleridge redivivus' becomes a real possibility. Here we see the closing of the process initiated by Lowes's *Road to Xanadu* (1927) and affirmed with modest clarity by Miss Coburn in *Inquiring Spirit: A New Presentation of Coleridge* (1951). Though there have been very few additions to the prose canon since the twenties, the methodical exploration of manuscripts has transformed and renewed our knowledge of Coleridge and our attitude to him and his work. The change is well summarised by Miss Coburn: 'In 1934 the Nonesuch Press compendium of Coleridge's prose and verse had seemed to suffice; thirty years later nothing less than a collected edition, as nearly complete as may be, seems adequate.'[1]

Every editor of Coleridge runs headlong into the fact that when Coleridge's mind is active, unity is always implicit. The unifying force of that 'tenacious & systematizing' mind is so pervasive as to defy all attempts to deal with his work a little at a time, to divide and conquer like an army occupying hostile territory or a conscientious legatee taking over as inheritance a huge ramshackle estate. To isolate any part of his work from all the rest, even for convenience or for the sake of method, for orderly distinction rather than division, is extremely difficult; and to index a Coleridge work a person almost needs to be Coleridge. Beyond the canonical and sub-canonical works with their intricate tendrillings in every direction, there are the manuscripts—letters, notebooks, marginalia, those folio volumes of miscellaneous material in the British Museum acquired from E.H.C., and the files and volumes of manuscripts and transcripts at Victoria College, Toronto. Like Mallory's Everest, they are *there*. A notebook entry, written when the lectures were at last finished, shows us Coleridge in relation to these materials:

[1] *Twentieth Century Views*, 7.

S.T.C. = who with long and large arm still collected precious
Armfuls in whatever direction he pressed forward, yet still took
up so much more than he could keep together that those who
followed him gleaned more from his continual droppings than he
himself brought home—Nay, made stately Corn-ricks therewith,
while the Reaper himself was still seen only with a strutting arm-
ful of newly cut Sheaves.—But I should misinform you grossly,
if I left you to infer that his Collections were a heap of incoherent
Miscellanea—No!—the very Contrary—Their variety con-
joined with the too great Coherency, the too great both desire &
power of referring them in systematic, nay, genetic subordination
was that which rendered his schemes gigantic & impracticable,
as an Author—& his Conversation less instructive, as a man/—
Inopem sua *Copia* fecit—too much was given, all so weighty &
brilliant as to preclude choice, & too many to be all received—
so that it passed over the Hearers mind like a roar of Waters—[1]

As he himself notices, the principle of unity in multeity obtains—not
ideally, to be sure, or in every instance, but as a constant dynamic
interinanimation that makes every fragment at least potentially re-
verberant; as though every item in this vast complex were held in a
'subtle Vulcanian Spider-web Net of Steel—strong as Steel yet subtle
as the Ether'[2]; as though every item were 'seeking, as it were *asking*'
for the self-realising relation that can declare that particular part an
integral element in the whole. In the sense that not every item is self-
subsistent, the manuscript material is fragmentary; in another and more
profound sense, the separate items are facets rather than fragments,
germs implying growth rather than broken pieces that bespeak dis-
order or death. To see how H.N.C. and Sara, and then T. M. Raysor,
pieced together the Shakespeare criticism from lecture notes, marginalia and scattered manuscripts, newspaper reports and personal
accounts is to grasp not only the difficulty but also the intricacy of the

---

[1] *Notebooks*, III, 4400; also printed *variatim* as 'L' Envoy' to *Literary Remains*, I, xiii-xiv.

[2] *Notebooks*, III, 3708. A central account of Coleridge's actual experience of association, the whole note was first printed by R. C. Bald in
his 'Coleridge and *The Ancient Mariner*', *Nineteenth Century Studies*, ed.
Davis, DeVane, Bald, Ithaca, 1940, 23-4; printed again by Humphry
House, Clark Lectures, 146-7.

procedure—a procedure that can seldom claim finality. The Shakespeare criticism can without undue difficulty be separated out. Not so the magnetic field of the notebooks. The editing of these, in scope, delicacy, and comprehensiveness, is a huge instance of the Coleridgean method called into life and shaped by the sheer nature and substance of the Coleridgean materials, themselves a continuous embodiment of Coleridge's intellectual, emotional, and imaginative activity.

III

Let us suppose that somebody wants to start reading Coleridge with the idea of getting to know his work in detail and as a whole. What, beyond what has already been written, can be offered by way of advice? What books may be profitably read in what order? For a start we can take warning from Coleridge himself. By the time he was revising *The Friend*—'the Main Pipe, from which I shall play off the whole accumulation and reservoir of my Head and Heart'[1]—he was well aware of the demands he would make on a reader.

> In the establishment of principles and fundamental doctrines, I must of necessity require the attention of my reader to become my fellow-labourer. The primary facts essential to the intelligibility of my principles I can prove to others only as far as I can prevail on them to retire *into themselves* and make their own minds the objects of their stedfast attention. But, on the other hand, I feel too deeply the importance of the convictions, which first impelled me to the present undertaking, to leave unattempted any honourable means of recommending them to as wide a circle as possible.[2]

A few years later, in a marginal note on Southey's *Life of Wesley*, he remarked upon the '*obtruded* purpose of the Friend or the Aids to Reflection; in which the aim of every sentence is to solicit, nay, *tease* the Reader to ask himself, whether he *actually* does or does not, understand *distinctly*? Whether he has however reflected on the precise

[1] CL, III, 145. *Cf*. III, 239: 'the outlet of my whole *reservoir* as well as of the living Fountain—till it shall be dried up'.
[2] *Friend*, I, 21: not in 1809–10.

meaning of the word, however familiar it may be both to his ear and his mouth?'[1] Yet these demands apply not only to the prose works, to whatever is more or less discursive, speculative, theoretical, metaphysical; they apply also to his poems. The immense importance of Coleridge's experience of making poetry of the first order—*The Ancient Mariner* particularly—can hardly be too strongly pressed: it is a shaping principle in his psychology, in his critical theory and practice, in his metaphysics, in his struggle with Kant's philosophy. If our sense of Coleridge's poetry is casual, shallow, or attenuated, we shall probably fail to experience in all his work the energy and specificity of his peculiarly tactile and lyrical intelligence.[2]

In constructing *Aids to Reflection* upon a series of 'Aphorisms', Coleridge defined the word *aphorism* as 'determinate position' (giving the etymology) and ended by saying that a 'twofold act of circumscribing, and detaching, when it is exerted by the mind on subjects of reflection and reason, is to *aphorize*, and the result an *aphorism*.'[3] In Coleridge's use, an aphorism is intended to initiate and guide further reflection. In this sense, three statements of Coleridge's may be of value to a reader.

> In all processes of the Understanding the shortest way will be discovered the last, and this perhaps while it constitutes the great advantage of having a Teacher to put us on the shortest road at the first, yet sometimes occasions a difficulty in the comprehension—/ in as much as the longest way is more near to the existing state of the mind, nearer to what, if left to myself on starting the thought, I should have thought next.—The shortest *way* gives me *the knowlege* best; the longest way makes me more *knowing*.[4]

[1] Part of marginal note on Southey's *Life of Wesley*, 1820, II, 166–78. In the same note Coleridge recalls that Joseph Hone had 'called my "Aids to Reflection" *a proper Brain-cracker*' (note 85).

[2] Richard Haven, *Patterns of Consciousness: An Essay on Coleridge*, 1969, explores the proposition that *The Rime of the Ancient Mariner* remains the central document even for his thinking: that in that poem Coleridge most fully embodied those patterns of experience which dominate his work both before and after (p. 18).

[3] *Aids to Reflection*, 18–19n.

[4] *Notebooks*, II, 3023.

Again, drawing a parallel between the growth of 'our cognitions' and the education of children, he writes:

> There is a period of aimless activity and unregulated accumulation, during which it is enough if we can preserve them in health and *out of harm's way*. Again, there is a period of orderliness, of circumspection, of discipline, in which we purify, separate, define, select, arrange, and settle the nomenclature of communication. There is also a period of dawning and twilight, a period of anticipation, affording trials of strength. And all these . . . will precede the attainment of a scientific M E T H O D.[1]

And finally, an acute insight into cognitive process altogether and also into Coleridge's distinctive way of getting to know.

> There is no way of arriving at any sciential End but by finding it at every step. The End is in the Means: or the Adequacy of each Mean is already its End. Southey once said to me: You are nosing every nettle along the Hedge, while the Greyhound (meaning himself, I presume) wants only to get sight of the Hare, and Flash—strait as a line! he has it in his mouth!—Even so, I replied, might a Cannibal say to an Anatomist, whom he had watched dissecting a body. But the fact is—I do not care two pence for the *Hare*; but I value most highly the excellencies of scent, patience, discrimination, free Activity; and find a Hare in every Nettle I make myself acquainted with. I follow the Chamois-Hunters, and seem to set out with the same Object. But I am no Hunter of *that* Chamois Goat; but avail myself of the Chace in order to a nobler purpose—that of making a road across the Mountain in which Common Sense may hereafter pass backward and forward, without desperate Leaps or Balloons that soar indeed but do not improve the chance of getting onward.[2]

Three things, it seems to me, are needed in reading Coleridge: a sense of the presence—or spell—of Coleridge's mind-in-action, of his

---

[1] *Friend*, I, 499.
[2] BM MS Egerton 2801, f 126: watermark 1822. Also printed in *Inquiring Spirit*, 143–4. Coleridge was fond of the chamois-hunting image: see for example *Sh. Crit.* II, 35, and *Friend*, I, 55 (quoted at pp. 42–3 below).

shaping activity; a tactile, rather than an abstractive, feeling for Coleridge materials; and, under the eye, materials fine-grained and intricate enough to '*tease*' us into paying close attention to the particular matters in hand and to hold us from 'the tendency to look abroad, *out* of the thing in question'.

No doubt, depending on the individual reader, more than one preliminary approach will be fruitful; but whatever the approach, early acquaintance with primary material is essential. Two selective editions commend themselves: Stephen Potter's Nonesuch edition of *Select Poetry and Prose of Coleridge* (1933), and I. A. Richards's *The Portable Coleridge* (1950).[1] Both offer a generous selection of poems, letters, notebook entries, and table talk, and both have topical sections devoted to politics, literary criticism, and 'Theologico-Metaphysical' writing. The Nonesuch edition is the more extensive (703 pages as compared to 568) and an unusual feature is the presentation of *The Ancient Mariner* in the first (1798) and final (1834) versions on facing pages. Richards's selection of poems is outstanding for its emphasis on 'late' poems, that is, poems composed after about January 1807, and his introduction includes the first serious critical notice of the late poems. Nonesuch gives more than twice as much space to letters as Richards does (Richards resolutely stops in October 1803 and gives only two letters of later date); both devote a large amount of space to literary criticism (224 pages in Nonesuch, 233 in Richards); and both are weak in marginalia. Both were published too early to have text or references consistent with the best edition of the letters, and the notebook entries are all from *Anima Poetae*; but that is a state of affairs a reader of Coleridge has to get used to for some time to come. Of the two collections, I prefer the Nonesuch edition, if only because it has almost one third

---

[1] Also 1950 (with some marginalia added), 1962, &c. Those who are sensitive to the physique of their books will persist in finding a copy of the 1933 edition in which the typically distinguished Nonesuch design is seen in a clean impression on a well-matched paper. *The Portable Coleridge*, originally published in cloth, has been current in paperback since 1961 at latest (New York, Viking Press). The 1950 edition had a large number of literal errors in the text, but these may have been corrected since.

more material and is a most agreeable book to handle; but Richards's introduction to the Viking edition is much too important to miss.[1]

To read through some such comprehensive selection will acquaint a reader with 'the great landmarks in the Map' of the man and will nourish an affectionate (or impatient) familiarity with some flowers and gems, and with some ruins and a certain amount of underbrush. In the preliminary phase of reading it is important to get a firm grasp of *The Ancient Mariner*, preferably without commentary, paying due regard to the revisions that occurred after 1798 and to the marginal gloss that first appeared (not quite complete) in 1817. *Christabel* and *Kubla Khan* will certainly cast their spell and rouse perplexity. Beyond the 'big three', the 'conversation poems' are important, and so is *Dejection: an Ode* (particularly in its relation to Wordsworth's Immortality Ode) and the poem *To William Wordsworth*. The 'late' poems make different critical demands, but several of them, particularly 'Youth and Age', 'Work without Hope', and the 'Epitaph', are moving, finely wrought, and accessible.

Given some emotional, psychological, and intellectual feeling for the country, the next step needs to be more resolute. William Walsh's *Coleridge: The Work and the Relevance* (1967) is (as far as I know) the only conspective account of the whole compass of Coleridge's manifold activity. With its clear explication and a penetrating commentary that shows (without over-arguing the case) how far many of Coleridge's central concerns are concerns for our own time, this book will sharpen the reader's perceptions for the next group of primary materials —Kathleen Coburn's *Inquiring Spirit: A New Presentation of Coleridge from his Published and Unpublished Prose Writings* (1951). This book, which seeks to remove Coleridge from 'the special property of "the *literati* by profession"', offers recondite materials (about one third of it hitherto unpublished) under the headings of psychology, education, language, logic and philosophy, literary criticism, the other fine arts, sciences, his contemporaries, society, and religion. The introduction is as good an introduction to Coleridge as it is to the most distinguished

---

[1] Similar selective editions have been published, primarily (like the Viking Coleridge) for university purposes, by E. L. Griggs, 1934; Elisabeth Schneider, 1951; Donald A. Stauffer, 1951; Kathleen Raine, (Penguin) 1957.

Coleridgean of our day; and the brief critical and bibliographical prefaces to the sections are incisive and useful. Altogether the book is indispensable, not merely for the quality and variety of materials collected in it, but as imaging forth of Coleridge as a very sensitive, perceptive, many-sided, and intelligent man. The book will make its demands of a reader, however; like most of Coleridge's concentrated writing it will not be easily mastered, and at first not all parts will strike with uniform force.

The reader should now be ready for one of the delights of Coleridge scholarship—John Livingston Lowes's *The Road to Xanadu* (1927, revised 1930, frequently reprinted in cloth and paperback). Subtitled *A Study in the Ways of the Imagination*, this great seminal study explores 'the enormous range of interlocked reading' and the personal observation and experience from which these poems arose. It is neither an account of the way the poems were written, nor an explication of their 'meaning'. What Lowes has done is to trace from the Gutch Memorandum Book (Notebook G) and any other available written source the verbal origins for words, phrases, and feelings that were finally embedded in the poems. His purpose is to find actual clusters of words that we can show by documentary evidence Coleridge certainly knew, and from these to examine the transforming, selecting, and shaping functions of imagination. A very learned textual and literary scholar, Lowes works in fascinated detail through the whole of Coleridge's writing (as it was then available to him), and through as much of his reading as he can relevantly bring to bear. Any reader who follows Lowes through his text and his copious notes *and* the 21 pages of closely printed Addenda and Corrigenda added in 1930 will be infected by Lowes's enthusiasm, will be familiar with almost all the mainstream and most of the backwaters of Coleridge documentation, and will have learned something about Coleridge's 'armed vision' and the 'armed vision' needed in Coleridge studies.[1] In the end, Lowes's psychology of poetic composition may seem less subtle than Coleridge's performance demands. Yet this voyage through Coleridge's oceanic reading, this exploration of the twilight realms of Coleridge's consciousness, is (because of the part the Gutch Memorandum Book plays in it) an

[1] The phrase 'armed vision' is from *Biog. Lit.*, I, 81.

invigorating introduction to the notebooks which we can now read
but which Lowes himself never saw. And *The Road to Xanadu* has gone
far to disarm the curious assumption that in Coleridge metaphysics and
abstruse learning did (or ever could) destroy the poet.

After that, two critical books may be ventured, both seminal:
Humphry House's *Coleridge: The Clark Lectures 1951-52* (1953) and
I. A. Richards's *Coleridge on Imagination* (1934). House's book had
better be read first. Here a rigorous scholar of fine sensibility offers a
unified view of Coleridge that takes serious account of his life and
temperament, the unpublished materials (especially notebooks), and
the poems. In what sense, he asks, is Coleridge both a great artist and a
great writer? House recognised that before a complete account could
be given much remained to be done, particularly in editing notebooks,
letters, and marginalia. But there is nothing tentative about his conception. His handling of minute primary materials is a model of tact and
precision; this book is as illuminating and compelling as it was when
first delivered to a large Cambridge audience twenty years ago.
Richards's book is of peculiar interest as a tribute by the man who
wrote those two reluctant harbingers of the New Criticism, *Principles
of Literary Criticism* and *Practical Criticism*. Compared with one or two
more recent studies of Coleridge's theory of imagination, this book may
seem exploratory (or self-exploratory) rather than definitive; but it has
been very influential, and it is well to pick up good influences at their
source.

At this point the reader might turn to *Coleridge: A Collection of
Critical Essays*, edited by Kathleen Coburn (1967), a selection of
fourteen critical observations written in this century. These cover a
variety of topics, and include part of I. A. Richards's introduction to
the Viking Coleridge, part of Herbert Read's often-reprinted *Coleridge
as Critic*, a sensitive note on patterns of sound and rhythm in *Kubla
Khan* by Elisabeth Schneider, and not more than three essays on *The
Ancient Mariner*.[1] At about the same time it would be well to read the
Shakespearean Criticism too, because by now (if not sooner) the *Biographia*

[1] Cited in n 2, p. 1, above. In the same Twentieth Century Views series,
James Boulger has edited a selection of essays on *The Ancient Mariner*,
1969.

Literaria will have started to loom above the threshold of attention. From a reader's point of view, the Shakespeare criticism leads to the *Biographia* and the *Biographia* to the Shakespeare criticism: together they form a single critical position with Shakespeare at one pole and Wordsworth at the other.

In the past thirty or forty years *Biographia Literaria* has received increasing attention, and so after a long period of quizzical neglect is recognised as a central document in the claim—now no longer seriously in question—that Coleridge is probably the greatest literary critic England has ever produced.[1] The book has had an unhappy history, and its history is almost a history of Coleridge's reputation. Hurriedly written under pressure, carelessly printed and delayed in publication, plagued by the publisher's error of judgement that led Coleridge to add material never intended for the book, contemptuously reviewed and in private rejected by Wordsworth, it had no hope of a second and considered edition in Coleridge's lifetime. Thirty years after first publication it came to a second edition in 1847, the text revised from a marked copy (now lost), enriched with notes and commentary, a biographical supplement by H.N.C. and a 180-page introduction by Sara Coleridge. That edition was reprinted in New York in 1848 and in Shedd's *Complete Works* in 1853, where it has been available ever since; but it was never reprinted in England. A plain text has been available in the Bohn edition since 1898 and in the Everyman edition since 1906.[2]

---

[1] As early as 1904 George Saintsbury had said in his *History of Criticism* (III, 230–1): 'So then, there abide these three, Aristotle, Longinus, and Coleridge. . . . Coleridge is the critical author to be turned over by day and by night. . . . Coleridge—not Addison, not the Germans, not any other—is the real introducer into the criticism of poetry of the realising and disrealising Imagination as a criterion.' Saintsbury's authority may have given impetus to Shawcross in preparing his edition of the *Biographia*, but at best indirectly; for despite Saintsbury's fine words, he clearly did not appreciate the scope or structure of the critique of Wordsworth, he ignored the doctrine of Imagination, and regarded the key passage on 'the poet, described in *ideal* perfection' (II, 12) as 'a soft shower of words, rhetorically pleasing rather than logically cogent'. See also n 1, p. 34.

[2] The Everyman edition with introduction by Arthur Symons was

Then in 1907, apparently out of a clear sky (unless with Saintsbury's oblique encouragement), the Oxford University Press published a two-volume edition by John Shawcross, brother-in-law of the Wordsworth editor Ernest de Selincourt: this was to replace 'the only annotated edition' of 1847, 'now long out of print'—an edition that 'as a whole . . . does not meet the needs of the reader of to-day.' It was more than thirty years before Shawcross's first edition was exhausted and a photographic reprint issued in 1939; then it was reissued in 1949 and with increasing frequency since then; but not until the early 1950s was an attempt made to begin to correct the numerous literal errors in the text. George Sampson's self-styled 'third edition' (Cambridge 1920) not only ignores Shawcross but reprints less than half the book; the only fresh edition since Shawcross's (George Watson's Everyman edition) does not attempt Shawcross's scope of commentary. Shawcross's biographical introduction is now out of date, but the extensive critical notes (incorporating much of the work of H.N.C. and Sara) are still valuable, and there is a welcome addition in the 1814 Bristol essays 'On the Principles of Genial Criticism' and three fragmentary essays on taste, on beauty, and on Poesy reprinted from *Literary Remains*. Shawcross was much preoccupied with Coleridge's borrowings from the German and took a more forthright view of literary influence than is any longer admissible; but he drew widely and carefully from Coleridge's published writings (as H.N.C. and Sara had not been able to do) in order 'to illustrate the continuity of his opinions'. This is the edition all Coleridge scholars have to use. It will serve until a better text, a more sensitive understanding of Coleridge's borrowings, and a firmer command of all the Coleridge materials (both primary and critical) come together in an acceptable modern edition.

George Sampson, in printing as the 'third edition' only Chapters 1–4 and 14–22, with the 1800 Preface to *Lyrical Ballads* and some other related documents added, accepted too literally Coleridge's deprecatory

---

replaced in 1956 by an edition by George Watson. Lightly annotated, but related to recent scholarship, this edition tried to clarify Coleridge's intention by omitting 'Satyrane's Letters' and the critique of Maturin's *Bertram*. Normalised spelling and punctuation neutralise the virtue of following the 1817 text (as Shawcross did not do).

description of the *Biographia* as 'so immethodical a miscellany', and assumed that all the gold could be extracted by simple excision.[1] The close of Chapter 13 and most of Chapter 14 have been so often reprinted in anthologies of critical texts that Sampson's assumption—and he was not the first to make it—was silently endorsed, and still among the uncritical is by no means dead. I have argued elsewhere, and see no reason to change my position, that although the book is no ideal of what Coleridge wanted it to be the *Biographia* is a unified work, not fragmentary, not disorganized; and that the unifying theme is Coleridge's need to arrive at a clear critical definition of William Wordsworth's art.[2] That the *Biographia* contains nothing beyond a perplexing (and

[1] The phrase 'so immethodical a miscellany' appears in the last paragraph of Ch 4 (I, 64)—a little early in the book for a summary judgment? Saintsbury is more likely to have encouraged Sampson than Shawcross: for he said it would be 'of no inconsiderable advantage, to subtitle this part [Ch. 14-22] . . . *A Critical Enquiry into the Principles which guided the Lyrical Ballads, and Mr Wordsworth's Account of Them*, to print this alone as substantive text, and to arrange all the rest as notes and appendices' (III, 207). Saintsbury had already done 'something of the kind' in his *Loci Critici* (1903), and Sampson completed the scheme by adding other documents that threw the emphasis upon *Lyrical Ballads*. Lytton Strachey said in a review of 7 Mar., 1908: 'The only fault to be found with Mr. Shawcross's commentary is that it is apt to take Coleridge a little too seriously.' In the Preface to *Anima Poetae* (1895) EHC said that the *Biographia*, like *The Friend*, 'never had [its] day at all'; and that continued to be the case until about 30 years after Shawcross's edition was published.

[2] 'The Integrity of *Biographia Literaria*', ESMEA, VI, 1953, 87–101. Although Coleridge said that 'the metaphysical disquisition at the end of the first volume . . . is unformed and immature' (*Table Talk*, 28 June 1833), I am not satisfied with the view that there is no logical connexion between the two volumes. For what Coleridge thought had gone adrift, see CL, IV, 874. In Feb., 1819 he told J. Britton: 'were it in my power, my works should be confined to the second volume of my "Literary Life", the Essays of the third volume of the "Friend", . . . with about fifty, or sixty pages from the two former volumes and some half-dozen of my poems.' (CL, IV, 925; *cf. Inquiring Spirit*, 202) But Britton was a stranger, and Coleridge was talking his way out of an invitation to give another series of lectures. There is no sign that this was

unsatisfactory) distinction between Fancy and Imagination, and some interesting biographical reminiscences is a view so commonly held that one of the most obvious 'uses' of the book has not been nearly as widely recognized as it should be: an unsurpassed critical analysis of the art and poetry of William Wordsworth.

Biographia Literaria remains a book for personal discovery: it reaches out far beyond the expected scope of biography, aesthetics, or the philosophy of poetry. Fortunately there is now help to be had in studies that draw the *Biographia* into close relation with the letters and notebooks, with *The Statesman's Manual*, the *Philosophical Lectures*, the *Theory of Life*, and the Shakespeare criticism. Richard Harter Fogle's *The Idea of Coleridge's Criticism* (1962) is an excellent topical study, and closes with an impressive Coleridgean critique of *Christabel*. J. A. Appleyard's *Coleridge's Philosophy of Literature: The Development of a Concept of Poetry 1791–1819* (1965) covers much of the same ground but in chronological sequence, and reaches some different conclusions.[1] Neither of these books is narrowly confined, any more than Coleridge was, to literary criticism: both take due notice of Coleridge's dominant religious and theological preoccupation from the earliest years, and of his social and political sense; and both pay due attention, as they must, to the quality and depth of Coleridge's psychological insight and understanding. Another book that brings Coleridge into a clear synthetic view is Richard Haven's *Patterns of Consciousness* (1969). This triad should be accurate, strenuous, and stimulating enough to arm the serious reader against the dismay that will strike him when he looks at the list of books and articles written on Coleridge since *The Road to Xanadu*. But at some time a much more strenuous piece of reading should be attempted: Thomas McFarland's immensely learned and important *Coleridge and the Pantheist Tradition* (1969).

Once this far out into the Coleridgean mental seascape we could

---

Coleridge's considered view at the end of his life, and few Coleridgeans would agree with him even if it were.

[1] Paul Deschamps, *La formation de la pensée de Coleridge 1771–1804* (Paris, 1964) offers the most accurate and detailed study of Coleridge's early intellectual development.

regard ourselves as a little salty but not quite yet ancient mariners. We need to turn back to the departure again: the letters and notebooks and marginalia—the really fine-grained primary materials that account for the steady refinement of Coleridge studies with their increasingly subtle recognitions and their clearer definition of the fruitful questions to ask. For the first two of these, new editions are now substantially in progress. Earl Leslie Griggs's *Collected Letters* (Vol I, II 1956; III, IV 1959) bring the account to the end of 1819; the last two volumes, announced as imminent in 1968, are to be published in 1971. Here are brought together in a careful transcription, from the original manuscripts as far as possible, all the letters that have survived in any form. This edition provides a far better text than we have had before; it adds many new letters and gathers in the little groups of published letters that had previously taxed the memory and ingenuity of scholars. Beyond 1819 we still turn to E. H. Coleridge's *Letters* of 1895 and Griggs's earlier *Unpublished Letters*, and fill in with the many other letters in manuscript and in a variety of printed sources. It is no gesture of ingratitude to say of the *Collected Letters* that the treatment of classical material is less than gratifying, that the bibliographical information is a little sketchy, that the interpolated biographical commentary is sometimes unsympathetic and importunate, and the indexing perfunctory. These are tokens of the magnitude of the task; and much the same can be said rather more strongly of Ernest de Selincourt's edition of the Wordsworth letters. Griggs's edition has extended, and will continue to extend, our knowledge and understanding of Coleridge far beyond anything a reader of the published letters could have expected thirty years ago. No student of Coleridge is well-advised to refrain from working in detail through these volumes. Here he will find much of the man as Lamb loved to see him 'in the quotidian undress of his mind'. He will also find much that is central to Coleridge's art and his thought, poured out (as his conversation was) with a large generosity of spirit, with a rare candour in self-revelation, with the startling virtuosity and exuberance of a great writer.

The notebooks, seventy in number, written to himself and for himself, are different from the letters in tune and texture. Their range is no less than the whole conceivable range of the man and his mind, and there is nothing elsewhere in his writing, formal or private, that does

not interlock with the notebooks. Two pairs of volumes of Miss
Kathleen Coburn's edition have already been published, in 1957 and
1961 (each volume has the text in one part, the notes in the other); a
third pair of volumes is now in the press. Vol II ends with the end of
1807, Vol III with the close of the last series of lectures in March 1819;
after that two more pairs of volumes and an index will follow. Until
the first volume of the *Notebooks* was published in 1957 we had known
about them only from the few revised extracts in Southey's *Omniana*
(1812) with some unacknowledged additions in *Literary Remains* I,
from the brilliant selection published by E. H. Coleridge as *Anima
Poetae* (1895), from Alois Brandl's imperfect transcript of the Gutch
Memorandum Book (1896), and Lowes's memorable exploration of that
Notebook in *The Road to Xanadu*.[1] The notebooks, as we are now
coming to see them in Miss Coburn's edition—transcribed with
scrupulous accuracy, arranged as well as may be (which happens to be
very well) in chronological order, provided with expository notes that
place the entries in the whole context of Coleridge's life and thought,
his reading and writing, his human and historical setting—provide
massive resources for discovering and rediscovering Coleridge in every
conceivable state of mind from the exaltation of intellectual triumph to
the nadir of humiliation and suicidal despair. These are a treasure-
house beyond any previous imagining—dramatic, human, profound,
immensely fertile. Surely there can never have been so complete and
intimate a record of the mind and nature of genius except perhaps
Leonardo's. They are volumes to be read again and again, for delight
and anguish as well as for study, as a tribute to the incorrigibility of the
human spirit and the mysterious power of imagination and reason.

The other recognizable group of manuscript material is the marginalia—the notes that Coleridge wrote in the margins and on the flyleaves
of his own (and other people's) books. These are very numerous and
many of them have been long in print in some form or other: H.N.C.
published a number of them in *Literary Remains*, Sara and Derwent

---

[1] Lowes intended a new edition of the Gutch Memorandum Book and
had collected extensive notes for this purpose. After his death, these
notes were inadvertently destroyed when his papers were received by
the Harvard University Library.

added some more, and most of these were reprinted by Shedd; Raysor revised and added to the literary marginalia in both his collections, and Miss Brinkley made additions and revisions over a wider area; a considerable number of sets of marginalia, more or less specialised, have been published in learned periodicals and elsewhere. The earliest extensive marginalia are rather later in date than we could have wished (there is little of substance before 1801) and a large proportion of them belong to the Highgate period. Covering a wide range of books and subjects, and ranging from terse reactions to long reflective monologues, they represent in many cases the day-to-day, even hour-by-hour, record of Coleridge's mind and sensibility in intimate relation to other minds. Many of the notes have never been published; many more have never been printed fully or accurately. As far as they can be dated with any certainty (for in many cases the same book was annotated over and over again, with notes on notes, corrections of first thoughts, new insights at a fresh reading) they stand parallel to the notebooks as a means of re-experiencing a perceptive mind in its heuristic and responsive energy. Written on so wide a variety of books and for such various purposes, the marginalia as a whole refuse to submit to any kind of topical or chronological arrangement. Some of the notes were written for other eyes to read, most of them not; but Coleridge considered them almost as part of his canon and hoped that at least some of them would be published.[1] Recent critical studies of Coleridge have recognised the importance of marginalia and have put some of them to very good use. But there is still a difficulty in finding reliable transcripts; and even when the originals can be examined, a satisfactory system of presentation and reference is often as hard to come by as an accurate reading. So they will be collected as completely and accurately as is at present possible into some volumes of the *Collected Coleridge*.

[1] For some account of the marginalia, see 'The Harvest on the Ground: Coleridge's Marginalia', UTQ, XXXVIII, 1969, 248–76; and for the dispersal of Coleridge's marked books, 'Portrait of a Bibliophile: 7, Coleridge', *The Book Collector*, X, 1961. To help readers trace separate publication of marginalia, the *New CBEL* entry for Coleridge has a separate division for 'Letters, Marginalia, and Fragments'.

The best biography of Coleridge is still James Dykes Campbell's *Narrative* (1894), expanded from the biographical introduction to his edition of the *Poetical Works*. Based upon his friend E. H. Coleridge's collection of books and manuscripts, this study is well-informed, perceptive, and unsentimental. The documentation is out of date, and we could now bring to bear a quantity of evidence that Campbell had no way of knowing. Nevertheless it is still a very good book to read; there is nothing yet to compare with it. Laurence Hanson's *Life of Coleridge: The Early Years* (1938) is an accomplished and sensitive piece of work, much fuller than Campbell's; but the book stops at June 1800 and has never been resumed. E. K. Chambers' *Coleridge: A Biographical Study* (1938) is at best an example of deft scholarly navigation through the manifold records of Coleridge's life. Unfortunately the documentation is elliptical and unhandy, the attitude imperially aloof, often scornful. This book does not make a Coleridgean's heart leap up. A reader still draws most of his sense of Coleridge's life from the letters and notebooks, and (in default of a biography more up-to-date than Campbell's and more humane than Chambers's) will turn to the records of his friends and associates: the journals and letters of Dorothy Wordsworth, the letters and records of Wordsworth and Lamb, of Tom Poole and Sara Hutchinson; of Southey, Godwin, the Wedgwoods, and Joseph Cottle; Humphry Davy and Daniel Stuart; De Quincey, Hazlitt, Matilda Betham, Julius Hare, F. D. Maurice, John Sterling, even Thomas Carlyle; and in the background the interminable but intelligently observant diaries of Henry Crabb Robinson. And there is the splendid record John Keats left of his one meeting with Coleridge on Hampstead Heath. The Armour and Howes collection, *Coleridge the Talker* (1940), draws a circle wide enough to include casual and obscure acquaintance. Twenty-five years after William Hazlitt, as a man of twenty, first met Coleridge, he could still recall the sound of Coleridge's voice.

> That spell is broke; that time is gone for ever; that voice is heard no more: but still the recollection comes rushing by with thoughts of long-past years, and rings in my ears with never-dying sound.

Those who have an ear can still hear that voice—in some of the poems,

in many letters, in the 1809–10 *Friend*, in the margins of books sometimes, in the notebooks constantly.

A scholar needs machines too. Students of the poems are grateful to
Sister Eugenia Logan for her *Concordance to the Poetry of Samuel Taylor
Coleridge* (1940) based on E. H. Coleridge's edition of the *Complete
Poetical Works*. As for bibliographies, E. H. Coleridge's bibliography of
the poems has already been mentioned (note 1, p. 13 above). The descriptive bibliography of Coleridge's works, like some other technical
branches of Coleridge scholarship, is in an imperfect state. The most detailed descriptive work was done by Thomas J. Wise in his *Bibliography
of Coleridge* (1913). For no reason of forgery or felony, the work is uneven
and unreliable, and misleading for its dogmatic tone. The Coleridge
descriptions in his *Ashley Library Catalogue* (1922–36) and in his *Two
Lake Poets* (1927) deal only with books in his own possession; some of
the descriptions are marred by self-deception. Pioneer though Wise
was in author-bibliography, his methods are less systematic and
complete than contemporary practice demands. George Healey's
bibliography of *The Cornell Wordsworth Collection* (1957), as far as it
includes Coleridge items, is a splendid model of precision and inclusiveness. John Louis Haney's privately printed *Bibliography* (1903),
technically less ambitious than Wise's work, is still much more useful,
inclusive, and reliable than Wise's scathing dismissal of the book would
suggest: it contains, among a number of interesting features, the first
attempt at a list of Coleridge's annotated books (a list that can now be
greatly extended) and is strong in American editions. The *New Cambridge Bibliography of English Literature*, III (1969) offers a fairly
complete but immethodical checklist of biographical and critical studies
to 1967, unhappily not innocent of errors and omissions. Richard
Haven will be publishing shortly a more thorough list (*Coleridge 1794–
1970: An annotated Bibliography*). *English Romantic Poets: A Review of
Research*, edited by T. M. Raysor, first issued in 1950 and revised in
1956, is now being rewritten: it can be expected to give a useful account
of 'the state of the art'.

But here, at the thought of checklists of textual, biographical, and
critical studies of Coleridge, the guide's heart fails: already so much has
been neglected in my account—about the philosophy, the relation to the

Germans, the 'Opus maximum' and the 'system', his social and political
writing, his journalism, his knowledge of Greek and Italian and music
and painting; his Biblical and theological studies, his excursions into
psychiatry, comparative religion, anthropology, the philosophy of
history. Here the reader must find his own way among the primary and
secondary materials with the stout heart of a pearl-diver and something
of the opportunist's swashbuckling zest. There are many memorable
books and essays; and there is much dross, and for the reader some
foot-slogging. But Coleridge, himself an avid reader of Jacob Boehme,
Hieronymus Fracastorius, Immanuel Swedenborg, and Giambattista
Vico, and a careful reader of reports on the slave trade, the poor laws,
the state of agriculture, and Animal Magnetism, would not be the person
to deny that 'a maggot may catch a Fish, and a Fish may have a
Diamond Ring in its Guts . . . or the Seal of Solomon'.[1]

IV

Coleridge himself has some good things to say about the readerly
virtues. A favourite maxim of his was: *'until you understand a writer's
ignorance, presume yourself ignorant of his understanding.'*[2] Jonathan Swift
said: 'When I am reading a book, whether wise or silly, it seems to me
to be alive and talking to me.' Many of the marginalia and notebook
entries show that it was the same with Coleridge.

It is often said, that Books are companions—they are so, dear, very
dear, Companions! But I often when I read a book that delights
me on the whole, feel a pang that the Author is not present—that
I cannot *object* to him this & that—express my sympathy &
gratitude for this part, & mention some fact that self-evidently
oversets a second. Start a doubt about a third—or confirm & carry

[1] BM MS Egerton 2801, f 57: watermark 1827. Printed in *Inquiring
Spirit* 202. *Cf. Notebooks*, II, 2784: 'What thousands of Threads in how
large a Web may not a Metaphysical Spider spin out of the Dirt of his
own Guts/ . . .'
[2] *Biog. Lit.*, I, 160. For variants, see *e.g. Notebooks*, I, 928; CL, III, 278.

a fourth thought. At times, I become restless: for my nature is very social.[1]

For the second essay in the 1818 *Friend* he chose a motto from Erasmus that enjoined the reader to 'sit down to a book . . . as a well-behaved visitor does to a banquet'. But Coleridge knew well that a good reader needs something more than good manners, and liked to point out something that he picked up from the *Mishnah* or from Donne's *Biathanatos*—that there are four kinds of readers:

1. Sponges, who absorb all they read, and return it nearly in the same state, only a little dirtied.
2. Sand-glasses, who retain nothing, and are content to get through a book for the sake of getting through the time.
3. Strain-bags, who retain merely the dregs of what they read.
4. Mogul diamonds, equally rare and valuable, who profit from what they read, and enable others to profit by it also.[2]

The virtues of the Mogul-diamond reader are explored elsewhere:

The conveyal of Knowlege by Words is in direct proportion to the stores and faculties of Observation (internal or external) of the person, who hears or reads them.[3]

What you have acquired by patient thought and cautious discrimination, demands a portion of the same effort in those who are to receive it from you.[4]

The reader, who would follow a close reasoner to the summit and absolute principle of any one important subject, has chosen a Chamois-hunter for his guide. Our guide will, indeed, take us the shortest way, will save us many a wearisome and perilous wandering, and warn us of many a mock road that had formerly led himself to the brink of chasms and precipices, or at best in an idle circle to the spot from whence he started. But he cannot

[1] *Notebooks*, II, 2322: Dec., 1804.
[2] *Sh. Crit.*, II, 39; *cf.* I, 221. The fullest version is in *Notebooks*, III, 3242, printed *variatim* in *Sh. Crit.*, I, 220–1. As for source-hunting, see *Notebooks*, II, 2375: 'I fear not him for a Critic who can confound a fellow-thinker with a Compiler.' The Erasmus motto is at *Friend*, I, 14; 15–16n.
[3] *Notebooks*, III, 4309.
[4] *Aids to Reflection*, 186.

carry us on his shoulders: we must strain our own sinews, as he has strained his; and make a firm footing on the smooth rock for ourselves, by the blood of toil from our own feet.[1]

We have encountered the Chamois-hunter figure before; we seem to be coming full circle. 'Alas!', he said in *The Friend,* 'legitimate reasoning is impossible without severe thinking, and thinking is neither an easy nor an amusing employment.'[2] Now, 'Thought and attention [are] very different Things—I never expected the former . . . from the Readers of the Friend—I did expect the latter, and was disappointed.'[3]

> In ATTENTION, we keep the mind *passive*: in THOUGHT, we rouse it into activity. In the former, we submit to an impression— we keep the mind steady in order to *receive* the stamp. In the latter, we seek to *imitate* the artist, while we ourselves make a copy or duplicate of his work. . . . [*S*]*elf*-knowledge, or an insight into the laws and constitution of the human mind and the *grounds* of religion and true morality, in addition to the effort of attention requires the energy of THOUGHT.[4]

If we are not prepared to make the first effort of attention and then engage in the activity of thinking, Coleridge's writing will remain for us 'for ever a sealed-up volume, a deep well without a wheel or windlass': this, he said, would have been the fate even of Shakespeare's 'inexhaustible mine of virgin treasure' but for the 'living comment and interpretation' of fine actors.[5]

In reading Coleridge we may often feel, as Coleridge felt in listening to 'the mockery of logic' by Hamlet and the clowns: that we are meeting 'the traditional wit valued like truth for its antiquity, and treasured up, like a tune, for use'.[6] When he chooses for his judge

> the earnest *impersonal* Reader
> Who in the work forgets me and the world and himself

[1] *Friend,* I, 55.
[2] *Ibid.*
[3] *Notebooks,* III, 3670: 3 Jan., 1810. The marginal note cited in n 1, p. 26 above also discusses this point.
[4] *Aids to Reflection,* 4n.
[5] *Sh. Crit.,* I, 186.
[6] *Sh. Crit.,* I, 33.

our minds turn towards his epitaph. But they turn also to that essay written for the *Encyclopaedia Metropolitana* in which he explores the need for *method*—method initiated and shaped by an intuition of the integral nature of the thing or matter under inquiry. When he counsels the reader of Shakespeare he also offers a paradigm for the reader of his own work.

> O gentle critic! be advised. Do not trust too much to your professional dexterity in the use of the scalping knife, and tomahawk. Weapons of diviner mould are wielded by your adversary: and you are meeting him here on his own peculiar ground, the ground of *Idea*, of Thought, and of inspiration.

2: Coleridge and Poetry:
I. Poems of the Supernatural

JOHN BEER

HOWEVER CRITICS have rated Coleridge as a poet, most have agreed that there is a superadded, even 'magical' quality about his writing in the year 1797-8. One is tempted to write of him as a man who had found himself on a green paradisal island which had been raised above the sea by some hidden volcanic action and which would be removed again, shortly afterwards, by the same mysterious agency. He sometimes wrote more subtly afterwards, or improved his work by new and vivid touches, but he did not again achieve the effortless enchantment which marked his best poetry in that year.

Literary miracles do not happen in quite such an arbitrary fashion, however. It would be truer to say that when the human mind is about to express itself in some new manner the onus often falls on single, fallible mortals, trying to resist the pressures to conform which pursue conservatives and revolutionaries alike, and that they may not be able to sustain the purity of their achievement for long. There will also be, in the previous tradition, a mass of hidden roots leading to their achievement.

Where should one look for the roots of Coleridge's achievement? Many have been found, often in the most recondite places, but some are so obvious that we might easily overlook them altogether. When T. S. Eliot was invited to write a biography of him for a National Portrait Gallery postcard many years ago, his first sentence ran: 'When five years old had read the Arabian Nights.'[1] This opening, despite its mannered appearance, shows considerable insight (and may, incidentally, shed some diffused light on Eliot himself, who was also a voracious childhood reader). For the Eastern tales, with their great vogue in the

[1] Quoted K. Coburn, *Twentieth Century Views*, 1.

eighteenth century, were in many ways a new literary force. Although the European romance-tradition might appear to offer a different way of apprehending human experience from that offered by the rationalist and legalist philosophy which dominated intellectual life, its devotion to Christian values made it also an indirect supporter of that order. It provided a means of relaxation, not a serious challenge. The Eastern tale, with its harsher climate and more direct invocations of magic, touched daemonic springs in the imagination which might simply be soothed and charmed to sleep by the blander European romances.

For Coleridge as a child, the experience of reading the *Arabian Nights* was not just a pleasant pastime. The volume came to exercise such a compulsive power over him that he was afraid to read it except under propitious conditions: 'I distinctly remember the anxious and fearful eagerness, with which I used to watch the window, in which the books lay—and whenever the Sun lay upon them, I would seize it, carry it by the wall, and bask, and read.' (CL, I, 347) His father, who belonged to a sober and godly tradition, burnt the books when he discovered their effect on his son; though it might have been better if he had been allowed to work through the experience in his own way, instead of having it left as an unresolved trauma. For his own part, Coleridge always maintained that he had gained from this reading, and that when his father had later tried to teach him about the wonder of the stars he was preaching to the already converted—'For from my early reading of Faery Tales, and Genii &c—my mind had been habituated *to the Vast . . .*' (*Ibid*, 354).

The taste for romance continued, and was perhaps stimulated further by finding himself an orphan and an exile at Christ's Hospital, where straightforward physical hunger and his obsessive enjoyment of reading combined to create a strange condition:

> Conceive what I must have been at fourteen; I was in a continual low fever. My whole being was, with eyes closed to every object of present sense, to crumple myself up in a sunny corner and read, read, read—fancy myself on Robinson Crusoe's Island, finding a mountain of plum-cake, and eating a room for myself, and then eating it into the shapes of tables and chairs—hunger and fancy![1]

[1] J. Gillman, *Life of Coleridge*, 1838, I, 20.

Coleridge in 1795, by P. Vandyke

Coleridge's reading at school was not confined to romances, of course. The imagination which had been awakened by them was led into further fields as Coleridge's intellect developed; he found himself exploring all forms of speculation which rendered the world a more magical place than contemporary rationalism allowed it to be. He 'conjured over Boehme' and translated the hymns of Synesius; years afterwards his younger schoolfellow Charles Lamb was to remember how he had heard him standing in the cloisters, unfolding 'the mysteries of Jamblichus or Plotinus . . . or reciting Homer in his Greek, or Pindar . . .'.[1]

This taste for poetry and metaphysical speculation was in no way removed from Coleridge's enjoyment of romance; rather it marked an attempt to give philosophical respectability to the effects of that enjoyment by proving that the strange effect of reality which the romance conveyed to the mind was not after all an illusion but did in fact tell us something important about the nature of 'reality'. But if this belief was the source of some of Coleridge's most valuable psychological insights it could in the short run relax his grasp on the objective reality of the particular situations which he had to face. His college debts, his subsequent enlistment as a dragoon and his ill-advised marriage were all examples of a recurrent failing which also showed itself in a propensity to fabricate a version of his past, present or future that did not altogether fit the facts. There was no cunning or malice in such fabrications, however: they were most often produced to meet some pressing need of the moment—to retain the affection or goodwill of a friend, or to convince a publisher that a promised work really would, in the end, be produced.

It would be wrong to imagine from this that Coleridge was not a practically-minded man. He could show penetrating insight into questions of politics or commerce and there were times when he made a career in political journalism. After his army experience he collaborated for a time with the more sober Southey as a lecturer in Bristol, then established his own journal, *The Watchman*. But the pressure of his intellectual and imaginative concerns, and the light which he thought they might throw on human nature, along with his desire to be a great

[1] Lamb, *Works*, ed. Lucas, 1903–5, II, 21.

poet, were always undermining his attempts to undertake a more orthodox career.

Even during periods when he was largely devoting himself to more mundane writing, the Eastern tales continued to work strongly in his imagination. Their descriptions of scenes conjured up by spirits were a stimulus for new departures in landscape poetry; and their sensuous scenes provided a medium for discreet exploration of the erotic. Thus James Ridley's *Tales of the Genii*, though always finally directed towards the inculcation of virtue under the guise of Allah, were full of arresting descriptions of pleasure. When Coleridge wrote of the Aeolian harp (in his poem of that name) that

> *Like some coy maid half yielding to her lover,*
> *It pours such sweet upbraiding, as must needs*
> *Tempt to repeat the wrong!*   (PW, I, 101)

he was probably drawing on Ridley's description of the carvings in the mansion at Shadaski, which included, among other scenes, 'coyly willing virgins; who seemed, even in the ivory in which they were carved, to show a soft reluctance'[1]—indeed, the whole poem, showing Coleridge and Sara at Clevedon, may contain some reminiscences of the main delight depicted in the carvings; that of 'the joys of sweet retirement with the favourite nymph' (I, 71). (When they finally left the cottage, a year later, he wrote a poem entitled 'Reflections on having left a Place of Retirement'.[2])

As we have mentioned, however, Coleridge's reading of romances was now no longer undertaken in pursuit of a straightforward absorption in pleasured imagination. His approach had become more sophisticated: he wanted to explain *why* romances should have exercised and continued to exercise such a hold on him, and why that hold should be so

---

[1] *Tales of the Genii*, 3rd ed. 1766, I, 70.
[2] 'Retirement' was, of course, a common ideal in the eighteenth century. Ridley's *Tales*, which were all, apparently, inventions, offer an unusual blend of qualities. Their dominating oriental exoticism shades off into touches of European romance, eighteenth-century taste and Western moral values. This may account for their particular appeal to writers who, like Coleridge, were still absorbing the new impact of the Eastern tale.

different from the sense of the world which was given by the rationalist society around him. It is a commonplace that the full experience of reading romance is like that of passing into a different world; what Coleridge wanted to investigate was the psychological truth within that commonplace. Against the current of eighteenth-century thought which allowed for such diversions simply as a relief from the more serious concerns of the everyday world, he was inclined to believe that the romance played a far more important part in human experience—and that it was, among other things, associated importantly with the religious sense.

This belief was linked with others, all of them forming a part of his reactions to the French Revolution. The meaningless bloodshed of the events in France, and the failure of his own limited scheme of 'pantiso-cracy', had convinced him that schemes for the amelioration of man-kind could come about only through a deeper understanding of human nature. Despite the enthusiasm of the people during the early stages of the revolution, later events had shown that a revolutionary act could not by itself change the wills of men to the extent that was needed for lasting improvement of society. Violence in such a context simply bred further violence.

If the revolution could not come about through a straightforward application of reason, was it possible to charm the wills of mankind in some other way? The idea led Coleridge back to his explorations of extra-rational phenomena. The late eighteenth century had shown deep interest in everything that had to do with 'genius', for example, seeing in such powers an element which might pass beyond ordinary human faculties and guard against the ultimate sterility of an 'age of reason'. The genius need not be an artist. He might be a scientist, penetrating the inward meaning of the universe, or a priest, bringing heaven before men's eyes, or a ruler, controlling his people not by physical coercion but by a wisdom which was also imaginative enough to appeal to their total nature and so educe a willing co-operation from them. In each case, the implication is the same. Men are most fully compelled, not by physical coercion, but by the imaginative power of the genius, which makes an irresistible and completely satisfying appeal to the whole man.

The full range of Coleridge's intellectual pursuits during these years

cannot be covered here; I have explored his early interest in religion
and mythology more fully in a previous study[1] and hope to take a harder
look at his psychological theories in a later one. It is enough to suggest,
briefly, that he was drawn towards the conception of a hidden tradition
of wisdom, emerging from time to time under various guises in the
religions and mythologies of mankind. In particular he was struck by
the fact that all religions, however wide their divergences, seemed to
contain two stable elements: a belief in God and a belief in immortality.
He was also interested in the association made by many mystical
thinkers between the sun and the ultimate nature of God, and in the
devotion paid to the sun in many ancient religions. One form of this
devotion, found in Egyptian hieroglyphics and other emblems all over
the world, showed itself in the recurring emblem of the sun, the serpent
and the wings, the sun expressing the central being of God, the serpent
the energy which goes out from it and the wings the love that returns to
it. This esoteric form of the Trinity seems to have appealed particularly
to Coleridge both as an image of the creative process and as a paradigm
for the explanation of human nature. According to it, human evil
would be seen as the result of energy being separated from its source,
and becoming consequently corrupt. If it is not renewed by the return
to its source, as imaged in the wings in the emblem, the state of corruption must continue. But when there is a flow of love between the
source of all love and the individual organism the broken cycle is
restored and human energies flourish again in their beauty. A fragment
for the poem *The Destiny of Nations* uses this pattern of ideas (and fore-
shadows *The Ancient Mariner*): Coleridge describes how Night is always
striving to

> *regain the losses of that hour*
> *When Love rose glittering, and his gorgeous wings*
> *Over the abyss fluttered with such glad noise,*
> *As what time after long and pestful calms,*
> *With slimy shapes and miscreated life*

---

[1] *Coleridge the Visionary*, London 1959. This study may be consulted
for amplification and further justification of many points made here
concerning Coleridge's intellectual interests, particularly in the
years before 1798. The present essay contains new material, however.

> *Poisoning the vast Pacific, the fresh breeze*
> *Wakens the merchant-sail uprising.*   (PW, I, 140)

But if some such esoteric explanation of human evil were true it also
followed that knowledge of it could not be left to reason alone: it
would be better grasped in the sphere of the imagination. And it was
therefore important that the human imagination should be nourished,
not starved. In the same poem Coleridge stressed the work of fancy
in keeping alive important forms of knowledge, using the image of
the Northern Lights which both guide the Laplander through the
winter darkness and remind him of the sun that will return. He went on
to justify this work of the imagination in explicit terms:

> *For Fancy is the power*
> *That first unsensualises the dark mind,*
> *Giving it new delights; and bids it swell*
> *With wild activity; and peopling air,*
> *By obscure fears of Beings invisible,*
> *Emancipates it from the grosser thrall*
> *Of the present impulse, teaching Self-control,*
> *Till Superstition with unconscious hand*
> *Seat Reason on her throne.*   (PW, I, 134)

He explained how some of the Laplander's own superstitions teach
important forms of the wisdom—as in the legends

> *with which*
> *The polar ancient thrills his uncouth throng:*
> *Whether of pitying Spirits that make their moan*
> *O'er slaughtered infants, or that Giant Bird*
> *Vuokho, of whose rushing wings the noise*
> *Is Tempest, when the unutterable Shape*
> *Speeds from the mother of Death, and utters once*
> *That shriek, which never murderer heard, and lived.*
>   (PW, I, 134)

Such superstitions keep alive pathos and the sublime: they teach,
through tenderness and fear, the ways of a universe in which those
emotions are centrally significant.

What is true of superstition in primitive society is true also, in more

civilized societies, of romance: it too keeps the mind open to possibilities which a dominant rationalism might otherwise hide.

Coleridge's thinking on this last point was at its height in the autumn
of 1797. On October 14th he wrote to Thelwall about the 'littleness' of
most human knowledge and emotions: 'the universe itself—what but an
immense heap of *little* things?' Something more was needed to induce
in him the sense of sublime:

> My mind feels as if it ached to behold and know something
> great—something *one and indivisible*—and it is only in the faith of
> this that rocks or waterfalls, mountains or caverns give me the
> sense of sublimity or majesty!—But in this faith *all things*
> counterfeit infinity!   (CL, I, 349)

A day or two later using much the same arguments, he wrote to Poole
that he could not agree with those who contended that the reading of
romances and fairy tales by children should be discouraged:

> Should children be permitted to read Romances, and Relations of
> Giants and Magicians, and Genii?—I know all that has been said
> against it; but I have formed my faith in the affirmative.—I know
> no other way of giving the mind a love of 'the Great', and 'the
> Whole'.—Those who have been led to the same truths step by
> step thro' the constant testimony of their senses, seem to me to
> want a sense which I possess—They contemplate nothing but
> *parts*—and all *parts* are necessarily little—and the Universe to them
> is but a mass of *little things*.   (CL, I, 354)

This defence of the romance as an educative force opens the way for a
view of art which might offer more play to romance elements than had
normally been allowed for in eighteenth-century literary orthodoxy.
Johnson's view that the function of art was 'to instruct by pleasing' is
here being given a new literalness: in Coleridge's view the romance is
not simply an aid to the transmission of moral truth; it conveys a truth
of its own which cannot easily be transmitted in any other way. And
when we compare the final phrase of the first extract ('in this faith *all
things* counterfeit infinity'[1]) with a fragment from an early notebook:

---

[1] The phrase 'counterfeit infinity', comes from Cudworth's *Intellectual
System*. See W. Schrickx, 'Coleridge and the Cambridge Platonists',
REL, 1966, VII, 80–1.

> great things that on the ocean
> counterfeit infinity
>
> (*Notebooks*, I, 273)

we can see how this line of thinking was leading Coleridge toward the writing of a romance in which 'great things . . . on the ocean' would play a leading part.

As often with the creative process, however, the journey to this particular version of the romance did not take place in a direct line. In 1797 Coleridge's thinking, which had become intimately involved with that of Wordsworth, had been concerned with a slightly different issue: that of the origin of evil and the relationship of emotions such as guilt and remorse to human actions in general. These questions had been central to the dramas which they had been composing: Wordsworth's *The Borderers* and Coleridge's *Osorio*. Since it was not clear that these dramas were likely to have a popular success—or indeed that they would ever be performed at all—one project which now preoccupied them was that of producing a work on the same theme which might enjoy a larger circulation and so enable them to earn some money by devoting themselves to the larger and more important works which, they agreed, ought to be the object of their main poetic labours.

The first idea for such a work was the projected prose-tale, 'The Wanderings of Cain'. It seems likely, from various pieces of evidence, that the walk on which this piece was planned took place in November 1797, and was also the occasion of the most dramatic event in Coleridge's poetic career: the composition of *Kubla Khan*.[1] If so (and for the purposes of the following tentative reconstruction I shall assume that it was) it could be argued that the idea of Cain helped to organize *Kubla Khan* and that the liberation of writing this poem in turn provided one of the necessary stages in the transition from the gothic glooms of the Cain drafts to the vivid positive colours of *The Ancient Mariner*.

[1] The date of the poem has been a matter of some dispute, partly because Coleridge in his later published note gave it as 'the summer of 1797'—which is very unlikely. The earlier Crewe MS note states that it was composed in 'the fall of the year, 1797', which is more possible, and M. L. Reed has recently argued persuasively (*Wordsworth: The Chronology of the Early Years, 1770–99*, 1967, 208–9nn.) that it was

There is some record of this November walk in an extract from a letter of Dorothy Wordsworth describing the scenery as they went:

[From Porlock] we kept close to the shore about four miles. Our road lay through wood, rising almost perpendicularly from the sea, with views of the opposite mountains of Wales: thence we came by twilight to Lynmouth, in Devonshire. The next morning we were guided to a valley at the top of one of those immense hills which open at each end to the sea, and is from its rocky appearance called the Valley of Stones. We mounted a cliff at the end of the valley, and looked from it immediately on to the sea.

(WL, I, (1967), 194)

From now on we are forced to speculate more, but various items fall into place. Shortly before this Coleridge had completed his *Osorio*, and in the letter to Thelwall just mentioned, described an alternation of moods, between one in which he could see a whole landscape as one entity, the expression of a single 'Almighty Spirit', and one in which he was most conscious of his own isolation. To illustrate the latter he had quoted from his tragedy the speech of his 'Moorish Woman' in response to a statement of a Priest concerning the owl ('Its note comes dreariest in the *fall of the year*'). She had replied by describing the beauty of the scene:

The hanging Woods, that touch'd by Autumn seem'd
As they were blossoming hues of fire and gold,

---

composed during the course of a visit to the Valley of Rocks in early November. It is noticeable that when Coleridge referred to the situation of the farmhouse he described it as 'between Porlock and Linton' (prefaces) or 'between Porlock and Ilfracombe' (Unpublished *Table Talk*, TLS, 10 May 1957, 293), but that when he speaks of the actual retirement, in a manuscript note, he says 'between Linton and Porlock' (quoted by E. K. Chambers, RES, 1938, XI, 78–80); this reversal of direction lends some weight to the idea that, while returning from the Valley, Coleridge was taken ill and forced to retire to the lonely farmhouse, while William and Dorothy Wordsworth continued on their way back (on their way possibly, despatching the 'person on business from Porlock' to bring supplies of some sort to Coleridge).

The hanging Woods, most lovely in decay,
The many clouds, the Sea, the Rock, the Sands,
Lay in the silent moonshine—and the Owl,
(Strange, very strange!) the Scritch-owl only wak'd,
Sole Voice, sole Eye of all that world of Beauty!—
Why, such a thing am I?—Where are these men?
I need the sympathy of human faces
To beat away this deep contempt for all things
Which quenches my revenge!

(CL, I, 350)

It is perhaps significant that Coleridge should have returned to that phrase, 'the fall of the year' when he later recalled the time of composition of *Kubla Khan*, the more particularly since this use of the phrase suggests that he may have been thinking of the contrast, in literal terms, between 'spring' and 'fall'—spring being the season in which the budding of the trees and nesting of birds make us conscious of 'the one Life' and helps us to see the unity of all things, while 'fall' is the season when the fall of the leaf reminds us of death and therefore exposes our sense of isolation and mortality to the bone.

If we imagine Coleridge and Wordsworth discussing the relationship between the phenomena of life and decay, the sense of sublimity, and the religious sense, as they passed along the wooded shores of the Bristol Channel to Linton, it would be natural for them to be reminded of a passage from Shaftesbury,[1] who ends one part of his rhapsody *The Moralists* by making one of his speakers exemplify the link between the sublime and the religious sense in terms of reactions to a landscape.

[1] Both poets speak of Shaftesbury in terms which suggest a deep influence: Wordsworth mentions Shaftesbury as 'an author at present unjustly depreciated' in his 'Essay Supplementary'; see also W. J. B. Owen, *Wordsworth as Critic*, 1969, 49n (on Shaftesbury and *Prelude VI*) and M. Rader, *Wordsworth: a Philosophical Approach*, Oxford 1967, 52–5; for Coleridge see CL, I, 214 and the discussion in R. L. Brett's *Third Earl of Shaftesbury*, 1951. The landscape near Porlock remained in Coleridge's mind as memorably sublime: cf., e.g., CL, I, 498 where he mentions 'the great rocky fragments which jut out from the Hills both here & at Porlock & which alas! we have not at dear Stowey!'

He describes the scene at the foot of Mount Atlas and talks of the effects of this rocky desolation and of dark wooded landscapes on the spirits of travellers:

Beneath the *Mountain's* foot, the rocky Country rises into Hills, a proper Basis of the ponderous Mass above: where huge embody'd Rocks lie pil'd on one another, and seem to prop the high Arch of Heaven.—See! with what trembling Steps poor Mankind tread the narrow Brink of the deep Precipices! From whence with giddy Horror they look down, mistrusting even the Ground which bears 'em; whilst they hear the hollow Sound of Torrents underneath, and see the Ruin of the impending Rock; with falling Trees which hang with their Roots upwards, and seem to draw more Ruin after'em. Here thoughtless Men, seiz'd with the Newness of such Objects, become thoughtful, and willingly contemplate the incessant Changes of this Earth's Surface. They see, as in one instant, the Revolutions of past Ages, the fleeting Forms of Things, and the Decay even of this our *Globe*; whose Youth and first Formation they consider, whilst the apparent Spoil and irreparable Breaches of the wasted Mountain shew them the World it-self only as a noble Ruin, and make them think of its approaching Period.—But here mid-way the *Mountain*, a spacious Border of thick Wood harbours our weary'd Travellers: who now are come among the ever-green and lofty Pines, the Firs, and noble Cedars, whose towring Heads seem endless in the Sky; the rest of Trees appearing only as Shrubs beside them. And here a different Horror seizes our shelter'd Travellers, when they see the Day diminish'd by the deep Shapes of the vast Wood; which closing thick above, spreads Darkness and eternal Night below. The faint and gloomy Light looks horrid as the Shade it-self: and the profound Stillness of these Places imposes Silence upon Men, struck with the hoarse Echoings of every Sound within the spacious Caverns of the Wood. Here *Space* astonishes. *Silence* it-self seems pregnant; whilst an unknown Force works on the Mind, and dubious Objects move the wakeful Sense. Mysterious *Voices* are either heard or fansy'd: and various Forms of *Deity* seem to present themselves, and appear more manifest in these sacred Silvan Scenes; such as of old gave rise to Temples, and favour'd the Religion of the antient World. Even we our-selves, who in plain Characters may read DIVINITY from so many bright Parts of Earth, chuse rather these obscurer Places, to spell out that mysterious Being, which to our weak Eyes appears at best under a Veil of Cloud.[1]

It is, as I have said, necessarily speculation to suppose that this passage from their admired Shaftesbury was in the minds of Wordsworth and Coleridge during the walk, but the speculation turns out to fit the main result of the tour in a curiously exact way. According to Hazlitt, Coleridge told him the following summer that he and Wordsworth were to have made the Valley of Rocks 'the scene of a prose-tale, which was to have been in the manner of, but far superior to, the *Death of Abel*, but they had relinquished the design'.[2] This projected tale was 'The Wanderings of Cain', and it is perhaps significant that the long fragment which survives opens, not in the Valley of Rocks, but in a dark forest, where Cain is making his way with difficulty, and where the darkness becomes a correlative for his own sense of guilt and oppression. While his son, the innocent child of nature, Enos, leads him into the moonlight, Cain searches restlessly for 'the god of the dead' (PW, I, 292).

A reconstruction of the conversations during the walk on which 'The Wanderings of Cain' was planned might run something like this. As Wordsworth and Coleridge walked along the path near Porlock, sometimes passing into dark woods, sometimes coming into view of the Bristol Channel, they talked of the relationship between fear, the dark places of Nature, and the sense of sublimity. Wordsworth's contribution to the discussion would draw heavily on his own recent experience, which had led him towards despair concerning politics and an isolation which, though giving him a sense of the sublime, was also in danger of becoming pride and contempt; from this he had learned to extricate himself by the cultivation of human sympathy.[3] Coleridge, for his part, would, in discussing the relation between sublimity and fear, associate it more naturally with the phenomena of genius. Genius, he would argue, differs according to whether it is associated with life or death.

[1] Shaftesbury, *Characteristics*, 2nd ed., 1714, II, 389-91.
[2] 'My First Acquaintance with Poets': *Works*, ed. Howe, XVII, 120.
[3] See 'Lines left upon a seat in a Yew-tree . . .' in *Lyrical Ballads*, for his poetic exploration of the idea in connection with a bright landscape seen from a dark wooded place.

The man whose genius is associated with a strong sense of life is happy and self-contained. He drinks of his own genius as at a self-renewing fountain and creates his works of art with the effortlessness of a sun rising and illuminating the entire landscape. But if his consciousness includes a strong sense of death, the nature of his genius becomes correspondingly different. The very objects which before reflected his sense of his own immortality and were splendid now become objects of fear to him. He becomes obsessed by savage and ruinous places which speak more directly to his new fears.

And with the range of his recent reading in mythology in mind Coleridge could go on to illustrate this phenomenon from an effortlessly remembered range of reference. This, he would argue, was the significance of the many traditions concerning Cain and his descendants. It was in Cain's murder of Abel that the sense of death in man had first been made actual; in killing his brother he had also become aware that he himself would one day cease to be. Adam in Eden had known the state of absolute genius: the sun-illuminated garden and the self-renewing fountain which reflected the light of the sun. But Cain found it more natural to seek out desolate places, whose gloom suited his new sense of death. Anything associated with his former sense of immortality was now an occasion of fear. When he and his descendants came to any place which reminded them of that lost glory they treated it with awe and respect and sought in some way to propitiate the power which they sensed there. Hence the ancient tradition that the sons of Cain became sun-worshippers and built the stone circles and the enclosed temples to the sun which were often found by rivers in ancient civilizations, and that the sons of Tubal-Cain devoted themselves to work in metals. Hence, too, the universal awe of great rocky places, which reminded men of their loss of paradise—whether they pictured it as a city of Atlantis, flooded by a Deluge, or as a paradise-garden laid waste by some great natural disaster—a volcanic eruption, or an earthquake unsettling great rocks.

If these ideas were running through their minds, it would be only natural for them to continue the theme as they visited the Valley of Rocks. Hazlitt, returning to the Valley with them the following summer described it as

. . . bedded among precipices overhanging the sea, with rocky caverns beneath, into which the waves dash, and where the sea-gull for ever wheels its screaming flight. On the tops of these are huge stones thrown transverse, as if an earthquake had tossed them there, and behind these is a fretwork of perpendicular rocks, something like the *Giant's Causeway*.[1]

Faced with this wilder landscape after the scenes of late autumn in North Somerset, it would be natural to think of it as a scene in which a man obsessed by the fear of death might feel himself strangely at home, since such scenes would at least give his fears objective embodiment. And why should one not write a prose poem about the state of mind of Cain as he wanders through various landscapes of this sort, sometimes obsessed by fear in dark cavernous places, sometimes finding a dreary but reassuring embodiment of the same fears in places where there is no life, yet where great forms continue to exist, reassuring him by their very presence?

If indeed cultivation of the sublime reflected a universal desire to regain a lost glory, a work of this sort might have a universal appeal. Gessner's *Death of Abel*, after all, had enjoyed an extraordinary success throughout Europe by its appeal to the universal sense of pathos; why should not an equivalent piece devoted to the universal human sense of the sublime achieve an equal popularity? Such a piece, moreover, could draw on the perceptions of both poets. Coleridge could use the same theme which he had recently employed in *Osorio*—that a sense of vestigial life in a moonlit and beautiful landscape might more successfully remind a man obsessed by death of a possible universe of life than all the normal manifestations of life by the light of common day. He would therefore give Cain the company of his child Enos, who retained a perception of the inherent beauty of life which was lost to his father Cain. And Wordsworth, in turn, would be given some opportunity for the expression of his own sense of the vividness with which natural human kindness could strike a man who had been obsessed by the desolation and despair of human life generally.

We may go on to suppose that this plan was in the minds of the two poets as they began their homeward journey, but that while passing

[1] 'My First Acquaintance with Poets', *Works*, ed. Howe, XVII, 120.

through Culbone Coleridge was seized with dysentery so fierce that he found it necessary to retire to a farmhouse for a time until he recovered. (Wordsworth later recalled that on their walks in Somerset he had sometimes been seized by pains which caused him to 'throw himself down and writhe like a worm on the ground'.) As it happens, the farm to which he retired could in itself remind him (seriously or humorously) of the obsessive theme of Cain and the ancient sun-worshippers. Its name, Ash Farm, might suggest some ancient and fiery disaster, and it was built as a foursquare enclosure by the side of a stream which could be heard rushing nearby. (Although the idea may seem a trifle tenuous, it receives unexpected support from the fact that when Coleridge tried to remember the name of the farm thirty years later he remembered it as 'Brimstone Farm'—which suggests that some such connection had been running in his mind.[1])

So, it follows, the scene was set, mentally as well as physically, for the composition of the poem *Kubla Khan*. Coleridge opened the volume of Purchas's *Pilgrimage*[2] and there his eye lighted on the words

> In *Xamdu* did *Cublai Can* build a stately Palace, encompassing sixteene mile of plaine ground with a wall, wherein are fertile Meddowes, pleasant Springs, delightful Streames, and all sorts of beasts of chase and game, and in the middest thereof a sumptuous house of pleasure.[3]

The most immediate point which would strike Coleridge in these circumstances would be the link between 'Can' and 'Cain', a connection which was already heavily reinforced by literary allusion. It was commonly supposed that the Tartars, who were still a byword for

---

[1] See 'Morchard Bishop', 'The Farm House of Kubla Khan', TLS, 10 May, 1957, 293, and D. H. Karrfalt, 'Another Note on Kubla Khan and Coleridge's retirement to Ash Farm', NQ, 1966, CCXI, 171-2.

[2] It is not inherently impossible that this book should have been on the shelves of a lonely farmhouse; equally, Coleridge and the Wordsworths might have carried the volume, despite its bulk, to help in planning their poem. But Coleridge had an extraordinary literary memory and it is also conceivable that he simply referred to the book in his mind's eye.

[3] *Purchas his Pilgrimage*, 1626, 418.

fierceness and cruelty in eighteenth-century England, were descendants of Cain (or possibly of Noah's lustful son Cham). To find one of these fierce kings building a gentle place of pleasure would naturally bring to mind the tradition that the descendants of Cain built enclosures sacred to the sun in a vain attempt to regain the glory of their lost paradise.[1] And this brought into play two themes: the image of the sun-enclosure by the sacred river (recorded instances of which include sacred places by the Nile in Egypt and the Alpheus in Greece) and the consciousness of death which Cain's crime brought into the world. These two themes are brought together in the lines which intervene between those describing Kubla Khan's 'decree' and those which amplify Purchas's description:

> *Where Alph, the sacred river, ran*
> *Through caverns measureless to man*
> *Down to a sunless sea.*

There is nothing in Purchas to authorize the introduction of the river, caverns and sea at this point, but it is essential to the structure of ideas in the poem that they should appear here, to describe the state of consciousness of this Tartar descendant of Cain. From many rivers sacred to the sun the Alpheus selected itself partly because its name contained the Aleph/Alpha element which recurs throughout literature and mythology to suggest the primal. The biblical reference to 'Alpha and Omega' is reinforced by Cabbalistic usage: Moses is called Alpha, and Fludd speaks of a fountain becoming infinite when it flows from dark Aleph to light Aleph.[2] But it had a further symbolic potency, also. The tradition that the river Alpheus ran underground to re-emerge as the fountain Arethusa in Sicily was the basis of a Greek love-myth, in which the ardent Alpheus was pictured as always seeking the female Arethusa. And this in turn could be related to Milton's statement that in Eden a part of the river which flowed through the garden returned to feed the central fountain, so that it was always self-renewing.

The river Alph of Coleridge's poem behaves differently, however. There is no Arethusa to complement it, no hint of any self-renewing

[1] See Berkeley's *Siris* (quoted, *Coleridge the Visionary*, 119).
[2] *Cf. Coleridge the Visionary*, 208–10; 342.

fountain: the river runs down through hollow caverns to a sea of death which is devoid of sun. It thus becomes a perfect image for Kubla Khan's basic death-consciousness, that very abyss in himself which urges to the construction of a place of pleasure as a refuge from it. Everything in the garden corresponds to what was known of ancient sun-worship: the circular enclosure itself, the bright streams shining to the sun, the incense which was burnt in its worship, the forests, their darkness relieved by sunny 'spots of greenery'. But the same images also convey a potent sense of immortality. Fraught by the prospect of death, this son of Cain surrounds himself by fertile ground, by an endless maze of rills, by incense (which whenever its scent is perceived gives one a sense of the timeless) and undying forests.

The fact that the Alph does not return as a fountain but runs down to a sunless sea has already suggested the flaw in this paradise, however. Whatever Kubla does, he cannot escape the fact that his paradise must inevitably be lost, just as Milton's was eventually forced to move down to the desolate sea,

> *pusht by the horned floud*
> *With all his verdure spoild and trees adrift*
> *Down the great river to the op'ning Gulf,*
> *And there take root an Iland salt and bare,*
> *The haunt of Seales and Orcs, and Sea-mews clang.*[1]

As it happens this Miltonic scene of desolation (which resembles in atmosphere Hazlitt's description of the Valley of Rocks) appears in *Paradise Lost* shortly after lines which correspond to the opening lines of Coleridge's poem, where Adam in a vision of the future of the world is shown all cities and empires, the first being

> *the destind walls*
> *Of* Cambalu, *seat of* Cathaian Can . . .[2]

The memory of Cambalu here probably helped to transform Purchas's 'Xamdu' into Coleridge's trisyllabic 'Xanadu', and the Miltonic note perceptible here persists throughout the poem, both in the general rhythm and in specific images. In the second stanza it becomes overt in

[1] *Paradise Lost*, xi, 831–5.
[2] *Ibid.*, xi, 387–8.

Wordsworth in 1818, by B. R. Haydon

a further verbal echo, when the words 'cedarn cover' recall both Satan, approaching the human race, just before the temptation, through a landscape of 'stateliest Covert, Cedar, Pine, or Palme'[1] and Adam's later cry,

> *Cover me, ye Pines,*
> *Ye Cedars, with innumerable boughs*[2]

as he seeks to avoid the light of the heavenly shapes after the fall. The 'woman wailing for her daemon-lover' is also reminiscent of the 'Syrian damsels' lamenting the fate of Thammuz in Milton's poem, while in the last stanza the Mount Abora of which the damsel with a dulcimer sings ('Mount Amara' in the Crewe manuscript)[3] looks back to the Mount Amara ('by some supposed true Paradise'[4]), which Milton presents as one of the types of *his* true Paradise, and the 'symphony and song' with which the poet would build his dome recalls the 'Dulcet Symphonies and voices sweet' with which Milton's daemons built their palace of Pandaemonium.[5]

All this points to a reading of *Paradise Lost* which would view the fall of Satan as an allegory of the fall of man's daemonic powers and as an archetype for the exile of Cain.

And these prepossessions, once again, indicate the true subject of the poem. The fact that this poem works through mythological forms does not mean that it is backward-looking; rather, it is a poem about the universal nature of genius, seen as a permanent feature of human experience—a phenomenon to which, we have suggested, Coleridge had devoted a good deal of thought and investigation in his attempts to understand the nature of man. The story of Cain becomes a symbolic explanation of evil as the misdirection of a daemonic force which is, in its pure form, the most necessary and beneficial of human powers.

Coleridge had, as we have seen, devoured many works dealing with the phenomena of genius; but of these one in particular seems to have

---

[1] *Paradise Lost* ix, 435.
[2] *Ibid.*, ix, 1088–9.
[3] Coleridge first wrote 'Amora' then changed it to 'Amara'. See T. C. Skeat, 'Kubla Khan', *British Museum Quarterly*, 1962–3, XXVI, 80.
[4] *Paradise Lost*, iv, 181–2.
[5] *Ibid.*, i, 712.

left a permanent and important impress, which is reflected directly in the poem. Most images in the poem hark back to sources in religion, mythology, and previous poetry; some, such as the 'milk and honey-dew', possess a large variety of sources. Two, however, stand out anomalously. It is not clear why there should be so much stress on the 'dome', which finds no mention in Purchas's original, nor why there should be the sudden dramatic change to a 'deep romantic chasm' in the second stanza. Although there are domes in previous poetry,[1] none strikes one with sufficient resonance to explain the usage here. For this we must turn back to a work which used 'genius' in a different sense: James Ridley's *Tales of the Genii*. Coleridge could not have escaped reading this work in his boyhood; and the happy accident that the eastern agents of the supernatural were referred to sometimes as 'genii' evidently helped to give the word some of the magical connotations which it always has in his writings. The work of human genius could be seen as having something of the same power to change a scene or create a wonder that was exercised in the exotic oriental tales.

In Ridley's book one of the most magical of scenes is the one that is produced by the Genius of Riches for the delectation of the merchant Abudah. The ground is of gold dust, the stones are pearls, the flowers seem formed of vegetable crystal, emeralds and amethysts, and the trees and shrubs are of silver and gold.

> At the farther end of the prospect he beheld a vast and expanded dome, which seemed to cover a whole plane [*sic*], and rose to the clouds. This dome shone so brightly by the reflection of the costly materials of which it was composed, that he could hardly look toward it. However, as it seemed most to take his attention, he advanced up to the dome.
>
> The dome, which was of entire gold, stood upon three hundred pillars of precious stones; one emerald formed the shaft of one pillar, one diamond the capital, and one ruby the pedestal; the intermediate spaces between the pillars were of crystal, one piece between each pillar; so that the inside of the dome was visible from all parts. The architrave was of solid

---

[1] S. C. Harrex, 'Coleridge's pleasure-dome in "Kubla Khan"', NQ, CCXI, May 1966, 172–3.

pearl, inlaid with curious emblems, composed of festoons of amethysts, topazes, carbuncles, rubies, emeralds, sapphires, and the most sparkling diamonds.[1]

Shortly afterwards Abudah enjoys a second adventure, this time under the aegis of the Queen of Pleasures. He is taken by boat through an even more lovely landscape: as it passes through 'the meanders of the current' he sees 'hanging rocks of different hues; woods of spices, and perfumes breathing sweetness over the cool stream' and many other delights, including the carvings described earlier. But when he tries to open the chest in the centre of the temple the scene is turned to darkness and thunder and broken by the shrieks of the feasters.

> . . . Some, already blasted by the lightning, withered away; others, the ruins of the temple falling in huge fragments, half buried in the earth; the rest in madness running to and fro in despair, tore each other to pieces.[2]

All that is left is the 'dungeon of lust', a cavern through which Abudah makes his way only with difficulty, first by a long descent through filth and stench, then by an equally difficult and slippery ascent. But when he finally appears in the open air he finds himself upon a mountain, where ten thousand voices cry out, 'Long live our sultan, whom the mountains of *Tasgi* have brought forth!'[3]

One further passage seems to contribute to Coleridge's poem. Hassan Assar, the Caliph of Bagdad, was also transported to a delightful landscape, where lofty trees 'formed natural temples to the deities of the place' and 'the adjacent mountains were partly covered with ever green and flowering shrubs'. Here he meets a beautiful houri whom he springs to embrace,

> She also, as animated by the same inclination and desires, hastened toward the embrace of the all-admiring *Hassan*; but, alas, ere the happy couple could meet, the envious earth gave a hideous groan, and the ground parting under their feet, divided them from each other by a dismal chasm.

[1] *Tales of the Genii*, 1766, I, 51–2.
[2] *Ibid.*, I, 77.
[3] *Ibid.*, I, 81.

> While the astonished pair stood on different sides of the
> gulph, viewing the horrid fissure and the dark abyss, wild notes
> of strange uncouth warlike music were heard from the bottom
> of the pit . . .[1]

Hassan learns that this has happened because he had shown himself to
be biased by 'the outward appearance of things'.

These passages help to indicate why there should be such a powerful
antithesis between the images of pleasure in the first stanza of the poem
and the images of destruction in the second, and why these should be
closely linked (with a certain apparent arbitrariness) through landscape
to the themes of peace and war, love and lust. The genii of Ridley's
tales work with the same combination of capriciousness and underlying
morality.

Nevertheless, it is Coleridge's own conception of genius which is
the ultimate ordering force in the poem; in these first two stanzas the
immense weight of influence from earlier literature is all directed and
channelled by that conception into a series of images which present the
two sides of the daemonic in man: the creative indwelling power which
enables him to construct mighty works of engineering or art on the one
hand, and the driving, possessing energy which may urge him on to
great works of destruction on the other. Even while Kubla is constructing his ordered place of pleasure the caverns and sunless sea echo
back to him his fear of death; in the second stanza the savageness and
flawed grandeur of the landscape are eloquent of instincts which may
in less propitious times take over and reduce the landscape to ruin. In
terms of love this danger is represented by the woman wailing for her
daemon lover—unable to regain him yet still longing for him. In terms
of human power the dominant image is that of the fountain, not here the
ordered sun-fountain of the paradisal garden, always returning to
renew itself, but the mighty fountain of destruction, hurling great rocks
into the air; and these portents point to a conclusion in which Kubla
hears voices telling of an ultimate destruction—'ancestral voices
prophesying war'.

Yet as soon as this climax has been reached the tone changes. The
next lines present a picture of the pleasure-dome achieved:

[1] *Tales of the Genii*, I, 135–6.

> *The shadow of the dome of pleasure*
> *Floated midway on the waves;*
> *Where was heard the mingled measure*
> *From the fountain and the caves.*
> *It was a miracle of rare device,*
> *A sunny pleasure-dome with caves of ice!*
>
> (PW, I, 298)

The new feature which is introduced in these lines is the 'caves of ice', which can be traced, at least in part, to Maurice's *History of Hindostan*. Coleridge had copied out of this book some lines describing a strange phenomenon:

> In a cave in the mountains of Cashmere an Image of Ice, which makes it's appearance thus—two days before the new *moon* there appears a bubble of Ice: which increases in size every day till the 15th day, at which it is an ell or more in height: then, as the moon decreases, the Image does also till it vanishes.
>
> (*Notebooks*, I, 240)

The image had evidently struck Coleridge as a fine one for the response of human nature when it responds to its own potentialities of enlightenment. Just as the image of ice, underground, responds perfectly to the phases of the moon, so nature, in moments of joy, harmonizes with the inward forces of the universe. The ice in the cave becomes an underground emblem of the force which is needed to balance the outward energies of nature if destruction is not to ensue. In human terms it also images the mixture of sensuousness and purity which Coleridge, following Milton, held to be the key to human happiness. So the sunny pleasure-dome and caves of ice suggest a balance between reason and sense which Coleridge believes to be attainable in this life—at least under certain conditions.

The contraries of dome and caves are however not the only ones to be held in reconciliation in this stanza, which represents a moment of miraculous harmony between several contending forces; the sunny dome and the caves of ice, the fountain and the caves, the dome and the waves are counterpoised into a pattern which includes all the great contraries of human experience: the ultimate physical contraries of heat and cold, light and darkness, pleasure and pain even, in the sunny dome and the caves of ice; and the metaphysical contraries, both between the vital infinity of springing energy and the deathful infinity of the spatial universe (the fountain and the caves) and between eternity and the flux of time (the shadow of the dome and the flowing river).

But although these six lines describe a miracle, it is a miracle of held tensions, an artistic aim, which, while offering a positive alternative to the negative dialectic between the first and second stanzas, contains in itself no means of achieving itself. Every great artist, in Coleridge's view, is trying to hold together the elements which fall apart in the contraries of Kubla Khan's achievement; instead of the destructiveness and death of that universe he wishes to achieve a state where there is no longer a destructive fountain matched by measureless caverns and a lifeless ocean, but a fountain echoed by caves in 'mingled measure'. But how can that vision be actively created or communicated?

If an answer can be given at all by Coleridge, the form which it would take is suggested in the last stanza of the poem, which resolves the dialectic between the first and second stanzas in a new and more vital fashion by using the sun-symbolism of the one stanza and the moon-symbolism of the other in a different way. Coleridge is here able to use an idea which he drew from Swedenborgianism and from familiar Egyptian mythology: that in this world sun and moon emblematize a fatal separation between heat and light and that if they were reunited we should again see the 'lost sun of eternity'. And since that lost sun would also reveal itself as the essence of humanity, it is appropriate that the poet's voice should finally pass into the first person ('Could I revive within me . . .'). In the second stanza the sunny hopes of the first stanza gave place to a sombre picture of dark heated lust and yearning love beneath a waning moon and this corresponds to a familiar mythological pattern, the most striking example being that of the story of Isis and Osiris in Egyptian mythology, where the world is seen existing always between destructive power (the hot sun or the overflowing Nile—both called Typhon) and the patient recreating power of the moon Isis. Isis is always seeking to replace the fiery Typhon by her lost Osiris, the sun-god who would be her true lover and in whom heat and light would be reconciled. It is the renewed marriage between Osiris and Isis which is figured in this last stanza. When we know that traditionally the dulcimer (or sambuca) was thought to be the female counterpart to Apollo's lyre, and when we discover from Apuleius that the 'Abyssinian maid' was almost certainly a priestess of Isis, the synthesis of sun-mythologies in the last stanza becomes clear. Coleridge is arguing that when the male and female principles harmonize, this makes possible the creation of true art. ('Great men', he once wrote, 'are always androgynous', *Table Talk*, 1 September 1832.) Given the restoration of the 'symphony and song' which come from reunion with the female principle (however mediated) he would be able to produce an art which would be like the sunny domes and caves of ice of the vision, but now produced into reality for all who are charmed into response. Throughout, the picture is of the inspired genius, and more particularly of Apollo, the inspired bard. It is Apollo, with his lyre, for whom the 'damsel with a dulcimer' would be a fitting complement: the Apollo who in mythology built a temple with his music; the Apollo who, when incarnate on earth, appeared with the flashing eyes and floating hair of a sun god.

When the great and complicated structure of ideas and images beneath its deceptively simple surface has been perceived, the poem assumes a different status from that of the impressionist and sensuous poem which it is often taken to be. In relation to Coleridge it seems like a trick played upon him by his own subconscious mind, which had presented him with a short poem to resolve all the themes and images which had so strenuously preoccupied him, yet resolved them into an image so arrogant that he would never be able to reveal its true significance, and would, in publishing the poem, be forced to take cover behind the term 'psychological curiosity'. For the practical critic it presents in an extreme form a problem which must often greet him in reading romantic poetry—that the total poem may not be readily available in the immediate verbal structure which appears on the page. There *is* a fine poem on the page: it moves to the incantation of its own mazy rhythms and turns sinuously in mazes of bright enchantment. But the total poem which is revealed when we explore those images turns out to criticize the self-indulgence of incantation for its own sake and to accept that incantation only as the necessary context for the projection of a more exalted and inclusive view of art.

As a total structure, therefore, *Kubla Khan* exhibits the paradoxes and contradictions of Coleridge's own personality and art. Despite his periods of indulgent sloth (apparent or actual), there was behind all his activities a strenuous urge to make sense of the universe in a way which would give full weight to human imagination. But the problem remained—*Kubla Khan* was (as he sub-titled it) 'a vision in a dream'. Was this vision the extreme projection of a central universal harmony, or simply a fantasy removed, not just once, but twice, from the real?

The dilemma could not be resolved in any simple manner; it remained to haunt Coleridge all his life. Nor was there any obvious point to which he could move, having written the poem. But it seems as if the experience of having written it at least had a liberating effect upon his literary art generally. During the period immediately following its composition Coleridge's work took on a new and more vivid quality: he also became more willing to experiment, less worried if his work did not have the final, consummate wholeness of achievement to which he was ultimately aspiring.

The poem immediately following, *The Ancient Mariner*, exemplifies these new qualities sharply. One can see its roots in many of Coleridge's earlier projects: his idea of writing a long poem on the Origin of Evil; the abortive 'Wanderings of Cain'; and, most important of all, perhaps, the idea (which, according to De Quincey,[1] had preoccupied him during the previous summer) of writing a poem 'on delirium, confounding its own dream scenery with external things, and connected with the imagery of high latitudes'. A major catalyst in precipitating the form of the poem was the idea of bringing together the ballad-mode and the matter of previous travel-accounts, making possible a journey-romance which could allow various features of Coleridge's thinking and imagining to co-exist without requiring any over-rigid intellectual structure. The symbolic structure could be indicated by the elements of the poem without having to be worked out in any fullness of detail, and the poem could therefore be used as an experiment without prejudicing future assaults on the central problem of reconciling reason and imagination. Wordsworth's suggestion that the incident of shooting an albatross might be the central 'crime', and the report of a neighbour, Mr Cruik-

[1] *Collected Writings*, ed. Masson, Edinburgh, 1889, II, 145.

shank, that he had dreamed of a spectre-ship worked by a crew of dead men, also took their part as early organizing features.

None of these features quite accounts for the precise series of incidents which takes place at the beginning of the poem, however, and it may be that in this respect we are closest to its inception when we look at a notebook entry[1] which seems to be recalling the excursion to the Valley of Rocks on which 'The Wanderings of Cain' was projected:

> Valley of Stones—& the three Ships in the Sun, the broad Sun /— Remember at Linton the Pilchard Merchant from Cornwall, who agreed that all the rest of the Catholic Religion would be abandoned / but they would never give up their Fast & Lent Days / No! Never give up Cornish Pilchards!

Why should these incidents have stuck together in Coleridge's mind? That mention of the sun, with the slight plangency of emphasis in its repetition as 'the broad sun', suggests an association with *The Ancient Mariner*, and its 'the broad bright sun'. It may be conjectured, therefore, that the whole passage recalls a sequence of events in which Coleridge and Wordsworth, having visited the sombre Valley of Rocks, with its stark shapes of stones, came out to the sea again and saw three ships out on the sea, brightly illuminated by the setting sun: a picture like this, whether seen as joyful or sinister, would join well with Coleridge's idea of Cain as haunted by emblems both of death and of a lost glory and act as a reminder that images of total joy as well as of fear, may suddenly leap into the mind. The encounter with the pilchard merchant, finally, would bring them back to a realization that for many men such ideas are meaningless, since they live largely in the context of their own immediate concerns. So the pilchard-merchant sees the decline and possible extinction of the Catholic faith finally as a matter

---

[1] *Notebooks*, I, 1535. The editor's note dates the entry 1799, but it does not follow that the incident took place then. R. C. Bald (*Nineteenth Century Studies*, ed. Bald etc., Ithaca, N.Y., 1940, 40) decided regretfully that it was most likely a reference to the expedition of May 1798, when Hazlitt pointed out to Coleridge a ship near Linton which reminded him of the 'spectre-ship'. But it is not necessary to assume that Hazlitt's single ship, seen against the setting sun long before they reached Linton, was one of the *three* mentioned here.

of whether people will give up the fast days on which they eat the Cornish pilchards which are his means of livelihood. Yet there is an innocence about such men and their delight in their everyday lives: never having been forced to face the extremes of human experience which might give them a sense beyond their immediate concerns, they are content to rest in immediate pleasures. If, on the other hand, they are faced by natural or moral disasters, they will have no equipment with which to meet them.

Such reflections on the difference of experience between men like the pilchard-merchant and those who, like Wordsworth and Coleridge, had been forced to take a harder look at human experience, would be relevant to the discussion of pleasure in *Kubla Khan*; it could also have set working the larger themes of *The Ancient Mariner*. For sailors, too, can be seen as men who are largely concerned with their own immediate pleasures; even if their voyages are not always undertaken 'in the broad sun' they are still plotted by charts, compasses and clocks which give them a sense of their own control of events. But supposing that such a sailor were to pass into greater tribulations, where he was the sole survivor among many dead men, and where all sense of time— indeed of journeying—gradually disappeared; could he pass through such a complete disorientation of the normal and not in some important way be changed?

It is this question which seems to lie behind the early incidents of the poem where the Wedding-Guest, the innocent man of sense, is interrupted by the 'experienced' Mariner, whose tale in turn involves the different fates accorded to himself, who through crime has been made to see the nature of the universe behind the humanly-imposed fictions of space and time and who must therefore live a 'life-in-death', haunted by, but not possessed of, what he has seen, and to his shipmates, whose attitude to his shooting of the albatross never rose above a 'superstition' associated always with their own comfort, and whose worst punishment would therefore be their own death.

From an early stage, the events and landscape of the poem lend symbolic depth to its meaning. It was a favourite idea of Coleridge's (an idea which he took over from previous philosophers) that human beings cannot endure unmodified exposure to the divine. Time and space are a creation of the divine mercy to shield human beings from the power of God which, without such protection, would be experienced as pure energy. So in this poem, the sailors curse the fortune which has brought them into the land of mist and snow, and are even ready to applaud the Mariner when his killing of the bird is followed by a breeze—but their pleasure is short-lived, for the breeze brings them into a region where they are becalmed and exposed to the full heat of the sun without alleviation.

The torments of the Mariner and his shipmates are symbolic of all such torments. The energies of the universe, existing now without proper connection to their source, become corrupt. Slimy things crawl on the sea. Strange and sinister fires are seen at night. And when a sail is at last seen, it contains only two nightmare figures, Death and Life-in-Death, who portray the coming fate—the first claiming the ship's crew and the second the Mariner.

As this fate is worked out, the Mariner is left alone with the corruption of the sea and the corruption of the bodies about him, each dead man cursing him with his eye.

Eventually, however, a change comes. Instead of the powerful sun, the moon takes command of the seascape, a body of light replacing one of heat. And while the Mariner is watching the watersnakes from the ship, he is suddenly seized by their beauty and blesses them. This action, which comes from his heart, is described by means of Coleridge's favourite fountain image:

> *A spring of love gushed from my heart,*
> *And I blessed them unaware.*

Immediately the spell begins to break. Once again an inward state is matched by the outward scene: in his relief he falls asleep and dreams of dew, and awakens to find that it is raining. More lights are seen in the sky, this time without sinister suggestion, and a wind blows up. Simultaneously, the dead men rise and begin to work the ropes of the ship, which actually moves on without the breeze having reached it. The climax of this episode comes at dawn, when the ghostly figures cease their work and gather round the mast to hymn the sun. But now the sun is no longer a wrathful sun: it is the lost sun in which heat is tempered by light. Likewise, the hymn is no ordinary chant but a direct exchange of light and music between the figures and the source of their life. At this point, the Mariner is being initiated into the central meaning of the universe as Coleridge conceives it, a universe in which all life is intended to be permeated by light and music:

> . . . *the one Life within us and abroad,*
> *Which meets all motion and becomes its soul,*
> *A light in sound, a sound-like power in light,*
> *Rhythm in all thought, and joyance every where.* . . .
> (*The Eolian Harp*, PW, I, 101)

The morning is quiet, but the Mariner's penance is not yet complete. After a time, the ship gives a sudden bound forward and he drops down, to hear two voices debating his condition, then wakes once more, to see the dead men still cursing him with their eyes. But now that spell is snapped. He turns, to see that the ship is nearing his own native country. In a final vision of beauty across the moonlit bay he sees each corpse surmounted by a spirit, which signals to the land.

From this dreamlike state the poem returns to reality with the arrival in a boat of the pilot, the pilot's boy and the Hermit. The fears voiced by the first two are countered by the assurances and prayers of the Hermit, a true priest of Nature who, like the later Christabel, offers his devotions in the forest. The Mariner begs him for absolution, whereupon he insists on hearing his story. As the Mariner recounts it, we learn that it is the first of many such recountings, for it is now the Mariner's fate to pass through all lands, like the Wandering Jew, seeking the chosen individuals to whom his story can be told.

There were several reasons why *The Ancient Mariner* succeeded where 'The Wanderings of Cain' had not. One was that the subject-matter enabled Coleridge to draw on his rich store of reading in travel-books, where the realistic narrative often passed into descriptions so vivid and exotic as to be hardly distinguishable from romance. John Livingston Lowes, in *The Road to Xanadu*, traced many images in the poem to their sources in earlier travel-books. At the same time, he was able to demonstrate that these images, when they re-emerged, were often magically transformed. A single example will suffice here. Father

Bourzes had described how, at sea, 'Vortices' sometimes appeared and disappeared 'like Flashes of Lightning' and how fish, also, left behind 'a luminous track'. Captain Cook had written of sea animals which were 'a beautiful, pale green, tinged with burnished gloss; and, in the dark . . . had a faint appearance of glowing fire'. Bartram, describing the yellow bream, had recorded that at the gills there was a little spatula 'encircled with silver and velvet black'. Each of these contributed a vividness to Coleridge's stanza:

> *Within the shadow of the ship*
> *I watched their rich attire:*
> *Blue, glossy green, and velvet black,*
> *They coiled and swam; and every track*
> *Was a flash of golden fire.*

—yet the stanza itself is much more that the sum of such parts.[1] *The Ancient Mariner* was written for money (to defray the costs of a walking tour, according to Wordsworth) and the poets were evidently looking for an arresting narrative. They also needed to find a way of writing poetry in a language which was adapted to popular speech. The most obvious form of popular poetry which lay to hand was the ballad, as handed down among the common people from generation to generation. The ballad-form which they came to adopt was not exactly that of the traditional form, however. It lacked the irregularities which one associates with the examples in, say, Percy's *Reliques*. It was the new German form of the long-ballad, as practised by Bürger in *Lenore*, which attracted them. Sir Walter Scott's translation, entitled *William and Helen* (1796), has many stanzas which are closer to the alliteration and rhythms of *The Ancient Mariner* than are those of the earlier ballads, *e.g.*

XLVII

> *Tramp! tramp! along the land they rode;*
> *Splash! splash! along the sea;*
> *The steed is wight, the spur is bright,*
> *The flashing pebbles flee.*

[1] See J. L. Lowes, *The Road to Xanadu*, 1927, 44–53, for the full account.

This form also enabled Coleridge to use a child-like openness of imagery and language, in harmony with his belief that the consciousness of the child expressed certain values which were easily lost in adult life.

But although this form of the ballad and travel-tale combined to give Coleridge the mode with which to create a great poem, it would be wrong to imagine from the deftly-handled shifts and turns of its narrative that the poem, even in its final form, is simply a dramatic and vivid poem with no contours beyond the closely-held plot. Just as *Kubla Khan* is a poem about the nature of human genius, so this one indicates the depths of reality which are revealed in the extremities of human experience.

Yet, as has been suggested, there is also a touch of the experimental about *The Ancient Mariner*, which eased Coleridge's labours. Within his supernatural framework he could state some of his favourite ideas and observe to what extent they were picked up by his readers—to what extent they 'worked'. Had he sat down to explore those ideas with more care the poem might well not have been written.

Something of the sort seems to have taken place, indeed, when he came to write the sequel, *Christabel*—a poem in which, as he later wrote, 'I should have more nearly realized my ideal, than I had done in my first attempt' (*Biog. Lit.*, II, 6). Here he set out to explore the relationship between the world of everyday prudential reasoning and the world of romance more fully.

The germ of the poem is to be found in an idea which Coleridge had been exploring for some time past—that of the redemptive power of the innocent 'child of nature'. An original feature of 'The Wanderings of Cain' would have been the part played by Cain's son, Enos, with his innocent vision of nature; in the surviving fragment it is he who leads his father out into the moonlight. And it is one of Coleridge's cherished ideas at this time that the moment when the innocent child of nature encounters the world of romance is in some manner the key-moment for an understanding of human existence. Thus 'The Foster-Mother's Tale', which is the story of a boy who never learnt to read or pray but who made himself an intimate with nature, ends with the incident where he

> . . . *seiz'd a boat,*
> *And all alone, set sail by silent moonlight*
> *Up a great river, great as any sea,*
> *And ne'er was heard of more . . .* (PW, I, 184)

In 'The Nightingale', likewise, Coleridge describes a 'gentle Maid' who finds it natural in the evenings to leave her home near an empty castle and go out into the overgrown castle-grounds

> *Even like a Lady vowed and dedicate*
> *To something more than Nature in the grove.* (PW, I, 266)

At the end of the poem, moreover, he drives the point home by describing how he has determined to make his own son Hartley 'nature's playmate', and how on one occasion, when he woke up in distress,

> *I hurried with him to our orchard-plot,*
> *And he beheld the moon, and, hushed at once,*
> *Suspends his sobs, and laughs most silently,*
> *While his fair eyes, that swam with undropped tears,*
> *Did glitter in the yellow moon-beam!* (PW, I, 267)

By doing this he had evidently hoped to give his child a rapport with the world of romance similar to that which is enjoyed by the heroine of his poem: her devotion to Nature gives her an immediate contact with the vital joy expressed by the nightingale, whose song, like Hartley's smile, is controlled by the light of the moon; she listens,

> *and oft, a moment's space,*
> *What time the moon was lost behind a cloud,*
> *Hath heard a pause of silence; till the moon*
> *Emerging, hath awakened earth and sky*
> *With one sensation, and those wakeful birds*
> *Have all burst forth in choral minstrelsy,*
> *As if some sudden gale had swept at once*
> *A hundred airy harps! And she hath watched*
> *Many a nightingale perch giddily*
> *On blossomy twig still swinging from the breeze,*
> *And to that motion tune his wanton song*
> *Like tipsy Joy that reels with tossing head.* (PW, I, 266)

This passage is a necessary key for an understanding of the opening of *Christabel*. Here too one sees a young girl going out into the forest at night, but the scene is altogether more sombre. Owing to the thin grey cloud that 'covers but not hides the sky', the full moon does not shine brightly, but 'looks both small and dull'; while the joyful chorus of the nightingale is replaced by the brooding note of owls. The joyful vitality of *The Nightingale* has given place to an atmosphere altogether more sinister—not evil, rather the minimal form of good. The benevolent energies of nature are at their lowest ebb—so that, if Christabel's discovery of Geraldine in the wood is another encounter between the child of nature and the world of romance, it is an encounter fraught with peril.

The sense is reinforced by subsequent events. Geraldine seems to be a figure of beauty and pathos—even to represent goodness—until the moment of her undressing, when, having dismissed the presence of Christabel's dead mother with a withering curse, she reveals the horror which her robe hides.

> *Behold! her bosom and half her side—*
> *A sight to dream of, not to tell!*
> *O shield her! shield sweet Christabel!*

The mystery of that horror is matched by the mystery of the spell which is cast by Geraldine when, having collected herself in 'scorn and pride' (the marks of a fallen angel) she lies down and takes Christabel in her arms.

What takes place during the night is not clear, except that it is in some sense a struggle for power: Christabel emerges with an obscure sense of sin—but also, apparently, as innocent as before she went to sleep, having been guarded by benevolent spirits, including her mother.

The nature of Geraldine may well owe something to *Tales of the Genii*, where the sultan Misnar intervenes to rescue a beautiful lady who is being attacked by four ruffians in the forest, to discover later that the whole situation was contrived, and that she was really an evil and ugly enchantress,[1] and where the virtuous Urad takes pity on a woman who knocks at her door and allows her to stay the night, only to find that she has been deceived:

[1] *Tales of the Genii*, I, 301–8.

As they prepared for their homely bed, *Urad* turning round, beheld *Lahnar's* breast uncovered, and saw, by the appearance, it was no female she was preparing to receive into her bed.[1]

Contemporary rumours that Geraldine was really a man in disguise no doubt owe something to stories of this sort, but the statement by the reviewer in *The Examiner*[2] that 'there is something disgusting at the bottom of his subject' is wide of the mark if it implies agreement with the writer who maintained that *Christabel* was 'the most obscene Poem in the English Language' (CL, 918 and n.). Coleridge is not repeating these stories in their original form but trying to extract from them some inner core of significance, connected with his own ideas about the relationship between innocence and experience. According to Derwent Coleridge, Geraldine was intended to be 'no witch or goblin, or malignant being of any kind, but a spirit, executing her appointed task with the best goodwill . . .'[3] and this affirmation can be reconciled with her behaviour in the poem by reference to the images of dull moon, drowsy cock and brooding owls which opened it. Like them, her energies are basically good but reduced to a low subsistence. And just as the Hermit of *The Ancient Mariner*, who prays in the midst of nature, at 'the moss that wholly hides / The rotted old oak-stump', also 'loves to talke with marineres / That come from a far countree', so Christabel, when she has taken Geraldine into her father's castle, and restored her with some of her mother's 'wild-flower wine', sees that in her full stature she is like a figure of old romance:

> *She was most beautiful to see*
> *Like a lady of a far countrée.*

Part One of *Christabel* was completed before Coleridge left Nether Stowey for Germany; he was never again to know a time of such untroubled creativity. His stay at Göttingen may have contributed to his later failures of creation, since he was there in contact with a tradition which encouraged more intense habits of analysis and systematization than suited his own particular type of speculation. Personally, also, the

---

[1] *Ibid.*, I, 206.
[2] No. 440, 2 June, 1816, 348–9.
[3] *Poems*, ed. D. and S. Coleridge, 1868, xlii, n.

period abroad had harmful effects, since it helped to undermine a marriage which hitherto, despite tensions and incompatibilities, had been reasonably satisfactory.

Certain effects of disenchantment are felt in the second part of *Christabel*, which was written some time after the return. This is not to say that the writing is not very fine: there is a psychological perceptivity about the new part which was less visible in the first. What is missing, however, is the interacting harmony of language which existed previously. The first part succeeded in creating a 'charm of words' which breathed out an atmosphere beyond itself through the subtle interplay of rhythm and imagery; in the second the working of Coleridge's analytic mind is more evident.

This is by no means inappropriate to the effect of the new section, of course, since as H. N. Coleridge later remarked in the *Quarterly Review*,[1] it can be called an attempt at 'witchery by daylight'. The opening lines bring into the open a factor which has been half-evident throughout: the castle in which Christabel lives is a 'world of death'. Since the death of Christabel's mother, Sir Leoline her father has been obsessed by the fact of death, and this has coloured his whole existence.

In such a world, according to Coleridge's theory, Sir Leoline will act like the death-obsessed Cain: he will still be strong and well-intentioned; but redemption from his obsession can take place only if the innocent child of nature undertakes a new encounter with energy (the descent of the wings leading to the elevation of the serpent). This is what in fact happens when Christabel brings Geraldine into the castle. But it is a dangerous meeting of forces, since innocence cannot encounter experience without receiving some stamp from it. The threat is made apparent when Christabel, at sight of Geraldine embracing her own father, remembers the revelation of the night before and responds with serpentine behaviour:

> *Again she saw that bosom old,*
> *Again she felt that bosom cold,*
> *And drew in her breath with a hissing sound . . .*

[1] 1834, LII, 29.

Later, when Geraldine looks at her 'askance', her look (which recalls Satan's 'scornful eye askance' (PL, vi, 149) and his 'eying askance' the innocent pleasures of Adam and Eve in Paradise (PL, iv, 504)) is not only serpentine, but also reminds us directly of that clouded moon at the beginning of the poem which was both 'small and dull';

> *A snake's small eye blinks dull and shy;*
> *And the lady's eyes they shrunk in her head,*
> *Each shrunk up to a serpent's eye . . .*

Throughout the poem as we have seen, evil has been represented in this way: it is the veiling and hiding of good. The minimal light of the clouded moon and the half-hidden eye of the snake both speak of a vision that has been obscured until it no longer controls human energies, which are left to the caprice of the passion of the moment.

It is impossible to know how Coleridge would have concluded the poem, but it seems clear that Christabel would finally have overcome the peril of the forces represented by Geraldine and that her victory, transforming her from dove into eagle, would have acted 'for the weal of her lover'. In the poem as we have it, the clearest grasp of the struggle is held by Bard Bracy who, without knowing exactly what is happening, sees in a dream the struggle symbolized. He dreams that he finds Christabel's pet dove distressed in the forest:

> *I stooped, methought, the dove to take,*
> *When lo! I saw a bright green snake*
> *Coiled around its wings and neck. . . .*

His proposed remedy is the natural bardic one—it is

> *With music strong and saintly song*
> *To wander through the forest bare,*
> *Lest aught unholy loiter there.*

Sir Leoline, however, mistakes the meaning of the dream and supposes that it is Geraldine who is in danger. For this situation, he has his own solution. Ignoring Bracy's suggestion, he promises to crush 'the snake' by force.

Sir Leoline is imprisoned by his world of death. There is little evidence of life in the woods around his castle, where the spring comes late in the year and, within the castle itself, death is triumphant. There is even a curious correspondence with Milton's Hell, which was also a citadel of violence, and itself described as a 'Universe of death'. As Satan passes out of Hell,

> *The Gates wide op'n stood,*
> *That with extended wings a Bannerd Host*
> *Under spred Ensigns marching might pass through*
> *With Horse and Chariots rankt in loose array. . . .*[1]

Similarly, when Christabel and Geraldine enter the castle, they pass through

> *The gate that was ironed within and without,*
> *Where an army in battle array had marched out.*

Eventually, one can see, this atmosphere of death would have disappeared from the castle, to be replaced by life—the 'one Life', but the way towards such a conclusion is by no means clear. Coleridge no doubt intended to create a sequence of events which would have depicted the dove in Christabel raising the serpent in Geraldine to recreate the cycle of love and energy which for Coleridge was the note of true 'life'; it is easier to say this than to suggest how it could have been done, however, particularly in a moral and literary context which demanded that Christabel should remain 'innocent' in a very literal sense. It was a problem which neither Coleridge nor the Victorians were to solve—that of creating an energy of sensuousness which should yet avoid the imputations of sensuality; of showing in what sense, if any, 'innocence' could ever redeem 'evil'. 'The reason of my not finishing *Christabel*', said Coleridge a year before his death, 'is not, that I don't know how to do it—for I have, as I always had, the whole plan entire from beginning to end in my mind; but I fear I could not carry on with equal success the execution of the idea, an extremely subtle and difficult one' (*Table Talk*, 6 July 1833).

In the case of *The Ancient Mariner*, which he *had* completed, the problem was a different one—to know exactly what it was that he had created in writing it. In one sense, the increasing isolation and sufferings of his own life made it seem more of a personal allegory than he

[1] *Paradise Lost*, ii, 884-7.

could have foreseen. Whereas he could say of Wordsworth, writing *The Prelude*, 'now he is at the Helm of a noble Bark: now he sails right onward . . .' (*Notebooks*, I, 1546), he compared himself on one occasion to a member of the ship's crew ('verily "I raise my limbs like lifeless *Tools*"') (*Notebooks*, II, 2557) and, in *Constancy to an Ideal Object*, wrote that without the sense of love the most paradisal scene

> *were but a becalméd bark,*
> *Whose Helmsman on an ocean waste and wide*
> *Sits mute and pale his mouldering helm beside.* (PW, I, 456)

When he made his first sea-voyage to Malta in 1804 his mind was constantly running on his earlier poem (as his notebooks show). At one point also his reflections were directly responsible for a later addition. Some 'sickly thoughts' involving a fantasy in which Mary Wordsworth had died and Wordsworth had taken Sara Hutchinson instead were accompanied by a description of the stars 'sinking in the Horizon' and of the 'Light of the Compass & rudderman's Lamp reflected with forms on the Main Sail' (*Notebooks*, II, 2001); this in turn gave birth to the lines which he added, along with the description of fear 'sipping' at the Mariner's heart:

> *The stars were dim, and thick the night,*
> *The steersman's face by his lamp gleamed white;*
> *From the sails the dew did drip—*

When he stepped ashore at Malta he wrote: 'Found myself light as a blessed Ghost' (*Notebooks*, II, 2100).

Yet, although it is possible, as George Whalley has done,[1] to set out a persuasive and sensitive case for reading *The Ancient Mariner* as a personal allegory, the identification ultimately breaks down. We have seen that he sometimes identified himself with the shipmates rather than with the Mariner—as he also did when he made his graceful and rueful reference to the poem in his own *Epitaph*, praying

> *That he who many a year with toil of breath*
> *Found death in life, may here find life in death!* (PW, I, 492)

---

[1] G. Whalley, 'The Mariner and the Albatross', UTQ, 1946–7, XVI, 381–98.

and it would perhaps be truer to say that he found many coincidences with the poem in his own later experiences which, though tragic in overtone, also delighted him by their tendency to confirm his implicit analysis of human experience there. That analysis had been devoted to distinguishing the 'natural man', who, like the shipmates, was always liable to fall into a mechanistic way of acting and thinking, from the enlightened one whose superior insight (which marked him off as a man at once haunted and blessed), initiated him into a full sense of life and its significance. The fact that at different times he found himself in both classes, confirmed the analysis even if it left open the further moral interpretation to be drawn.

His own indecisions about the final nature of his poem are reflected in the changes which he made to it at different times. The first main revision was carried out in 1800 and seems to have been motivated partly by a desire to accommodate the poem more to the character of *Lyrical Ballads* as a whole by removing some of the more unusual antique words, smoothing one or two of the expressions and removing some dramatic touches. For the edition of 1817, on the other hand, Coleridge restored some of the more dramatic expressions and cast the whole poem more boldly in the form of a dramatic romance, providing it now for the first time with a series of prose glosses in the margins. These make it a more mannered poem than the original and serve to distance it from the writer as well as from the reader. On the other hand they also increase the dramatic effect, an effect which has been brought out by some of Coleridge's best critics.[1]

What Coleridge was evidently trying to do during these years was to objectivize the imaginative effect of the poem as much as possible and to present it as a 'poetic romance' which could be read as an exercise in the supernatural without too much inquiry into the seriousness or effectiveness of his assault on ultimate truth in the poem. In doing so he was tacitly accepting and reinforcing what had in fact been the attitude of his audience up till then, and preparing for a nineteenth-century public which would group it, with his poem 'Love' (a more

[1] E. E. Bostetter, *e.g.*, reads the poem as a presentation of nightmare (*The Romantic Ventriloquists*, Seattle, 1963); William Empson as a poem about causeless guilt (CQ, 1964, VI, 298–319).

straightforward romance) as favourite anthology-pieces. In his *Table Talk* he himself grouped the two poems together: '"The Ancient Mariner" cannot be imitated, nor the poem, "Love". *They may be excelled; they are not imitable.*'[1]

In making this assertion Coleridge was stating a final attitude to the poem which stressed the imaginative achievement at the expense of the structure of meaning. A similar point was made in a conversation with Mrs Barbauld, who objected that the poem 'had no moral':

> As to the want of a moral, I told her that in my own judgement the poem had too much; and that the only, or chief fault, if I might say so, was the obtrusion of the moral sentiment so openly on the reader as a principle or cause of action in a work of such pure imagination. It ought to have had no more moral than the *Arabian Nights'* tale of the Merchant's sitting down to eat dates by the side of a well and throwing the shells aside, and lo! a genie starts up, and says that he *must* kill the aforesaid merchant, *because* one of the date shells had, it seems, put out the eye of the genie's son. (*Table Talk*, 31 May 1830)

This desire for a more arbitrary plot may carry a personal note: in so far as he could be said to have killed his own genius in youth, this could not be seen as a wilful action, even at the level of the Mariner's act. The visitations of genius, it seemed, were hardly relatable to any moral dispensation: looking back he could trace no crime which could be regarded as an equivalent for what he had suffered. But there is a more important implication: he was also assigning the whole realm of imagination to the sphere of mystery.

This move is echoed in his thinking about the supernatural generally. He was no longer ready to believe that the supernatural could yield certain knowledge of the transcendental, that one could learn something important about the nature of the universe from one's experiences in reading romance. Nor, on the other hand, could he wholly abandon the idea. He deleted from a copy of the *Biographia Literaria* a passage describing the Imagination as 'a repetition in the finite mind of the eternal act of creation' and wrote a recantation of his once-held faith

[1] T. Allsop, *Letters, etc. of S. T. Coleridge*, 1836, I, 95.

in the 'Heaven-descended Know Thyself',[1] but in the same breath he continued, 'Ignore thyself, strive to know thy God!'—which still left open the possibility that the divine might correspond to what was revealed so arbitrarily and capriciously in the visitations of human genius.

There was a further turn to the screw. It *might* be so—but if so, what sort of universe was it which could deprive him of the strange indwelling music which had possessed him (or so it seems) continuously from the time when he composed *Kubla Khan* to the point when he left England for Germany? When he had come to describe this experience at the climax of the letter to Sara Hutchinson which became *Dejection: An Ode*, he was already using terms more psychological than before, seeing it as dependent upon a state of personal happiness:

> *O pure of Heart! thou need'st not ask of me*
> *What this strong music in the Soul may be . . .*
> *Joy is that strong Voice, Joy that luminous Cloud—*
> *We, we ourselves rejoice!*
> *And thence flows all that charms or ear or sight,*
> *All melodies the Echoes of that Voice,*
> *All Colors a Suffusion of that Light.*   (CL, II, 798)

Many years later he declared that if he had the opportunity of hearing good music more often it might produce the right conditions for completing *Christabel*. But more than any other factor he believed that the necessary condition of further creation was love—that love which would have united the possessing genius with the tender heart, which would have made him an Apollo with his lute, partnering the Abyssinian maid with her sambuca and so creating a 'symphony and song' to which the creations of his imagination would effortlessly rise. And since he had never known that love he could argue that the crucial experiment had never been made.

To this extent the romance-experience remained a powerful presence with him, so that it is not surprising to find it repeating itself in his later poetry. In *The Garden of Boccaccio*, composed in 1828, he describes once again a scene of pleasure in romance and, once again, finds romance mysteriously turning into 'reality'. This ultimate experi-

[1] See *Coleridge the Visionary*, 37 and n.

ence of romance, when we pass into the scene which is described and find ourselves part of it, comes in this poem as a result of looking at a tapestry depicting scenes from Boccaccio:

> *I see no longer! I myself am there,*
> *Sit on the ground-sward, and the banquet share,*
> *'Tis I, that sweep that lute's love-echoing strings,*
> *And gaze upon the maid who gazing sings:*
> *Or pause and listen to the tinkling bells*
> *From the high tower, and think that there she dwells.*
> *With old Boccaccio's soul I stand possest,*
> *And breathe an air like life, that swells my chest.* (PW, I, 479)

Although the feeling for romance is as strong as ever here, however, Coleridge is no longer willing to suggest any sure link with the supernatural in a literal sense. Like *The Ancient Mariner*, the whole sphere of romance is now assigned to a realm of its own: his former sense that the imagination reveals the eternal is neither affirmed or denied.

The proper image for himself now, therefore, is not that of the sun-god charming all men into a harmony by his revelations of the eternal; in a letter of 1820 he lights upon a more sombre image:

> . . . I have often thought, within the last five or six years, that if ever I should feel once again the genial warmth and stir of the poetic impulse, and referred to my own experiences, I should venture on a yet stranger and wilder Allegory than of yore—that I should *allegorize* myself, as a rock with it's summit raised above the surface of some Bay or Strait in the Arctic Sea 'while yet the stern and solitary Night Brook'd no alternate Sway'—all around me fixed and firm methought as my own Substance, and near me lofty Masses, that might have seemed to 'hold the moon and stars in fee,' and often in such wild play with meteoric lights, or with the Shine from above which they made rebound in sparkles or disband in off-shoots and splinters and iridescent needle-shafts of keenest Glitter, that it was a pride and a place of Healing to lie, as in an Apostle's Shadow, within the Eclipse and deep sub-stance-seeming Gloom of 'these dread Ambassadors from Earth to Heaven, Great Hierarchs' and tho' obscured yet to think myself obscured by consubstantial Forms, based in the same Foundation as my own. (UL, II, 262)

In this image, the emphasis has shifted from that of radiant and inspired man to one of man as primarily *bulk* (though it is a bulk which, he makes clear, has been raised by a hidden fire). This new allegory of his existence makes him primarily an object figure, existing under the illumination of Arctic lights and heavenly bodies to which he responds by reflections from his own surface of crystals and glittering spars.

Coleridge's later poetry is the product of this shift in his sense of himself. As a result, the supernatural implications of his earlier poems are softened down and the dominant mode is that of the romance, presented within an affirmation of the supremacy of human love which may or may not be given metaphysical significance according to the reader's own beliefs.

For this reason, however, most modern readers, living in an age which has rejected the general nineteenth-century view of affectionate love as a key to the meaning of human existence, find their enjoyment of Coleridge's poems accordingly restricted. If they find a way forward in appreciation it is likely to move through an appreciation of one particular facet of his poetry: its expression of a private music (both visual and aural) which corresponds to various facets of his sensibility.

Some of the characteristics of that music have been indicated earlier: a rhythm which works always towards the suggestion of incantation, and an imagery which twists and turns between the vivid and the crystalline, the sensuous and the tender. All this, when handled, as in the supernatural poems, with a flair for the dramatic and a child-like openness of manner goes to constitute the 'Coleridgean style'—a style which, to quote his remark again, can be excelled but not imitated. No-one else could achieve the precise blend of qualities which, in his best work, always reminds us (even at the moment when we may be tempted to dismiss some passage as pandering overmuch to the child-consciousness) that we are dealing with a highly sensitive and intelligent man.

Although the Coleridgean music is available to all who care to immerse themselves in his writing until they are attuned to it, however, it may still seem, within the context of contemporary poetry, like the music of a man singing on a rock in the Atlantic, his voice heard in snatches of calm but destined to be later, and inexorably, hidden by the pressing noise of the waves around it. Yet a different experience is available to the reader—when, as in the exploration of *Kubla Khan*, the surrounding sea shrinks away and what seemed like a rock is seen to be the summit of an Atlantic mountain, from the top of which Coleridge is surveying a country of human experience which for us is normally submerged. It is a strange moment in one's reading experience: the incantation of the poem ceases to be the containing force of the poem and becomes a subsidiary aid, while the images perform a silent dance and take up new positions, no longer the landscape of a never-never land, but the structuring symbols of a great dialectic in which imagination and reason play equally important parts.

In this respect, our reading of *Kubla Khan* is crucial to our reading of Coleridge generally. Its projection of a large visionary speculation within a context of incantation corresponds to much that lies buried in his own thinking and writing, and explains why he so often gives the impression of living areas of his life in an alternative universe. John Sterling found it a disturbing impression:

> It is painful to observe in Coleridge, that with all the kindness and glorious far-seeing intelligence of his eye there is a glare in it, a light half unearthly, half morbid. It is the glittering eye of the Ancient Mariner.[1]

But we cannot come to terms with it unless we notice, in addition to the kindness and intelligence which are the immediate characteristics of his writing, that glare, which is the mark of a man who has been possessed by the possibility of reaching an inclusive vision of the universe and who has damaged himself by his single-mindedness in pursuing it. Coleridge in other words, was *not*, precisely, his own Ancient Mariner: the tragic paradox of his career was at once more splendid and more banal. In seeking permanent access to the 'life in death' which was the Mariner's brief glimpse of a universal harmony, he had damaged the springs of his own vision and condemned himself to spend certain tracts of his life, like one of the Mariner's own 'shipmates', in the 'death in life' of more mechanical labours.

But whatever he later lost he could not lose the memory of his former aspirations. He might actively conspire with his readers to turn his

[1] *Essays and Tales*, 1848, I, xxv.

poems of the supernatural into more straightforward and acceptable romances, but somewhere within him there remained a created land-scape which, once having been impressed by the daemon, must always exist: somewhere a voice would continue to sing of Mount Abora. For that reason, more than for any other, he was for his contemporaries, and is still for us, a numinous figure.

3: Coleridge and Poetry:
II. The Conversational and other Poems

A. R. JONES

T HE IMPRESSION that the English Romantic poets were primarily concerned with sensory perception, particularly in their attitude towards landscape, stubbornly persists, probably because of the nineteenth century's insistence that they were poets of the countryside, that is, poets celebrating nature as opposed to the towns, and more particularly because of their success in establishing the texture of their poetry by embodying vision in images of sensory perception. The ambiguities of the verb 'to see' are notorious; we say that we see an argument as readily as we see the landscape. The English Romantic poets were quick to exploit this ambiguity as, indeed, they were to manipulate the vague concept of Nature. Where previously poets had talked, loosely, of holding a mirror up to Nature, they more frequently use Nature to mean the mirror itself.[1] The sense of sight is elevated to the capacity for insight and the theory of perception gives way to vision, the idea of the creative imagination.

Many of the most powerful and characteristic Romantic poems are concerned with recreating and synthesizing certain landscapes of mind and very few with the immediate apprehension of sensory experience. Indeed, the Romantic imagination is most effective when the poet is withdrawn from the world of perception and deprived of sensory experience. Then the poet may inhabit completely the landscape of mind. The climactic vision of *The Prelude* is that, when having climbed Snowdon overnight in order to see the sunrise from the summit, Wordsworth sees the mists, moon, hills, and hears the roar of waters but

---

[1] But see M. H. Abrams, *The Mirror and the Lamp: Romantic Theory and the Critical Tradition*, New York, 1953.

beholds 'the emblem of a mind / That feeds upon infinity.' For Wordsworth the 'serene and blessed mood' is one of complete withdrawal when,

> . . . *even the motion of our human blood*
> *Almost suspended, we are laid asleep*
> *In body, and become a living soul :*

Shelley and Keats are hardly more concerned with immediate sensory
perception. 'I cannot see the flowers at my feet' Keats asserts, but,
nonetheless, continues the stanza by describing the scent, colour and
texture of the blossom he cannot see, and Shelley's imagery is notor-
iously less concrete, the patterning of his poems more abstract, than
anything to be found in Keats.

   Yet, as M. H. Abrams demonstrates in his essay 'The Correspondent
Breeze',[1] the invisible forces of the mind are one of the most powerful
and recurring images in English Romantic poetry, and in addressing the
'wild West Wind', Shelley was, in effect, presenting his variation on a
theme already well established. The mode of correspondences, images
that unite the landscape of perception and the landscape of mind, was
well established by Wordsworth and Coleridge and is too often taken
for granted in the poetry of the younger Romantics, and, perhaps, too
readily overlooked, even now, as being central to the poetic procedures
of Romantic poetry as a whole. Yet Wordsworth goes to some pains in
the opening paragraphs of *The Prelude* to confirm this correspondence :

> *For I, methought, while the sweet breath of heaven*
> *Was blowing on my body, felt within*
> *A correspondent breeze, that gently moved*
> *With quickening virtue, but is now become*
> *A tempest, a redundant energy,*
> *Vexing its own creation. Thanks to both,*
> *And their congenial powers, that while they join*
> *In breaking up a long-continued frost,*
> *Bring with them vernal promises, the hope*
> *Of active days urged on by flying hours . . .*[2]

[1] M. H. Abrams, 'The Correspondent Breeze: A Romantic Metaphor',
The Kenyon Review, XIX, 1957, 113–30. Reprinted and rev. *English
Romantic Poets*, ed. M. H. Abrams, Oxford, 1960.
[2] *The Prelude*, I, 33–42.

The breeze, thought of presumably as belonging to spring, corresponds to the tempestuous energy of mind, that thaws the 'long-continued frost' bringing creative movement and renewal to the world of nature as to the dormant, 'long-confined', interior life of the poet. The most characteristic and memorable passages in *The Prelude* are undoubtedly those in which mental, moral and psychological crises are so fully embodied in action and incident that we experience the growth of the poet's mind without making too precise a distinction between the inner world of thought and feeling and the outer world of immediate perception. The least satisfactory passages in the poem are those in which Wordsworth, standing aside from the direct dramatization of action and incident, reflects on the meaning and the moral to be drawn from them. Too often in these reflective passages he breaks down the blank verse into the kind of rhetoric that characterizes his poetry in and after *Ode to Duty* and *The Happy Warrior*, and too frequently he confuses meditation with didacticism. He is most powerful and convincing when the correspondence is fully contained, when the world of mind is embodied in images of sensory perception (thus fulfilling T. S. Eliot's demand for an 'objective correlative') and least effective when he abandons this correspondence and speaks editorially.

Although Wordsworth and Coleridge seem to share so much, Coleridge, by contrast, being so ruthlessly selfconscious, is most successful and most himself in his meditative, reflective poems that chart the landscape of his own inner world without mediation of the world of perception. His most concrete imagery is to be found in his supernatural poems, where he explores the darker areas of human consciousness. In his aptly named conversational poems the subject is unashamedly Coleridge, but then, if Wordsworth is the greater poet, there is little doubt that Coleridge had the more attractive, more powerful mind (whatever mind means in that context). There is always the suspicion that Wordsworth's great creative period was possible only because he was so unselfconscious, so unaware of the source and implications of his poetry, and that his decline after 1805 was to some extent accounted for by his increasing self-awareness. If there is anything in such a suspicion, then the contrast between the two poets is sharpened, for Coleridge was so often 'hurt' into poetry by the need to express new areas of consciousness, that this becomes his predominant poetic mode. In the group of poems known as the 'conversational' poems, Coleridge is preoccupied with the search for identity, thus anticipating one of the major themes of modern literature. If he found self-consciousness painfully inhibiting in his many attempts to organize his work and life, it certainly finds uninhibited expression in these poems which are also firmly though unobtrusively organized. Indeed, the shaping spirit of the creative imagination is nowhere displayed to better advantage.

The poems generally grouped under the heading of conversational poems are *The Nightingale, This Lime-Tree Bower My Prison, The Eolian Harp,* and *Frost at Midnight,* although *Fears in Solitude,* and *Dejection* cannot be left unaccounted for in any discussion of Coleridge's poetic achievement. Together with some of the shorter poems these form a body of poetry, closely related in style and subject, which can be considered separately from *The Ancient Mariner, Kubla Khan* and *Christabel* as a distinct, outstanding and too often neglected contribution to the continuity and development of English Romantic poetry. The idea of continuity should be stressed because in so many ways these poems, such original productions in themselves, draw heavily from the immediate past, on the poetry of Collins and Cowper in particular. Coleridge is building on the firm tradition of the epistolary style which established itself in English literature at least as early as Ben Jonson and which in the later eighteenth century became the main vehicle of expression for poets such as Cowper. Humphry House in his Clark Lectures establishes the connection between Cowper and Coleridge with a firm authority:

> The importance of Cowper to the poetic environment in which Coleridge grew up is perhaps greater and more marked than that of Collins, and in the long run certainly greater than that of Bowles. . . . Cowper was the great example of a poet using blank verse, freely, easily, for personal purposes, as the metre of conversational matter and a conversational vocabulary. . . . In the Conversational poems Coleridge is carrying on where Cowper left off. The autobiographical element is given deeper psychological analysis, and the thought about it carries over into what

is properly metaphysical poetry. The informal method is kept; but everything has greater impact; the imagery leaves Cowper's direct statement; the descriptive passages are more intricately and closely knit to their psychological effects; the description is more minute, delicate and various in correspondence with the more minute and various states of mind on which it bears. Above all, the language of some of the poems, particularly 'Frost at Midnight', has the verbal concentration on which great poetry always depends, and Cowper so obviously nearly always lacks.[1]

The tone and manner of these poems are their most immediately obvious feature; G. M. Harper calls them 'Poems of Friendship',[2] a description that at least suggests the easy intimacy that Coleridge establishes with his readers, drawing them into the poems as friends into a familiar circle of select and chosen company. Yet the tone of these poems should not be allowed to beguile the reader into valuing them for their charm alone or into underestimating the tough, intellectual and spiritual problems that each poem confronts. Indeed one of the vital aspects of these poems is the way in which they demonstrate the workings of Coleridge's subtle and powerful intelligence.

In *This Lime-Tree Bower My Prison* and *The Nightingale*, Coleridge establishes what is to become the characteristic manner of this group of poems as a whole. *This Lime-Tree Bower My Prison* is addressed to Charles Lamb, his old school-friend, and commemorates a visit paid by Lamb to Coleridge who 'met with an accident, which disabled him from walking during the whole time of their stay'. Coleridge, left behind while Lamb, Wordsworth and Dorothy go out walking, follows them in his imagination as they proceed from the 'hill-top edge' down into the 'roaring dale', emerging again into the 'wide, wide Heaven'. He anticipates Lamb's pleasure in the scene before turning to describe the place where he is sitting. His last description is of the rook flying

---

[1] Humphry House, *Coleridge, The Clark Lectures 1951–2*, 1953, 71–3; Cowper's poem *The Task* is the point of comparison he uses.
[2] 'Coleridge's Conversation Poems', *Spirit of Delight*, New York, 1928, reprinted *English Romantic Poets*, ed. M. H. Abrams, Oxford, 1960, 144–57.

homewards in the dusk and he wonders whether Lamb also saw it or
heard it 'creeking'. The whole poem seems artless and charming and
there is no doubting Coleridge's selfless affection as he accompanies his
friends in imagination in their walk, or his faith in the power of Nature
to exert a beneficent influence in times of crises and desolation—an idea
expanded by Wordsworth in *Tintern Abbey*. Yet, nonetheless, the reader
must wonder whether the walk imaginatively taken by Coleridge does
not, like so many of Coleridge's journeys, conceal a symbolism tactfully
but firmly asserted. Coleridge is always deeply introspective, constantly
watching and analysing the workings of his own mind, particularly
when engaged in the act of creation; he is aware of the 'world without'
but also of the 'still more wonderful world within' and his poetry
establishes an easy commerce between nature and mind.[1] The MS
version of the poem that he sent to Southey in July 1797, opens more
abruptly than the final version. In particular, the final version expands
the opening eleven lines to twenty-eight while, at the same time,
suppressing elements in this MS version that opens,

> *Well, they are gone, and here I must remain,*
> *Lam'd by the scathe of fire, lonely and faint,*
> *This lime-tree bower my prison! They, meantime,*
> *My Friends, whom I may never meet again*
> *On springy heath, along the hill-top edge*
> *Wander delighted, and look down, perchance,*
> *On that same rifted dell, where many an ash*
> *Twists its wild limbs beside the ferny rock*
> *Whose plumy ferns forever nod and drip*
> *Spray'd by the waterfall. But chiefly thou*
> *My gentle hearted* Charles! *thou who had pin'd . . .*

There is no mention in the final version of his being 'Lam'd by the
scathe of fire', a reference, as he explained to Southey, to the fact that
'dear Sara accidentally emptied a skillet of boiling milk on my foot,
which confined me during the whole time of C. Lamb's stay'. There is
also no mention of his being 'lonely and faint' though this may well be

---

[1] But see Dorothy Emmet, 'Coleridge on the Growth of the Mind',
rep. K. Coburn, *Twentieth Century Views*, 161–78.

inferred from the description of the lime-tree bower as 'my prison' that still stands in the final version. Yet the whole development of this opening in its final version has been radically changed. The tone is more contemplative, the movement of the verse less brisk but more suggestive. In particular the description of the 'rifted dell' has undergone a number of significant changes, indicated by its now being described as the 'roaring dell':

> *The roaring dell, o'erwooded, narrow, deep,*
> *And only speckled by the mid-day sun;*
> *Where its slim trunk the ash from rock to rock*
> *Flings arching like a bridge;—that branchless ash,*
> *Unsunn'd and damp, whose few poor yellow leaves*
> *Ne'er tremble in the gale, yet tremble still,*
> *Fann'd by the water-fall! and there my friends*
> *Behold the dark green file of long lank weeds,*
> *That all at once (a most fantastic sight!)*
> *Still nod and drip beneath the dripping edge*
> *Of the blue clay-stone.*

The 'plumy ferns' of the MS have now become 'long lank weeds'; the 'many an ash' gives way to concentration on 'that branchless ash,/ Unsunn'd and damp'; the ferns that 'forever nod and drip' in the MS version, 'all at once (a most fantastic sight!)/ Still nod and drip' in the final version. The descent into the dell in the final version has become the dominant image; in the MS version he imagines his friends merely looking down into the dell whereas in the final version they 'wind down' into its depths, emerging, eventually, into the 'wide wide Heaven'. Without pressing the image of the dell too hard or too far (Coleridge seems to be constantly inviting allegorical interpretation as here with his contrast between dell and Heaven), he is at some pains to draw parallels between his own imprisoned position in the lime-tree bower, the descent into the dell with its branchless ash, and the picture of Lamb,

> *In the great City pent, winning thy way*
> *With sad yet patient soul, through evil and pain*
> *And strange calamity!*

Moreover, just as Lamb and his friends in this imaginary journey find their way out of the dell into the 'wide wide Heaven', that is also the 'wide landscape' where they sense the presence of the 'Almighty Spirit', so Coleridge feels himself to be released from his prison, and experiences a parallel ascent which culminates in his blessing the homeward-bound rook (a blessing comparable to the Mariner's blessing of the water-snakes). A. Gérard sees the structure of this poem to be typical of the 'conversation' poems and describes their 'general framework' as being a 'heartbeat rhythm of systole and diastole, contraction and expansion, in which the poets' attention is wandering to and fro between his concrete, immediate experience and the wide and many-faceted world of the non-self'.[1] Yet Humphry House, in his Clark Lectures, had anticipated A. Gérard's point when in his discussion of *Frost at Midnight* he notices the typical rhythm of the poem as one of contraction and expansion and also that the centre of the poem 'is the Ego, the "I" —the seeing, remembering, projecting mind—the man sitting in a cottage room at night. From the room the mind moves out, by stages, first to the physical contest of weather and sound, then to the village, then to the world—"all the numberless goings-on of life". Next with a swift contracting transition, . . . it comes in again in the fire.'[2] What A. Gérard describes as 'Romantic egotism . . . not as an abstract concept, but as a living source of inspiration', Humphry House places in a more convincing context of Coleridge's practice and theory of poetry but, more importantly, he sees that the movement of the mind not only gives these poems their structure but that it is the subject of the poems. Analysing *Frost at Midnight*, Humphry House writes,

> Not only do the movements of the mind give the poem its design and unity; but the poem as a whole leaves us with a quite extra-ordinary sense of the mind's *very being*, in suspense, above time and space; the mind with all its powers of affection and memory, and its power of reading nature as the language of God.

Poetry differs from other writings because of what Coleridge describes

[1] 'The Systolic Rhythm: The Structure of Coleridge's Conversation Poems', EC, July 1960; rep. K. Coburn, *Twentieth Century Views*, 78–87.
[2] *Coleridge, The Clark Lectures 1951–2*, 79–81.

as 'that pleasurable emotion, that peculiar state and degree of excitement that arises in the poet himself in the act of composition'.[1] His affection for Lamb is undoubtedly the controlling power that shapes Coleridge's 'peculiar state and degree of excitement' in *This Lime-Tree Bower My Prison* and that lends this poem its grace, elegance and harmony of address. But at the same time as we are impressed by this power of affection, we are also conscious of an 'extraordinary sense of the mind's *very being*, in suspense, above time and space', that 'arises in the poet himself in the act of composition'.

We can see the MS version of the poem's beginning as no more than a blunt summary which opens out in the final version into a statement of great subtlety and power, involving us in the full associative range of experience set up, but also immersing us in the universal implications balanced in Coleridge's mind against the particular circumstances. In other words, in touching on one part of his experience—in this case the pleasure of Lamb's visit and the frustrations of not being able to accompany him on the walk—Coleridge immerses us in his whole mental landscape, where to touch on a part necessarily involves the whole. The associational process of mind, while fully controlled, is essentially emblematic, particularly in so far as Coleridge reads 'nature as the language of God'. It is in this respect that the landscape, outward and visible, becomes the world of mind, of thought, feeling and spirit, perceived in the act of creative imagination. 'The poet himself in the act of composition', realizes in language that world where the universal is perceived in and through particulars.

The general framework of the poems may be described as one of expansion and contraction, or of systole and diastole, but the most prominent feature of their structure is surely the reversal that characterizes all of them. The first section of *This Lime-Tree Bower My Prison* is Coleridge's imaginative creation of the walk taken by Lamb and his friends (to line 43) and the final section demonstrates the way in which this act of creative imagination adds an entirely new dimension to Coleridge's own situation; imagination and reality, at first seen as quite discrete—the imagined walk, and the Coleridge who finds freedom and

[1] *Sh. Crit.*, II, 50, but see House, *Coleridge*, 149ff.

creative movement through imagination, and the reality of Coleridge
confined and imprisoned in the lime-tree bower—interpenetrate until
the final section of the poem demonstrates these two dimensions as
being inseparable.

A comparison between an earlier 'effusion', *The Eolian Harp*,
written in August 1795, and a later poem *The Nightingale*, dated April
1798 and the only poem to be described by Coleridge as a 'conversation'
poem, not only shows the maturity of the later poem but also the way in
which he established what becomes a characteristic procedure. *The
Eolian Harp* opens with an apostrophe to 'My pensive Sara!' and even
in this poem we can, unfortunately, see with all the wisdom of hind-
sight what Coleridge means by describing their relationship as the
bringing together of two minds 'so utterly contrariant in their primary
and organical constitution'.[1] Sitting with Sara at dusk, he is quickly
taken up with ideas and associations moving in ever widening circles
until with his speculations regarding the relation between man, nature
and God, the poem has become wholly inclusive in scope. The opening
of the poem is characteristically awkward leading to the fanciful idea
of the significance of Jasmin and Myrtle,

> *our Cot o'ergrown*
> *With white-flower'd Jasmin, and the broad-leav'd Myrtle,*
> *(Meet emblems they of Innocence and Love!)*

Even the style of the opening lines has that stilted quality that reminds
the reader of the strong eighteenth-century tradition on which he is
relying. More importantly, perhaps, the opening of these poems recalls
Coleridge's comment on Dryden, 'Dryden's genius was of that sort
which catches fire by its own motion; his chariot wheels *get* hot by
driving fast.'[2] We can see how, after a somewhat uncertain opening, his
imagination 'catches fire' with the image of the scent from the beanfields,

> *How exquisite the scents*
> *Snatch'd from yon beanfield! and the world so hush'd!*
> *The stilly murmur of the distant Sea*
> *Tells us of silence.*

[1] I. CL, II, 832, Letter to Southey, July 1802.
[2] *Table Talk*, 1 November, 1833.

The poem from this point quickly moves us into the image of the Eolian Harp itself, a traditionally eighteenth-century concept used here with a subtlety and complexity peculiarly Coleridge's own to establish both the passivity and the creative energy of the human mind,

> *O! the one Life within us and abroad,*
> *Which meets all motion and becomes its soul,*
> *A light in sound, a sound-like power in light,*
> *Rhythm in all thought, and joyance every where—*[1]

which leads him to put forward somewhat breathlessly the suggestion

> *And what if all of animated nature*
> *Be but organic Harps diversely fram'd,*
> *That tremble into thought, as o'er them sweeps*
> *Plastic and vast, one intellectual breeze,*
> *At once the Soul of each, and God of all?*

The concept of harmony between the mind and the world of nature, and between nature and God establishes a universal 'rhythm in all thought', made possible by the sense of what Coleridge here describes as 'joyance', that state of excitement, of concentrated, increased, awareness, that is a necessary part of the act of creative imagination.

Coleridge's thought habitually reaches out for theistic, neo-Platonic conclusions; a realization, probably derived from the Cambridge Platonists,[2] of the one-ness of the world, a universal power, 'plastic and vast', 'at once the Soul of each, and God of all'. The cosmic gesture of such metaphysical inclusiveness affirmed in this image is blighted by the 'mild reproof' of Sara's strict orthodoxy and the poem is reversed in the last paragraph, the brilliance of its imaginative daring relegated to 'these shapings of the unregenerate mind', its ethical implications written off as 'vain Philosophy's aye-babbling spring'. This reversal destroys the whole balance of the poem that even textually loses the self-confidence that enabled Coleridge in the body of the poem to establish a flexible,

---

[1] These lines first appeared in 1803 and are not part of the original poem of 1795, but they strengthen the idea of 'the One Life'.
[2] See R. L. Brett, *Fancy and Imagination*, 1969, 39–41, and 'Coleridge's Theory of the Imagination', ESMEA, II, 1949.

informal and wonderfully natural style in which thought and language come together with delicate precision. The vision of an harmonious universe achieved in the first section of the poem is not, however, altogether balanced by the sectarian piety of the close. Yet, nonetheless, it is not easy to see how Coleridge could have developed the thought of the poem further. At least as it stands, the poem is a testimony to the comprehensive nature of the poet's theism as compared with the poverty of orthodoxy. Moreover, although the idea of Sara requesting Coleridge to 'walk humbly with my God', indicates her ignorance of the true nature of the man, his fear of the 'unregenerate mind' is not so groundless. Coleridge realized that the power of the mind was not by any means always at the service of beneficent forces but that the creative imagination could and sometimes did bring potent evil to the light of day; it is in the power that he seems to realize particularly in the unfinished *Christabel* when he more than hints at a world subverted by the powers of darkness. In a way that never seems to occur to Wordsworth, Coleridge is sensitive to the ambiguous moral implications involved in creative imagination and in particular to the paganism and evil in a world of nature not securely bound to the world of God, or in the unconscious, nightmare world of man not fully under the control of a morally trained consciousness. It is this awareness that makes him most vulnerable to the rebuke from Sara, 'Meek Daughter in the family of Christ!', and that more than anything else accounts for the sudden disappointing collapse of the poem.

The Nightingale is a fully accomplished poem, intimate, graceful and deceptively complex. In *This Lime-Tree Bower My Prison*, Coleridge withdraws into the mental landscape of memory and re-creation because of enforced inactivity; in *The Eolian Harp* he has retreated into the private world of Sara and himself at dusk from which his imaginative vision travels outwards to embrace the world of God, man and nature, and from which he is recalled by Sara. In *The Nightingale* Coleridge's senses are again confined but this time by night and stillness. In the darkness he first recalls the 'vernal showers / That gladden the green earth' of the daylight world but his attention is arrested by the song of the nightingale. He recalls the traditional attitude towards the bird that associates it with melancholy,

> *With the remembrance of a grievous wrong,*
> *Or slow distemper, or neglected love,*
> *(And so, poor wretch! filled all things with himself,*
> *And made all gentle sounds tell back the tale*
> *Of his own sorrow)*

Yet Coleridge, who opens the poem by establishing his reluctance to let such a day with William and Dorothy Wordsworth slip into night, is determined to find further happiness in the darkness for

> *My Friend, and thou, our Sister! we have learnt*
> *A different lore: we may not thus profane*
> *Nature's sweet voices, always full of love*
> *And joyance!*

In contrast to the traditional nightingale as a symbol of frustrated love, shame and melancholy, Coleridge offers 'the merry Nightingale'

> *That crowds, and hurries, and precipitates*
> *With fast thick warble his delicious notes,*
> *As he were fearful that an April night*
> *Would be too short for him to utter forth*
> *His love-chant, and disburthen his full soul*
> *Of all its music!*

Having overturned the traditional, poetic symbolism of the nightingale by insisting on the quite different reality of experience, Coleridge introduces a description of a deserted castle, a gentle maid and a wild grove where many nightingales have made their home. The landscape he describes is curiously Gothic,[1] the nightingales' song oddly 'wanton', an attribute from the traditional poetic symbolism he has already rejected. T. S. Eliot deploys this symbolism in *Sweeney Among the Nightingales* and again in 'A Game of Chess', the second section of *The Waste Land*, we learn of

> *Philomel, by the barbarous king*
> *So rudely forced; yet there the nightingale*

---

[1] Said to refer to Enmore, castle of the Earl of Egmont, the Maid being the daughter of the Earl's agent. Coleridge, like Wordsworth, was in the habit of using real incidents as the basis for his poems.

> *Filled all the desert with inviolable voice*
> *And still she cried, and still the world pursues,*
> *'Jug Jug' to dirty ears.*

In Coleridge's poem, the nightingales certainly

> *answer and provoke each other's song,*
> *With skirmish and capricious passagings,*
> *And murmurs musical and swift jug jug,*

but the immediate point he wishes to make is concerned with the way
in which the song of the birds seems to turn night into day and thus
follows on from Coleridge's evident reluctance to bring a happy day to
an end. The attitude of the 'gentle maid' toward the nightingale grove is
certainly sacramental, 'like a lady vowed and dedicate', but at the centre
of this description is the nightingales' relation to the moon which is
similar to the relation between the 'Eolian harp' and the wind,

> *She knows all their notes,*
> *That gentle Maid! and oft, a moment's space,*
> *What time the moon was lost behind a cloud,*
> *Hath heard a pause of silence; till the moon*
> *Emerging, hath awakened earth and sky*
> *With one sensation, and those wakeful birds*
> *Have all burst forth in choral minstrelsy,*
> *As if some sudden gale had swept at once*
> *A hundred airy harps!*

The idea of hearing a pause of silence is rather like Milton's notorious
darkness visible. Yet the function of the image is clear enough, the
birds responding to the moon, silencing their song when it is hidden but
bursting out in 'choral minstrelsy' when the moon re-appears, as at
daybreak, the day-time birds break into the dawn chorus. Similar to the
Eolian harp, the birds are passive until the moon shines when they break
into a gale of song. Thus the image establishes a similar world of
harmony to that described in *The Eolian Harp*, the mood is one of
'joyance' or 'tipsy Joy',[1] the necessary mood of excitement in which

---

[1] A strange echo of Comus's first speech 'Meanwhile welcome joy and
feast,/Midnight shout and revelry,/Tipsy dance and jollity.' (*Comus,*
102–104.)

awareness is heightened, and the creative imagination embraces the whole world of mind and animated nature. The relation between the nightingales and the moon is paralleled with an anecdote in the last section of the poem concerning Coleridge's son Hartley who, waking distressed from a nightmare, was carried by his father into the orchard. When Hartley saw the moon he stopped crying and began to laugh 'most silently'. This incident would seem to suggest that the discordant distress within the child's inner world was changed to happiness and harmony when confronted with the moon. His description of the harp and the wind on the strings is interchangeable with the psychological effect of changes of mood within the individual—this is made perfectly clear with the idea of trembling into thought—and similarly his description of the effect of the moon awakening 'with one sensation' the earth and the sky, clarifies the relationship between the inner landscape of mind and the outer landscape of nature. The Eolian harp and the moon are both inanimate yet the harp turns wind to music and harmony and the moon reflects the light of the sun. The analogy between the harp and the moon is clear enough but most important is the analogy between them and the creative mind. Lit by the power of 'joyance' the mind reflects beauty and love in terms of the natural world or, like the harp, turns the movement of experience into the wonder of poetry.

When 'joyance' is absent the mind is no longer creative but, like the harp and the moon, merely inanimate, or at least, a passive rather than a vital force. In *The Nightingale* Coleridge discusses the traditional, accepted symbolism of the nightingale and even advises the poet to draw his images from the world of nature rather than the world of books, but he does not mention the traditional analogy of poet and nightingale. (He also does not admit the way in which he draws on books. His nightingale is much indebted to Milton's 'that on yon bloomy spray / Warblest at eve, when all the woods are still' in his Sonnet I, not to mention 'the wakeful nightingale' in Eden, or his use of the Miltonism 'What time' in line 76.) Yet the poem is a conversation between poets and is as much concerned with poetry as with anything else. Certainly Coleridge draws on his direct experience, though one vastly changed in its re-creation. The child Hartley is associated with the process of the creative mind, though here also the incident seems to have been transformed. In his notebook Coleridge describes this incident thus:

> Hartley fell down & hurt himself—I caught him up crying & screaming—& ran out of doors with him.—The Moon caught his eye—he ceased crying immediately—& his eyes & the tears in them, how they glittered in the Moonlight![1]

In the poem Coleridge describes the child as suffering 'some inward pain . . . one infant's dream—' but notices the way in which his 'tears,/ Did glitter in the yellow moon-beam!'—a 'glittering eye' he shares with the Ancient Mariner. Thus the happiness of the child is restored by the light of the moon, though in this case the child, no poet, is nonetheless one who has been brought up as 'Nature's play-mate'. Moreover, Coleridge clearly agreed with Wordsworth in the belief in the special power of childhood to respond spontaneously to natural phenomena and to that extent the child experiences naturally (like the nightingale) what the poet can only experience in a state of heightened awareness.

In these poems Coleridge is prepared to accept the world of nature in all her moods. In *The Eolian Harp*, the mood is one of fulfilment and Coleridge asserts,

> *Methinks, it should have been impossible*
> *Not to love all things in a world so fill'd.*

The mood of *The Nightingale* is less fanciful, more withdrawn and more characteristically streaked with melancholy. Even so, he asserts,

> *In Nature there is nothing melancholy.*

Nevertheless, he is conscious that in bringing up his son as 'Nature's play-mate' he is ensuring that the boy's mind will be stored with precious and ineradicable stores of happy associations,

> *But if that Heaven*
> *Should give me life, his childhood shall grow up*
> *Familiar with these songs, that with the night*
> *He may associate joy.*

[1] *Notebooks*, I, 219. This may, of course, describe a similar occasion rather than the actual incident.

In *This Lime-Tree Bower My Prison* he is insistent on the power of nature to influence happiness. At the beginning of the poem he rejects his confinement because, he says,

> *I have lost*
> *Beauties and feelings, such as would have been*
> *Most sweet to my remembrance even when age*
> *Had dimm'd mine eyes to blindness!*

The feeling of being 'lonely and faint' is clearly in these lines in which he imagines himself into a Miltonic old-age and blindness. Later, when the poem returns to contemplate the bower, he reproves himself for this feeling of being totally isolated,

> *Henceforth I shall know*
> *That Nature ne'er deserts the wise and pure;*
> *No plot so narrow, be but Nature there,*
> *No waste so vacant, but may well employ*
> *Each faculty of sense, and keep the heart*
> *Awake to Love and Beauty!*

Indeed, he seems to congratulate himself on not being able to accompany Lamb and his friends *because* it gave him the opportunity to

> *lift the soul, and contemplate*
> *With lively joy the joys we cannot share.*

Altogether in this poem he moves tentatively towards the conclusion which he believes he may be able to share with Lamb,

> *my gentle-hearted Charles, to whom*
> *No sound is dissonant which tells of Life.*

Again Coleridge is expressing a belief often thought of as being peculiarly Wordsworthian. *Lines Written Above Tintern Abbey* develops all these movements of thought and lays particular stress on the knowledge that 'Nature never did betray / The heart that loved her,' as well as on the power of memory associated with nature to restore the human spirit. Thus the experience of nature is valued in both Coleridge and Wordsworth not only for the sense

> *Of present pleasure, but with pleasing thoughts*
> *That in this moment there is life and food*
> *For future years.*   (*Tintern Abbey*, 64–6)

Yet even so Coleridge's poems are sociable in a way that Wordsworth's never are; the tone of the conversational poems is always that of good talk among friends, each poem permeated by the power of affection. We are made aware not only of Coleridge talking but also of the person to whom he is talking. Wordsworth, by way of contrast, is always the solitary; we seldom have the sense of another's presence and even, as in *Lines Written Above Tintern Abbey* when he turns to address his sister, or in *The Prelude* when he addresses Coleridge, there is little sense of their presence in the poems themselves except as listeners. In *This Lime-Tree Bower My Prison* we are not only aware of Lamb's presence but Coleridge tries to see the walk through the eyes of his friend; in *The Eolian Harp* we are as much aware of Sara as of Coleridge; and in *The Nightingale* his affection for the Wordsworths sustains the whole poem so much so that he is able to introduce the homely incident of Hartley's distress without breaking in any way the continuity of the poem.

Both *This Lime-Tree Bower My Prison* and *The Nightingale* are wonderfully achieved poems, subtle in the modulations of tone and rhythm and impressive in the decorous way in which they grow by steady accretion as one movement of the poem parallels the next. Perhaps their most obvious feature, however, is the way in which the poems, in spite of the apparent casualness with which one idea leads to another, achieve a firm sense of organic growth and unity. The most personal and most lovely of all these conversation poems, however, is undoubtedly *Frost at Midnight*. No other poem shows Coleridge to better advantage. As a poem it has all those qualities so evident in *This Lime-Tree Bower My Prison* and *The Nightingale*, in particular the tone of informality, the sense of place, the positive outgoing relation with the world of man and nature, and the feeling of unity in 'multeity'. Yet it is more closely organized than any of them, more complex in its movements, quicker and more familiar in its effects. W. L. Renwick, who otherwise demonstrates little obvious enthusiasm for Coleridge whom he clearly sees as a Wordsworthian creation, insists that there 'is no better conducted poem in the English language than "Frost at Midnight"'.[1] On the whole W. L. Renwick's judgements are grudging, petulant even, but in describing *Frost at Midnight* he seems to have pointed to just that decorous quality that characterizes the poem.

Quite clearly in *The Eolian Harp* there is a real element of self-reproach but even in *This Lime-Tree Bower* the tone is broken by an unnecessary note of self-pity. Apart from imagining himself as old and blind in that poem, he also refers to his friends out walking as gone for ever, friends 'whom I never more may meet again'—where the 'never more' and 'again' reinforce superfluously an already over-dramatized sentiment. Even in *The Nightingale* he cannot prevent himself it seems from wondering whether he has a future at all—'But if that Heaven / Should give me life,'—and is perhaps somewhat final and excessive in bidding the birds and his friends farewell, as if he suspects that perhaps he will not last the night. These elements are not by any means obtrusive or in themselves at all objectionable, but they are indicative of Coleridge's tendency to dramatize himself in Hamlet-like poses as if none too sure that the love and sympathy he extends to others will be returned. Yet *Frost at Midnight*, the most introspective and personal of these poems avoids any hint of self-dramatization. It is intensely meditative, the product of what he calls 'the self-watching subtilizing mind' and it would not have been altogether surprising, if he had struck a Hamlet-like pose at least somewhere in the poem. In point of fact, however, the sense of stillness and calm with which the poem begins pervades the whole poem which closes, as it opens, with a sense of quiet serenity. Although he is concerned with isolation, withdrawal from the world into 'abstruser musings', and although he is concerned with minutely recording the movements of his own mind, he has successfully objectified the experience without once losing the informal, even homely tone of voice by which a particular individual communicates in recognizable accents and by which an intangible but quite definite relationship is established between that individual and his readers. The power of

[1] *English Literature 1789–1815*, The Oxford History of English Literature, Oxford, 1963, ch. VI, 155.

affection that gives this poem its tone is that felt by Coleridge for his son Hartley, 'my babe so beautiful' but the theme of the poem, as Humphry House points out in his lucid analysis,[1] is the movement of the mind. He follows the various changes in the poem and notes the way in which it grows into 'unity and seriousness' with Coleridge marrying mind and language to convey faithfully 'the way the wind is behaving'. However, Humphry House does not for his purposes bring out the parallels central to the poem as a whole, which depends on the contrast between Coleridge's childhood and growth and the imagined, hoped-for childhood and growth of his son Hartley.

In the opening paragraph Coleridge notices how the quietness disturbs his thought,

> *And vexes meditation with its strange*
> *And extreme silentness,*

which recalls the 'pause of silence' when in *The Nightingale* the moon is hidden and the birds cease their singing. In this silence the outside world of nature and man is described curiously as being 'inaudible as dreams'. Yet in this mood his mind focusses on the 'film which fluttered on the grate' and he seizes on this as an image of his own mind at that moment fluttering and idling purposelessly. His footnote reminds us, however, that these films 'are called *strangers* and supposed to portend the arrival of some absent friend' and this association is sufficient to transport him back in time and space to his own schooldays at Christ's Hospital, when he also remembers watching the film on the grate and at that time remembered his birth-place and how the next day he waited excitedly, unable to study, for the absent friend's visit foretold by the film. From this memory within a memory his mind returns to the room in which he is and focusses on the sleeping baby. The poem is set at midnight, as the title says, a time when one day ends and another is about to begin. Having, therefore, moved back in time to his own childhood, he now moves forward in time to the future he imagines for his son. Whereas he was brought up in the town, away from nature, seeing 'nought lovely but the sky and stars', he determines that Hartley shall experience all that is lovely in nature and

[1] *Coleridge, The Clark Lectures 1951–2, 79–83.*

> see and hear
> *The lovely shapes and sounds intelligible*
> *Of that eternal language, which thy God*
> *Utters, who from eternity doth teach*
> *Himself in all, and all things in himself.*
> *Great universal Teacher! he shall mould*
> *Thy spirit, and by giving make it ask.*

The most obvious contrast between Coleridge's upbringing and that he wishes for his son is the contrast between being 'reared / In the great city pent mid cloisters dim' and being raised in a landscape of 'lakes and sandy shores, beneath the crags / Of ancient mountains'. The contrast is really that of being 'reared' in a world of artificiality and being brought up naturally to 'wander like a breeze'. However, underlying this fairly trite romantic contrast is another of far greater significance to Coleridge. In the original 1798 version Coleridge had made it quite clear that his strong, if childish, belief in what the film portends is a 'most believing superstitious wish'. By suppressing these lines Coleridge dims somewhat the contrast between the pagan superstitions that played such a strong part in his formative years and the hope that his son will grow up familiar with nature, the book of God, the 'great Universal Teacher'. Coleridge's strong belief in a God, 'Himself in all, and all things in himself', has been sustained at least as far back as *The Eolian Harp* where he affirms his belief in a God 'At once the Soul of each, and God of all'—which stands in spite of Sara. Looked at from this point of view the relationship between father and son is enriched, for the son becomes the embodiment of his father's redemption. The relationship between the son and nature is clearly sacramental, nature being the 'eternal language of God'. The 'unregenerate mind' that Coleridge fears in *The Eolian Harp* therefore plays its part also in this poem and is specifically linked with the atavistic folklore and superstition, the manifestations of an age-old paganism that he knows to be so powerfully operative within his own mind and experience and which lies on him as heavily as the curse lies on the Ancient Mariner in a poem that gives powerful though ambiguous expression to paganism *and* Christianity. In the original 1798 version of the poem this is reinforced by the close of the

poem in lines subsequently deleted. Humphry House is quite right in
believing that ending the poem as it stands in the final version 'was one
of the best artistic decisions Coleridge ever made. For not only is the
present ending one of the finest pieces of descriptive writing in the
language, intricate and yet at the same time sparsely clear, compressing
so much of the moods of various weather; but it also perfectly rounds
the movement of the mind which has been the poem's theme,'

> *Therefore all seasons shall be sweet to thee,*
> *Whether the summer clothe the general earth*
> *With greenness, or the redbreast sit and sing*
> *Betwixt the tufts of snow on the bare branch*
> *Of mossy apple-tree, while the nigh thatch*
> *Smokes in the sun-thaw; whether the eave-drops fall*
> *Heard only in the trances of the blast,*
> *Or if the secret ministry of frost*
> *Shall hang them up in silent icicles,*
> *Quietly shining to the quiet Moon.*

This passage closes the final version with grace and loveliness and comes
in its context like a benediction completing the circle of thought from
'secret ministry' of frost back to the same ministry. Humphry House's
objection to the original conclusion is that it introduced new material
into the poem, 'the vista of new domestic detail was opened', and that
the poem merely stopped rather than ending. Yet, however justly
abandoned, the original ending has a quite distinct interest of its own;
originally the poem ended,

> *Or whether the secret ministry of cold*
> *Shall hang them up in silent icicles,*
> *Quietly shining to the quiet moon,*
> *Like those, my babe! which ere tomorrow's warmth*
> *Have capp'd their sharp keen points with pendulous drops,*
> *Will catch thine eye, and with their novelty*
> *Suspend thy little soul; then make thee shout,*
> *And stretch and flutter from thy mother's arms*
> *As thou wouldst fly for very eagerness.*

This original ending is clearly reminiscent of the end of *The Nightingale* where Hartley is taken into the orchard to see the moon. On this imagined occasion, however, the child shouts and struggles from his mother's arms as if to fly towards the icicles. However, the word 'flutter' must recall the film in the grate which is described as 'fluttered' and 'still flutters' and which becomes an image representing Coleridge's 'idling Spirit' as well as recalling the superstition concerning the arrival of some absent friend. It may be, therefore, that the repetition of the word here indicates an attempt by the baby to move away from the 'unregenerate mind' of his parents, away from superstition and paganism in order to embrace the ministry of nature, recognizing the fallen nature of man.

Whether or not such weight can be borne by this passage, there seems little doubt that artistically the poem was vastly improved by the revisions made after 1798. Equally there can be little doubt that the revisions tended to suppress to a large extent those elements of self-examination when in comparison with his son, Coleridge suspects that his own mind is potentially evil and degenerate. In the final version which is so strongly impressive because of the confidence with which Coleridge follows the movements of his mind, perhaps this underlying lack of confidence is already growing. One other indication that Coleridge is not so confident in the powers of his own mind as the poem itself would lead us to believe is his reference to the ministry of frost. The opening lines of the poem tell us,

> *The Frost performs its secret ministry*
> *Unhelped by any wind.*

The frost is distinct, therefore, from the Eolian harp which produces harmony only when caressed by the wind. Perhaps, therefore, the poet's isolation is already more pressing than the poem would otherwise suggest; the act of creative imagination is always seen as a reciprocal movement of the kind suggested by the harp or by the nightingales and the moon, the moon itself being a symbol of the reflective mind. Yet clearly Coleridge begins his poem by suggesting a complete separation between mind and nature, the frost separate, outside and indifferent to other forces. Curiously when the image of the 'secret ministry of frost'

returns in the last paragraph of the poem, it does so in conjunction with
the image of 'the quiet Moon', suggesting, perhaps, by this conjunction that a reciprocal relation has been re-established in much the same
way as the father re-establishes a fruitful redemptive relationship with
his son, and the son is imagined as re-establishing a natural, sacramental
relationship with God and nature which his father now is aware of being
denied. If Coleridge in his poem moves outward towards the world of
man and nature, he does so either by a process of mind 'inaudible as
dreams' or through recreating memories from the past, one memory
unlocking another.

Frost at Midnight is undoubtedly the finest of these conversational
poems; it was, perhaps, influential in stimulating Wordsworth to write
Lines Written Above Tintern Abbey, into which so many Coleridgean
themes are woven, and if Wordsworth's is the greater poem, Coleridge's
is the more human, more moving testimony of a man speaking to men.
If, however, there is anything at all in these pointers concerning Coleridge's awareness of a more suspect, more disturbing area of mind than
the poem immediately reveals—and certainly these pointers are
marginal, perhaps at best straws in the wind—we can at least show
in *The Ancient Mariner*, in *Kubla Khan* but particularly in *Christabel*, a
serious, daemonic concern with areas of consciousness, or subcon-
sciousness, that would fully justify Coleridge's fear of the 'unregenerate
mind'. In a sense these poems turn dream to nightmare and make it all
too audible.

We must also recall that if *Frost at Midnight* leads on to the complete
loss of confidence celebrated, if that is the word, in *Dejection*, in *Fears
in Solitude* written in April 1798, the month he also wrote *The Nightingale*, his concern and fears are associated with war and the threat of
invasion, but his passionate humanity cannot conceal the possibility
that the cause of his anxiety may be more deeply rooted in his own
psychology. The beginning and the close of the poem are reminiscent
of the landscape of *The Nightingale* but the middle sections are nearer
to the impassioned rhetoric of his early political poems than to the
conversational poems as a group. He sees himself as he undoubtedly
was, a meditative man who found joy and 'Religious meanings in the
forms of Nature'. Yet he is moved strongly by the horrors of war:

> *My God! It is a melancholy thing*
> *For such a man, who would full fain preserve*
> *His soul in calmness, yet perforce must feel*
> *For all his human brethren—O my God!*
> *It weighs upon the heart, that he must think*
> *What uproar and what strife may now be stirring*
> *This way or that way over these silent hills—*

There is no doubting his sincerity in attacking his age for its love of war or for its disregard of religion; his horror of war is strongly conveyed, his attack on the French and his calling on his countrymen to resist the enemy are powerfully urged. Yet we are left wondering in this the longest of these poems whether he does not protest too much and whether the 'meditative joy' of the solitary is as securely rooted as the poem's opening suggests. The tirade is perhaps too shrill, too long, too direct not to leave the reader with the feeling that he is seizing too readily the invasion alarms to express feelings whose source lies deeper than the occasion suggests. The argument of the poem is also disconcerting in that a passionate pacificism, an attack on the inhumanity of war itself, quite suddenly turns to an appeal to his countrymen to take up arms against the French. The poem lacks that degree of organization that characterizes the other conversational poems as indeed it also lacks that particular informality of tone that brings poet and reader together. Coleridge was aware of the poem's deficiencies, its unevenness of pace and tone, and in a note on an autograph MS of the poem wrote, 'N.B. The above is perhaps not Poetry—but rather a sort of middle thing between Poetry and Oratory—*sermoni propriora.*—Some parts are, I am conscious, too tame even for animated prose.' Certainly the body of the poem recalls his earlier declamatory style and there is too little of what Coleridge in the lovely closing paragraph of the poem calls 'conversing with the mind . . . a dance of thought'. Yet if this poem as a whole lacks those qualities we value in the other conversational poems, at least we are made aware of the disciplined activity of mind that produced these other poems and how precariously they were achieved. Nonetheless, the poem does close on a vision of unity in which nature, love and man are embraced in one comprehensive gesture,

> *—by nature's quietness*
> *And solitary musings, all my heart*
> *Is softened, and made worthy to indulge*
> *Love, and the thoughts that yearn for human kind.*

This is just the united vision that he failed to achieve only four years later, a failure made all too clear in *Dejection*.

Although *Dejection* is described by Coleridge as an Ode, its relation to the conversational poems is clarified by the fact that in its original form it was written as a verse-letter to Sara Hutchinson, dated 'Sunday Evening, April 14, 1802'. Even without this knowledge, however, Coleridge is clearly in the poem engaged intensely in 'conversing with the mind' and the whole poem is so shot through with personal memories that it must be grouped with the conversational poems. The poem raises unusual textual difficulties in so far as the version printed and treated as the *textus receptus* is significantly different from the text sent to Sara Hutchinson, which did not come to light until 1937.[1] There are strong personal reasons why Coleridge could not publish the verse letter and, therefore, good reasons why we cannot accept the *textus receptus* as the final version but only as a version acceptable for publication. The fact that the verse letter is more than a hundred lines longer than the printed version undoubtedly aggravates the problem of text. The verse letter is intimate, addressed to 'O dearest Sara', and central to it is his love for Sara and in particular his concern in case she should be ill and he, absent from her, should know of her illness and yet be unable to go to her and comfort her,

> *Thy Delights*
> *Far off, or near, alike I may partake—*
> *But O! to mourn for thee, and to forsake*
> *All power, all hope, of giving comfort to thee—*
> *To know that thou art weak and worn with pain,*
> *And not to hear thee, Sara! not to view thee—*
> *Not sit beside thy Bed,*
> *Not press thy aching Head,*

---

[1] E. de Selincourt, 'Coleridge's "Dejection: an Ode"', ESMEA, XXII, 1937; but see Humphry House, *Coleridge, The Clark Lectures 1951–2*, 133ff.

> *Not bring thee Health again—*
> *At least to hope, to try—*

He bitterly regrets writing her a complaining letter, 'which even to bodily Sickness bruis'd thy Soul', knowing that she would blame herself rather than him. He associates her with the Wordsworth circle and all it represents for him, though even brief visits are now painful to him because they serve to emphasize the misery of his life otherwise,

> *To visit those, I love, as I love thee,*
> *Mary, and William, and dear Dorothy,*
> *It is but a temptation to repine—*
> *The transientness is Poison in the Wine,*
> *Eats out the pith of Joy, makes all Joy hollow,*
> *All Pleasure a dim Dream of Pain to follow!*
> *. . . . .*
>
> *Wherefore, O wherefore! should I wish to be*
> *A wither'd branch upon a blossoming Tree?*

He is grateful for his children except when they remind him of the happiness that might have been his, at which times he half-wishes they had never been born. Twice he return to his life with his wife, what Shakespeare describes as the dark house and the detested wife,

> *My own peculiar Lot, my house-hold Life*
> *It is, and will remain, Indifference or Strife.*
> *. . . . .*
>
> *I speak now of those habitual Ills*
> *That wear out Life, when two unequal Minds*
> *Meet in one House and two discordant Wills—*
> *. . . my coarse domestic life has known*
> *No Habits of heart-nursing Sympathy.*

These references to his home-life contrast painfully with his return home as described in *The Nightingale* and his return at the end of *Fears in Solitude* to

> *my own lowly cottage, where my babe*
> *And my babe's mother dwell in peace!*

He assures Sara that there was a time when he was capable of Joy, but he now realizes that the hopes and dreams of that earlier time merely seemed to be but were not his and now each new misfortune

> *Suspends what nature gave me at my Birth,*
> *My shaping, spirit of Imagination!*

The emphasis is not on his loss of creative imagination but on a changed state of mind that is no longer capable of sustaining 'ill-tidings' without it affecting, suspending, his shaping spirit of Imagination. The loss of his ability to feel as well as see is also directly connected with Sara and the Wordsworth circle following as it does a reference to *Peter Bell*,

> *A boat becalm'd! dear William's Sky Canoe!*
> *—I see them all, so excellently fair!*
> *I see, not feel, how beautiful they are.*

Similarly, in this version, his realization that the source of joyance is within the mind is introduced by lines echoing Wordsworth's *Simon Lee* at the climax of which occur the lines,

> *So vain was his endeavour*
> *That at the root of the old tree*
> *He might have worked for ever.*

Coleridge could not have forgotten these lines when writing

> *It were a vain Endeavor,*
> *Tho' I should gaze for ever*
> *On that Green Light that lingers in the West!*
> *I may not hope from outward Forms to win*
> *The Passion and the Life, whose Fountains are within!*

Similarly, the lines that bear such weight of meaning in the printed text are in the verse-letter the opening of the last paragraph which is a most moving celebration of Sara's happiness, not in any sense related to his own despair,

> *O Sara! we receive but what we give,*
> *And in our life alone does Nature live*
> *Our's is her Wedding Garment, our's her Shroud—*
> *And would we aught behold of higher Worth*

> *Than that inanimate cold World allow'd*
> *To that poor loveless ever anxious Crowd,*
> *Ah! from the Soul itself must issue forth*
> *A Light, a Glory, and a luminous Cloud*
> *Enveloping the Earth!*

There is no doubt that the verse-letter is a poem of love and of deep feeling rather than a despairing celebration of the loss of imaginative vision. Coleridge contrasts his own unhappiness with the happiness of Sara and the Wordsworths, but the burden of the poem in this version is carried by his love for Sara and his happiness in celebrating her joy. In the numerous echoes from Wordsworth's poems that run through the verse letter he finds a common language, as it were, that draws him and Sara more closely together. As in all the conversational poems, Coleridge tries to see through the eyes of his friends, to put himself in their place and see from their point of view. This is part of the selflessness of the man; he is occasionally given to self-pity and this also is part of the man that must be accepted.

In the published version all the personal references have been suppressed and the loss is such as to change the temper of the poem entirely. As it was published the poem is rightly celebrated for the subtlety and intensity of Coleridge's self-analysis, for his despair, and for his comments on the relation between the mind and the world of nature. The echoes from Wordsworth, and in particular of his *Ode on the Intimations of Immortality*, the first four stanzas of which Coleridge must have seen on his visit to the Wordsworths in March 1802, have led critics[1] to suppose that the poem as a whole is an answer to the questions,

> *Whither is fled the visionary gleam?*
> *Where is it now, the glory and the dream?*

If this were so, then the theme of Coleridge's poem would be his rejection of the Wordsworthian belief in the efficacy of imaginative recreation—which was also his belief in the earlier conversational poems—and a despairing affirmation of the subjectivity of the creative

[1] See *e.g.* Mary Moorman, *William Wordsworth. The Early Years 1770–1803*, Oxford, 1957, 528.

imagination, the loss of which is irrecoverable. In fact, even if this is one of the themes of the published poem, the interest and power of the poem undoubtedly still reside in Coleridge's intense preoccupation with the workings of his own mind. The poem's epigraph, taken from the *Ballad of Sir Patrick Spens*, refers to the 'deadly storm' portended by the fact that the new Moon holds the 'old Moon in her arms' and the poem is organized around a series of contrasts between the new and the old, and scrupulously records the changing weather of the mind. In the first stanza the night is tranquil but in stanza VII we learn that the wind 'long has raved unnoticed', a storm that continues to the last stanza, VIII. The tranquillity of the opening is not, however, the peace and calm of the earlier conversational poems but the restless impatient movement of despair; it is not a creative, harmonious spirit but a discordant destructive one. This in the context of these poems is made clear by the image of the Eolian harp,

> *—the dull sobbing draft, that moans and rakes*
> *Upon the strings of this Æolian lute,*
> *Which better far were mute.*

He invited the winds to blow so that he may be moved in spirit, relieved of the 'dull pain' and brought back to vital life. The comparison with the agony of the Ancient Mariner when becalmed is clear enough; but he and Coleridge are suffering that death-in-life which is a prominent feature of despair. In this poem as in *The Ancient Mariner* we have a complete embodiment of that state of mind in which the world of nature is seen but not felt,

> *A grief without a pang, void, dark, and drear,*
> *A stifled, drowsy, unimpassionate grief,*
> *Which finds no natural outlet, no relief,*
> *In word, or sigh, or tear—*

He realizes that the source of all beauty, feeling and sympathy are within the human heart and that

> *—from the Soul itself must issue forth*
> *A light, a glory, a fair luminous cloud*
> *Enveloping the Earth—*

> *And from the soul itself must there be sent*
> *A sweet and potent voice, of its own birth,*
> *Of all sweet sounds the life and element.*

Nature, the language of God, is now a closed book to him, for his misery has driven out 'joyance', that state of heightened awareness when sight becomes insight into the harmony of all things. Joy is the inheritance of the pure and he has been utterly disinherited,

> *—Joy that ne'er was given,*
> *Save to the pure, and in their purest hour,*
> *Life, and Life's effluence, cloud at once and shower,*
> *Joy, Lady! is the spirit and the power,*
> *Which wedding Nature to us gives in dower*
> *A new Earth and new Heaven,*
> *Undreamt of by the sensual and the proud—*
> *Joy is the sweet voice, Joy the luminous cloud—*
> *We in ourselves rejoice!*

The most impressive aspect of the poem is the startling way in which Coleridge with detached precision shows such understanding of his own desolation and the honesty with which he confronts the humiliation and self-hatred that have destroyed his life. His afflictions now suspend his 'shaping spirit of Imagination' and in using 'suspends' we must assume that he had not entirely lost that sense of joy necessary to animate his soul and the inanimate world of nature. In stanza VII he puts behind him 'Reality's dark dreams' and listens to the wind. Presumably the link between this and the previous stanza is his reference to imagination that still is accessible to him, if only fitfully, although the transition is really neither quite clear nor particularly elegant. The reference to 'viper thoughts' is curiously unprepared for anywhere in the poem. The wind is itself creative but in a melodramatic, Jacobean sense, is tragic, bombastic and tells of 'groans, of trampled men, with smarting wounds'; in a different key the wind also tells the tale of a little child who 'hath lost her way'. Coleridge seems to identify with both aspects of the wind's creation, its dramatic hysteria and its quieter pathos, though the child also moans and screams in an attempt to make her mother hear. Thus this creative storm serves only to heighten Coleridge's sense of total isolation, too aware of man's misery, too lost to find any way home. The poem ends with a wish that this storm which brings misery, destruction, and loss to him, will endow his friend with restorative vision, 'wings of healing', and that she will enjoy the real tranquillity he once knew. Above all, however, he wished that she may learn joy and and that she may 'ever, evermore rejoice'.

This published version of the poem has an impressive formality which is constantly being undermined by the sheer flexibility of rhythm and tone in the language itself. It is tightly organized, even cryptically structured, but it lacks the warmth of love and concern that are so characteristically present in the verse-letter. In many ways the published poem is the finer poem, but there can be no doubt as to which of the versions brings the reader closest to Coleridge. Indeed, in these conversational poems it is in the end the expression of a particular kind of personality that we value. So we admire the Coleridge of *Dejection: An Ode* but prefer to keep company with the Coleridge of the verse-letter. With Coleridge, at least in the conversational poems, to admire the achievements of the poet is also to admire the humanity of the man. In this way Coleridge enjoys a distinctive kind of immortality. Even in his epitaph the spirit of the man is still present, 'he who many a year with toil of breath / Found death in life, may here find life in death'. It is characteristic that he should describe himself by his initials and that he should wish to be remembered as a poet 'or that which once seem'd he'. His humility never deserted him, but the achievement of his poetry is considerable. His conversational poems introduce many of the major themes of English Romantic poetry, while at the same time establishing immediate continuity with Cowper and the eighteenth century. In these poems he created a medium of expression both subtle and lucid, capable of prosaic statement and of imaginative vision of great power; above all he created a medium capable of conveying the genial, candid and eventually disillusioned genius of S.T.C.

4: *Coleridge and Criticism:*
I. Critical Theory

J. A. APPLEYARD

I

THOUGH HE wrote in 1840 (in an essay for *The Westminster Review*) John Stuart Mill was confident even then that a man could understand the nineteenth century by grasping the different viewpoints of its two great seminal minds, Jeremy Bentham and Samuel Taylor Coleridge. He put the difference this way: of any asserted fact or principle one could imagine Bentham asking 'Is it true?', whereas Coleridge would be likely to ask 'What does it mean?' The utilitarian question, Mill thought, implies self-confidence, objectivity, and clear and perhaps too simple criteria for determining truth. The Coleridgean response assumes that the mere existence or assertion of a fact or a principle is itself part of the problem, that the belief of people that something is true is already a phenomenon that has meaning and has to be explained.

Coleridge enjoyed dichotomies (indeed Hazlitt thought it was a constitutional weakness of his mind to be always wandering back and forth between alternatives), and would perhaps have found this one just, not because he was unconcerned about truth, but because the question about meaning is a roomier one and can accommodate different kinds of significance: what is affective and personal, social and historical, subjective values as well as what is objective and universal, above all what Mill accused Bentham of overlooking: 'the entire unanalyzed experience of the human race'. Bentham's attitude has its advantages, however: to judge is easier than to bear the burden of painful self-consciousness involved in always questioning after meaning. Coleridge—poet, political economist, literary critic, philosopher, theologian—habitually saw too much that had to be taken into account, and lived most of his life before he became at all confident about his ability to make even partial and provisional explanations. The development of his theories about literature is best seen against the background of Mill's question, as a series of attempts to create a theoretical structure adequate to his experience of poetry. The imperative arises, of course, because available theories do not account for the full meaning of the experience. What Coleridge had to do was to invent a point of view and a vocabulary equal to his experience. What in fact he probably accomplished was to shape the point of view from which most twentieth-century English and American readers think and talk about poetry. That accomplishment is the subject of our study here.

Of course the alteration of a later generation's consciousness is not the work of one man. Coleridge is as much sharer in as creator of the changes which literary theory went through between the neoclassic age and our own. Indeed a strong case has been made, by René Wellek[1] and lately by Gian N. G. Orsini,[2] that few of Coleridge's ideas were original and that the most significant among them were borrowed from the German romantics. It was an imputation Coleridge was himself particularly sensitive about and, the sceptical will say, with good reason. But when it is a question of an age reacting against the rigidities of an earlier viewpoint, within a culture so nearly homogeneous as that of the European eighteenth century, and with the common catalyst of the French revolution, then discerning the originality of current ideas and assigning priority among them becomes a quite delicate task. Coleridge freely admitted his general indebtedness to Kant, Schelling and the Schlegels. Frequently he took over phrases and whole passages *verbatim*. But it matters greatly to what purpose. No one who reads the early notebooks and letters can doubt that most of Coleridge's substantive ideas about literature were in his head long before he started borrowing from the Germans, and even the undoubted borrowings seem to have served largely to help on his own thinking, frequently to flesh out a surmise with the aid of a more precise terminology. Indeed Coleridge quite typically does scant justice to the exact meaning a term or an idea had for its originator; with Kant especially he scavenges for

[1] *Immanuel Kant in England 1793–1838*, Princeton, 1931.
[2] *Coleridge and German Idealism*, Carbondale, Illinois, 1969.

notions and distinctions which he uses for purposes entirely his own. To concentrate too much attention on the question of originality and priority is to miss seeing that Coleridge was the main interpreter, at least in the area of English literature, of that profound shift in consciousness which separates the Enlightenment from the nineteenth and twentieth centuries, that shift of which romanticism was only the most obvious phenomenon.

It remains paradoxical that, though Coleridge has this undoubted eminence as the metaphysician of English romanticism, it is somewhat difficult to recommend to the student the books and essays in which he will find this philosophy coherently set down. Kathleen Coburn has said that the literary form most characteristic of Coleridge is the fragment. His most interesting ideas often exist only in notebook entries or in letters. Of his lectures we have hardly any manuscripts, mainly secretaries' accounts or second-hand reports. His most substantial and best known prose work, the *Biographia Literaria,* is unread and largely unreadable. Coleridge himself called it an 'immethodical miscellany'. By itself it can give no adequate impression of his ideas, and indeed much harm has been done by anthologizing its supposedly key chapters as evidence of romantic literary theory. Coleridge has to be taken whole, and the development of his ideas traced from point to point, in order to see the significance of them at their maturity. What is said here is intended as a guide to that task.

II

The most convenient way of seeing Coleridge's philosophical development is in terms of a dichotomy roughly parallel to the one Mill suggests, except that now the two parts of the dichotomy have to be taken as conflicting states of mind competing for Coleridge's loyalty, creating a tension he would attempt to transcend. On the one side are experience, feeling, poetry, religious enthusiasm, a sense of the relationships among things and of the oneness of experience; on the other side are empirical science, logic, reason, literary convention, unitarianism and religious scepticism, and a sense of the disparateness and unrelatedness of things. The gap between was painful to a person who had grown up dreaming and wondering, unquestioning about genies and fairies, 'habituated to the Vast' (CL, I, 354), feeling 'the omnipresence of all in each' (*Notebooks* II, 2371). The outcome of the struggle between opposing viewpoints was perhaps predictable, but the philosophical resolution of the apparent disparity took Coleridge many years.

'Oneness' and 'joy' are the terms which sum up the experience of the one side of the dichotomy. It is the point of view of the poetry of the years before 1800. From Bishop Berkeley or from the seventeenth-century German mystic Jacob Boehme, Coleridge absorbed the idea of nature as the language of God, 'one mighty alphabet', 'a living Thing/ That acts upon the mind.'[1] The idea is an ancient one and links Coleridge with the whole neo-platonist tradition, whose fundamental aspiration was to offer an explanation of—indeed to provide the means of achieving —the unity of all being and consciousness in the divine. 'My mind feels as if it ached to behold and know something *great*—something *one and indivisible*', Coleridge writes in a letter of 1797 (CL, I, 349), and from 1800 on we regularly discover in his notebooks various plans for 'the one work' which would be a systematic verification of all philosophical and theological knowledge. It seems to have been Coleridge's habit to think in terms of these great syntheses. When the vision failed, 'intellectual *exsiccation*' followed, and the ode *Dejection* is the painful record of this loss of the 'shaping spirit of Imagination' (PW, I, 366). In the poem the only cure in prospect is the inward joy of the pure of heart, which is an energy powerful enough to animate the world of natural forms about us.

It is not accidental that Coleridge linked this sense of oneness and the joy which it inspired with the poet's creative powers. It was the experience of Wordsworth's poetry, he says, that started him thinking about the imagination. 'I was in my twenty-fourth year, when I had the happiness of knowing Mr. Wordsworth personally, and while memory lasts, I shall hardly forget the sudden effect produced on my mind by his recitation of a manuscript poem' (*Biog. Lit.*, I, 58). What impressed

---

[1] *The Destiny of Nations*, PW, I, 132; *This Lime-Tree Bower*, CL, I, 335. See also *Frost at Midnight*.

Coleridge was the 'union' of feeling and thought, the 'balance' of truth of observation and imaginative modification of detail, the lustre and sparkle restored to common things and incidents—in other words the power of imagination to unify, integrate and enliven. Thus the central element of Coleridge's mature literary theory reaches back for its foundation to the qualities which even in Coleridge's youth defined one side of the dichotomy he struggled to overcome.

III

The other half of Coleridge's mind is under the influence of men like Locke, Hume, Priestley, Davy and Godwin: empiricists, experimentalists, even atheists. In the last decade of the eighteenth century, science, dissent, and political radicalism were the fashion. The philosophical version of this attitude that Coleridge knew best was the associationist psychology of David Hartley's *Observations on Man* (London, 1749). The principle that ideas recall other ideas by reason of similarity, contrast, contiguity in space and time, or causal relationship, is as old as Aristotle. When the British empirical philosophers—Hobbes, Locke, Hume—took as their premise that there was nothing in the mind except data from external sense impressions arranged in more or less complex combinations, the association of ideas achieved the status of law, particularly in Hume, for whom it was the principle by which discrete perceptions were unified.[1] Hartley's contribution was to provide a physiological explanation of the process in terms of neural vibrations linking the sense receptors with the medullary substance of the brain, and—perhaps more importantly—to put the psychological data into a larger vision of inevitable progress towards greater spiritual happiness and a final state of 'theopathy', the experience of the contemplation of God.

The apparent empiricism, the rationality, the implications of social

[1] *Cf.* the three articles on associationist literary criticism by Martin Kallich: ELH, 12, 1945, 290–315; SP, 43, 1946, 644–67; MLN, 62, 1947, 166–73.

amelioration drew Coleridge to Hartley's views. In the middle 1790s there are several notebook entries and letters testifying to his enthusiasm, and in 1796 he named his eldest son Hartley (he was to name his younger son Berkeley). But the defects of such a mechanical and covertly materialistic point of view were not long in coming to light, and Coleridge's interest in Hartley did not survive his initial immersion in 'metaphysics' during the winter of illness and self-examination of 1800–1801. The specific object of his study then was Locke and the relationship of thoughts to things, and the heresy Coleridge entertained was that perhaps there was some utility in the metaphor of 'constituent Ideas' existing in the mind; this would get beyond 'the nonsense of vibrations' and the mechanism of associationism without having to resort to the extremity of innate ideas (CL, I, 626; CL, II, 696). Coleridge's doubts were significant. The trouble with associationism was that it did not 'tell in the heart'. He needed to bring into unity more than just the phenomena of sensation.

Coleridge could never have accepted the mechanism and materialism of associationist psychology and still have remained faithful to his own experience. But the rejection of this part of Hartley's philosophy turned out to be compatible with a powerful and almost undetected influence which other parts of the associationist theories had on Coleridge. The direction of British empiricism had led to ever more materialistic theories of knowledge; but it also led to an increasing emphasis on the *viewpoint* of the knowing subject as the unifying centre of the act of knowledge.[1] Earlier realistic epistemologies assumed the correspondence of the knower with the known; associationism produced as one of its consequences a shift in emphasis towards the integrative activity of the knower over against the atomistic and particulate existence of all sensory impressions. Various mental faculties were distinguished and examined; different tasks were assigned to each. The result was to throw the responsibility for the most profound or complete knowledge onto the *right kind* of mental act, onto something like intuition rather than analysis and judgement. Metaphors of creativity and generation replaced metaphors of recording, dissecting and recon-

[1] See Ralph Cohen, 'Association of Ideas and Poetic Unity', PQ, 36, 1957, 464–75.

stituting. The mirror became the lamp.[1] Thus the paradox that the quest for an experiential account of the knowledge process produced both the neural vibrations of the physiological psychologists and the various descriptions of creative imagination shared by Coleridge and his contemporaries.

IV

In the eighteenth century imagination meant something like the power of visualizing images of things absent or distant; at most it meant, as it did for Hume,[2] the faculty which combines in unusual and fantastical ways the elementary stock of ideas furnished by the senses, according to the laws of association. The term was now and then distinguished from *fancy*. When Coleridge came to make the same distinction, he gave to *imagination* the considerably greater burden of being the creative and unifying power which his analysis of the mind's activities required. In the notion of imagination the need for 'oneness' and joy comes together with a sufficiently psychological account of the process to satisfy both the poet and the philosopher in Coleridge.

The distinction is stated quite clearly in a letter of 1802 (CL, II, 864–6). Coleridge had as a very young man fallen under the influence of the sonnets of William Lisle Bowles, finding in them a welcome contrast to the tired conventional wit and ornamentation of the fashionable poetry of the age: Bowles was among the first who 'combined natural thoughts with natural diction', he 'reconciled the heart with the head' (*Biog. Lit.*, I, 16). But now Coleridge changes his view, and finds in the poems he once admired that natural objects interesting in themselves are overlaid with moral significance. Bowles has failed to see that Nature has her own proper interest, that each thing has a life of its own, that we are all *one life*. 'A Poet's *Heart* and *Intellect* should be *combined, intimately* combined and *unified*, with the great appearances in Nature—and not merely held in solution and loose mixture with them, in the shape of forced similes' (CL, II, 864). In

[1] See M. H. Abrams, *The Mirror and the Lamp: Romantic Theory and the Critical Tradition*, New York, 1953.
[2] Kallich, SP, 43, 1946, 656.

trying to explain the basis for this unification of heart, intellect, and natural object, Coleridge speaks of the 'logic' of a poem, as profound in its kind as the logic to be found in the *Organon* of Aristotle. Finally he reaches the point where he attributes the mere linking of objects and their moral or spiritual significance to 'Fancy, or the aggregating Faculty of the mind', whereas the perception of each thing as having a life of its own and yet as a part of the one life is the work of '*Imagination, or the modifying, and co-adunating* Faculty' (CL, II, 865-6).

What this means is clarified somewhat by a passage in a letter written two years later, where Coleridge discusses the achievement of Wordsworth as 'the first and greatest philosophical Poet—the only man who has effected a compleat and constant synthesis of Thought and Feeling and combined them with Poetic forms, with the music of pleasurable passion and with Imagination or the *modifying* Power in that highest sense of the word in which I have ventured to oppose it to Fancy, or the *aggregating* power—in that sense in which it is a dim Analogue of Creation, not all that we can *believe* but all that we can *conceive* of creation' (CL, II, 1034). Thought, feeling, music, and poetic forms are the elements which the imagination somehow unites and—special stress is put on the word—modifies. The process is not spelled out, but it is in a faint way analogous to God's creative act.

The last remark is significant. It points to the large implications latent in the project of describing the psychology of poetic creativity. Coleridge begins here by tackling a purely poetic problem, occasioned by his analyses of Bowles and Wordsworth and his need for a clearer self-understanding as a poet. The solution involves distinguishing imagination from fancy, but the most he will or can say here about the imagination is that it *modifies* the elements of the poetic process. The analogy of creation, however, sets loose connotations of a kind of activity and a level of responsibility for the imagination far beyond what the word 'modifying' would ordinarily suggest. Coleridge was to find that the scope of the imagination's task tended to escalate in elusive ways; in fact, the central problem of the later *Biographia* is largely the result of the ambitious role the imagination was accorded as the vehicle of the entire spiritual and intellectual being.

This process of inflation is part of the phenomenon Raymond

Williams[1] has pointed out, the shift in sensibility between the eighteenth and nineteenth centuries which resulted in the redefinition of a whole set of words—*art, culture, imagination* among them—so as to give an account of the split that was felt between the shapeless phenomena of experience—the everyday world of dull and mechanical mind—and the form which the insightful and creative mind could discern in or impose on the alien flux. The dichotomy served multiple purposes: it was one of the humanist's defences against both the physical sciences and the social conditions industrialism had created. In a more subtle way, it was a means of dealing with (perhaps because it had been itself one of the causes of) the experience of the death of God: the lost religious significance of things and events outside us might be recovered inside the sacred imagination (another instance of the associationist by-product whereby the subjective viewpoint replaced the formerly objective order of things as the source of the unity of knowledge). This is the real significance of the creation analogy: it points the direction which the idea of imagination would take in Coleridge, beyond the relatively simple task of unifying the elements of poetic composition, towards the vastly more significant function of shaping the deepest meaning of existence. But in 1802 or 1804 Coleridge's view of the imagination was not yet so ambitious.

V

The anti-scientific and anti-industrial bias in this point of view and the resulting need to affirm some kind of vital and spiritual power as the source of true significance are both clearly exemplified in another distinction closely paralleling the fancy/imagination one: the distinction between *mechanical* form and *organic* form. Coleridge first mentions it in a lecture in 1811, where he seems to have taken it literally from A. W. Schlegel.[2] *Mechanical* form is the result of copying: the

[1] *Culture and Society 1780–1950*, 1958.
[2] Wellek, *A History of Modern Criticism: 1750–1950*. New Haven, 1955–. It is not clear to what extent the basis for the distinction already existed in Coleridge's mind. See J. A. Appleyard, *Coleridge's Philosophy of Literature*. Cambridge, Mass., 1965, 106–18.

product appears 'as if it had come out of the same mould with the original' (*Sh. Crit.*, II, 131), a 'predetermined form' has been impressed on the material like a shape given to wet clay (*Sh. Crit.*, I, 198). *Organic* form, on the other hand, 'is innate; it shapes as it develops itself from within, and the fulness of its development is one and the same with the perfection of its outward form' (*Sh. Crit.*, I, 198).

The machine versus the living plant or animal body. The latter is characterized by a germination in which the teleology of the whole governs the relationship of the parts, by a process of growth 'from within', by assimilation of alien elements to its own substance; and the result is a unity in which the parts are interdependent on each other as reciprocally ends and means.[1] The model is clear enough, but its application to the making of poems leaves unanswered questions. Just how does the poem's form develop itself 'from within'? There is a determinism about a plant's growth from seed to flower to fruit that seems impossible to reconcile with the 'modifying' work of imagination. Perhaps it is best to take the distinction as bearing on the *result* more than on the *process*. In the context of the lecture, the passage referred to Shakespeare's genius in making the speeches of his *dramatis personae* seem to arise naturally out of the character of each speaker. Thus a unity of impression superior enough to resist analysis in conventional terms is explained by attributing it to the power of the original idea and the skill of the poet in developing it. The connotations of vitality, spontaneity, teleology, naturalness, and so forth, are significant in themselves for what they say about the cultural value this viewpoint places on the poet's art, but they are encomiastic rather than descriptive so far as the actual process of creativity is concerned.

VI

Between the autumn of 1811 and the spring of 1814 Coleridge gave several series of lectures on literary topics. The definition of poetry occupied much of his attention. In one version: 'It is an art (or whatever

---

[1] Abrams, *The Mirror and the Lamp*, 171–5.

better term our language may afford) of representing, in words, external nature and human thoughts and affections, both relatively to human affections, by the production of as much immediate pleasure in parts, as is compatible with the largest sum of pleasure in the whole' (*Sh. Crit.*, II, 41). The initial assumption here is the classical theory of *mimesis:* poetry *represents* 'external nature and human thoughts and affections'. Its task is not simply reportorial, for it treats these subjects 'relatively to human affections', perhaps an obvious but nonetheless an important qualification, for it suggests though somewhat vaguely the transforming process which the poet's own sense of value works on his material. The goal is immediate pleasure, as much in each of the parts as is compatible with the design of the whole; this application of organic unity seems to be intended to distinguish poetry from works of analysis or description. The opposite of poetry is science, Coleridge says in another lecture (and the opposite of prose is metre); the object of science is the communication of truth, the object of poetry is the communication of pleasure (*Sh. Crit.*, II, 49).

If we ask what this pleasure is, it seems to be a mental excitement in response to the objects the poet is representing, and to the way he modifies them in the process. Coleridge speaks of 'more than ordinary sensibility' on the part of the poet which occasions 'a more than ordinary sympathy' with objects of nature and events in human life. This in turn is united with 'a more than ordinary activity of the mind in general', especially of fancy and imagination. The object here is 'intellectual pleasure' (*Sh. Crit.*, II, 50-1). What this is can be seen in greater detail in a passage from a subsequent lecture where we can suppose that the reader's pleasure will be a mirror image of the poet's. Coleridge is discussing 'poetic genius' on which the adequate definition of poetry 'in its highest and most peculiar sense' must ultimately rest: it

> sustains and modifies the emotions, thoughts, and vivid representations of the poem by the energy without effort of the poet's own mind,—by the spontaneous activity of his imagination and fancy, and by whatever else with these reveals itself in the balancing and reconciling of opposite or discordant qualities, sameness with difference, a sense of novelty and freshness with old or customary objects, a more than usual state of emotion with

> more than usual order, self-possession and judgement with
> enthusiasm and vehement feeling,—and which, while it blends
> and harmonizes the natural and the artificial, still subordinates
> art to nature, the manner to the matter, and our admiration of the
> poet to our sympathy with the images, passions, characters, and
> incidents of the poem.   (*Sh. Crit.*, I, 150)

Two things are notable here about the imagination and the fancy. Their
own activity consists in balancing and reconciling opposite or discordant qualities—a more precise dialectic account of the 'modifying'
or 'coadunating' function, consistent with the work of integrating
experience that brought the imagination into prominence in the first
place, and related to the image of the organism as the model of the
unity that results.[1] At the same time the imagination and the fancy
thrust our attention away from themselves and towards nature, the
matter, images, incidents, and so forth, of the poem.

Coleridge's idea of 'representation' requires both these moments in
the activity of the imagination, a point sometimes lost sight of when the
creativity of that faculty is unduly stressed. As early as 1802 he wrote a
remarkable description of how the poet (Shakespeare was again his
example) 'thinks' himself into the thoughts and feelings of persons in
circumstances quite different from his own:

> For all sounds, and forms of human nature he must have the *ear*
> of a wild Arab listening in the silent Desart, the eye of a North
> American Indian tracing the footsteps of an Enemy upon the
> Leaves that strew the Forest—; the *Touch* of a Blind Man feeling
> the face of a darling Child.   (CL, II, 810)

The images convey more strikingly than Coleridge's discursive analyses
the relationship between the poet's imagination and his subject. The
third image especially illuminates the double mode of the imagination's
activity: it strains to know its subject, yet knows it only according to its
own mode of knowing.

These lectures preserve a collection of Coleridgean fragments, not
only textually but intellectually as well. Certain theories emerge clearly,

---

[1] Abrams points out that 'coadunate' is an eighteenth-century biological term for unified growth. *The Mirror and the Lamp*, 169.

but the most interesting speculative ideas are the ones made in passing and never fully developed. Coleridge's format was somewhat against him, but we may suspect that his own ideas about literature were not yet adequately worked out. The occasion to do so presented itself when he began the *Biographia Literaria*.

VII

In May 1815 Coleridge set out to write a preface about the principles of literary criticism for an edition of his poems. By the end of September he had finished the twenty-two chapters of his *Biographia Literaria*; or *Biographical Sketches of My Literary Life & Opinions*. It is a puzzling book, part intellectual biography, part philosophy of literature, tediously digressive in places, padded out with letters from a German tour and a reprinted review of Maturin's verse drama *Bertram*. Simplified of its oddities it appears to fall into two parts: the account of Coleridge's literary opinions in the first volume, and the extensive criticism of Wordsworth in the second.

Coleridge bases the growth of his own ideas about literature on the lessons he learned from three men. From James Boyer, who taught him when he was a boy at Christ's Hospital, he claims to have learned that poetry has a logic of its own, severe, complex, and subtle. But it was in the contemporary poetry of William Lisle Bowles that he first encountered genuine and credible emotion, and a simple style purged of the artificial diction that had been the convention. The greatest influence Coleridge attributed to Wordsworth: 'It was the union of deep feeling with profound thought; the fine balance of truth in observing, with the imaginative faculty in modifying the objects observed; and above all the original gift of spreading the tone, the *atmosphere,* and with it the depth and height of the ideal world around forms, incidents, and situations, of which, for the common view, custom had bedimmed all the lustre, had dried up the sparkle and the dew drops' (*Biog. Lit.*, I, 59).

The consequence of reading Wordsworth was the train of speculation that led to the conviction that fancy and imagination were two quite separate faculties, and not just different in degree (*Biog. Lit.*, I, 60–61). Coleridge does not immediately move to an explanation of his notion of imagination. He wants to proceed more or less chronologically, and so he devotes four chapters to a criticism of associationist psychology and an account of his own extrication from its grasp. Another chapter follows, on the influences he has undergone from the idealist philosophers. This brings him to Schelling, to a rather terse expression of his indebtedness to the German philosopher and some defensive remarks about plagiarism, and finally to a profoundly complex and obscure attempt to render the substance of Schelling's metaphysics of absolute consciousness.

Coleridge seems to realize himself that his ideas were dying under the weight of the theory which was supposed to elucidate them. He interrupts his exposition in the thirteenth chapter with a 'letter from a friend' advising that he defer the necessarily lengthy theoretical account to a later work. Instead he gives as a shorthand summary of what would have followed the celebrated definitions:

> The IMAGINATION then, I consider either as primary, or secondary. The primary IMAGINATION I hold to be the living Power and prime Agent of all human Perception, and as a repetition in the finite mind of the eternal act of creation in the infinite I AM. The secondary Imagination I consider as an echo of the former, co-existing with the conscious will, yet still as identical with the primary in the KIND of its agency, and differing only in *degree,* and in the *mode* of its operation. It dissolves, diffuses, dissipates, in order to recreate; or where this process is rendered impossible, yet still at all events it struggles to idealize and to unify. It is essentially *vital*, even as all objects (*as* objects) are essentially fixed and dead.
>
> FANCY, on the contrary, has no other counters to play with, but fixities and definites. The Fancy is indeed no other than a mode of Memory emancipated from the order of time and space; while it is blended with, and modified by that empirical phenomenon of the will, which we express by the word CHOICE. But equally with the ordinary memory the Fancy must receive all its materials ready made from the law of association.
>
> (*Biog. Lit.*, I, 202)

After thirteen chapters of preliminaries we are left to make our own way with the aid of these puzzling remarks.

The difficulty focuses on the distinction between the primary and the secondary imagination, and we notice one element of the difficulty at once: the primary imagination has a far more ambitious function than was attributed to the whole imagination in Coleridge's earlier distinction of it from fancy. Here it has become the faculty of all human perception, the end product of that tendency towards escalation noticed in the earlier analogy with divine creation. It is this grand vision of the primary imagination which makes it so perplexing to try to explain its relation to the secondary imagination. The latter seems to be the faculty of artistic creativity, yet its status as an 'echo' of the agent of ordering perception seems incompatible with the dignity Coleridge has continually attributed to the aesthetic imagination. In fact the description of the secondary imagination is hard to recognize here; its functions seem curiously analytic ('dissolves, diffuses, dissipates, in order to recreate') and its only familiar duty is to unify. Recording and modifying seem to have escaped notice.

It may be that it is impossible to interpret Coleridge's remarks here satisfactorily. There is some reason to think that he had second thoughts himself and considered removing the sentence about primary imagination.[1] If so, his doubts are understandable. The whole motive for the distinction of imagination from fancy in his earlier thinking had been to identify a faculty which could account for the integrative and intuitive aspects of the poet's creativity. With Schelling Coleridge got more than he wanted: a theory in which the imagination becomes the vehicle by which nature and mind are identified in Absolute Idea. Just why this should have tempted Coleridge is not clear; possibly it was a response to that subliminal need noted earlier for a guarantee that the human spirit could still put together convincing explanations of what men had once relied on religious faith to accomplish. Whatever the reason Coleridge could not be content with the vast power attributed to

[1] Shawcross refers to Sara Coleridge's remark in the 1847 ed. of *Biog Lit.* that the sentence was 'stroked out in a copy of the *Biographia Literaria* containing a few marginal notes of the author' (*Biog. Lit.*, I, 272).

imagination in the categories borrowed from Schelling. That system led to pantheism, he later realized, and the god of pantheism he could not take seriously (CL, IV, 883, 873–6). The enigmatic definitions of the thirteenth chapter seem to stand or fall with the Schellingian preliminaries. Coleridge himself could not accept the theories on which they were based, and he never referred to the primary/secondary distinction again.

VIII

The second volume of the *Biographia* is devoted to a criticism of Wordsworth's poetic theories. The point of view is remarkably free of the speculative obscurities of the final chapters of volume one. The notion of imagination is simpler and recalls the earlier explanations of the imagination/fancy distinction.

Coleridge's point of departure is the preface Wordsworth wrote for the second edition of *Lyrical Ballads* (1800). Though the preface grew out of many conversations between the two and is 'half a child of my own Brain,' Coleridge had for some time suspected 'that somewhere or other there is a radical Difference in our theoretical opinions respecting Poetry' (CL, II, 830). The disagreement centres on Wordsworth's theories about poetic diction, especially with two notions: first, that the proper language of poetry is a selection of the language really spoken by men in the incidents or situations of common life, since such language is the result of their being in touch with what is permanent and beautiful in nature; and, second, that there is no essential difference between the language of prose and the language of poetry, the truly important distinction being instead that which separates artificial diction from the language which conveys the truth and passion of men in real life.

Coleridge's dissent to both of these propositions seems uncharacteristic at first. On the first point he argues that for some purposes the language of men in the incidents of ordinary life might be justifiable, perhaps in dramatic poetry, but that as a rule the proposition is too categorical, one in fact that Wordsworth himself does not always observe. He denies the supposition that the language of men in ordinary situations is more closely in touch with what is permanent and beautiful in nature. On the contrary the rustic's speech is likely to conceal beneath colloquialisms the fact that he has fewer and less subtle ideas to convey. His language is influenced too much by accidents of birth and education, whereas in poetry, according to Aristotle, 'apparent individualities of rank, character, or occupation must be *representative* of a class' (*Biog. Lit.*, II, 33). The argument is curiously classical; Aristotle is not frequently invoked elsewhere to support Coleridge's position.

As to the second proposition, Coleridge argues, strenuously but somewhat beside the point, that metre and linguistic compression are natural to the poem, since they result from the attempt to balance spontaneous passion and voluntary control. Wordsworth had never denied the appropriateness of metre to poetry, only the *essential* difference between the language of prose and that of metrical composition (synonymous, for Wordsworth, with poetry). Coleridge seems to be staking a lot on the distinction he had just before made between a poem and poetry—'a poem of any length neither can be, or ought to be, all poetry' (*Biog. Lit.*, II, 11)—which is apparently the difference between a finished work in the medium of verse and the successful communication of peak states of imaginative excitement whether in prose or verse —a point of view consistent with his earlier science/poetry and prose/ metre distinctions. But to narrow the argument to the relationship of metre and 'poem' in this sense, and assert the natural connection of the two, seems to trivialize Wordsworth's position and Coleridge's response.

The real reason for Coleridge's discontent with Wordsworth's position may lie in his suspicion that his friend was insufficiently convinced of the active role of the imagination in the poetic process. After all, in putting together *Lyrical Ballads* they had had quite dissimilar intentions. They agreed on two points, that poetry could excite by its 'adherence to the truth of nature', and that subjects could be made interesting and novel 'by the modifying colors of imagination'. But Wordsworth's poems were to explore the first idea, and Coleridge went off in the direction of the supernatural and the 'willing suspension of disbelief' (*Biog. Lit.*, II, 5–6). That Coleridge should now distrust the apparently simple project of finding the true language of poetry in the situations of common life is not surprising; it is too accidental a source to satisfy his grand conception of the imagination's role in the poet's work: 'The poet . . . brings the whole soul of man into activity . . . He diffuses a tone and spirit of unity, that blends, and (as it were) *fuses*, each into each, by that synthetic and magical power, to which we have exclusively appropriated the name of imagination.' (*Biog. Lit.*, II, 12) In the same way Wordsworth's views on metre evoke in Coleridge a fear of 'prosaisms' (*Biog. Lit.*, II, 62), of too much attention to 'observation' rather than meditation (*Biog. Lit.*, II, 64), and remind him again of the lifeless exteriority of mechanical form compared to the vitality of organic growth from within:

> 'Could a rule be given from *without*, poetry would cease to be poetry, and sink into a mechanical art. It would be μόρφωσις, not ποίησις. The rules of the IMAGINATION are themselves the very powers of growth and production. The *words*, to which they are reducible, present only the outlines and external appearances of the fruit. A deceptive counterfeit of the superficial form and colors may be elaborated; but the marble peach feels cold and heavy, and *children* only put it to their mouths.' (*Biog. Lit.*, II, 65)

Coleridge returns to the testimony of his own experience, and to familiar notions evolved years earlier, as sources for his arguments against Wordsworth's naturalism. Both men searched for permanence, but Wordsworth seemed to Coleridge to locate it too readily in what was transitory and accidental. Fidelity and sensitivity to the way things are were qualities important to Coleridge's understanding of the poet too (the wild Arab passage, for example), but equally important, and perhaps even preponderant, was the conception of the imagination's shaping and transforming power. Somehow it does more than unify impressions and feelings into vivid awareness, as Wordsworth's imagination does. The images of creation and organic unity always seem to be straining towards some greater significance, which Coleridge can never adequately convey.

IX

That significance is adumbrated to some extent in the first of the essays in *The Statesman's Manual,* written in 1816. The subject is the Bible as the best guide to the principles of political science. Central to Coleridge's argument that amid the isolated facts of history we should look for permanently valid principles, is the distinction between *reason*, which gives 'knowledge of the laws of the WHOLE considered as ONE', and *understanding*, which is 'the science of a *phaenomena*, and of their subsumption under distinct kinds and sorts (*genus* and *species*). Its functions supply the rules and constitute the possibility of EXPERIENCE; but remain mere logical *forms* except as far as *materials* are given by the senses or sensations' (*Statesman's Manual*, Appendix, v). The distinction is Kant's but Coleridge gives slightly different values to the terms, using them, as frequently, in the sense of the traditional distinction in Western thought between the discursive and intuitive faculties.

The imagination is now described as holding a middle position between understanding and reason: it is 'that reconciling and mediatory power, which incorporating the Reason in Images of the Sense, and organizing (as it were) the flux of the Senses by the permanence and self-circling energies of the Reason, gives birth to a system of symbols, harmonious in themselves, and consubstansial with the truths of which they are the *conductors*' (*Ibid.*, 35). The characteristic product of the imagination is the *symbol*. Unlike an allegory, which is 'but a translation of abstract notions into a picture-language which is itself nothing but an abstraction from objects of the senses', a symbol 'is characterized by a translucence of the Special in the Individual or of the General in the Especial, or of the Universal in the General. Above all by the translucence of the Eternal through and in the Temporal. It always partakes of the Reality which it renders intelligible; and while it enunciates the whole, abides itself as a living part in that Unity of which it is the representative.' (*Ibid.*, 37) The work of the imagination now seems to be not so much to fuse opposite or discordant qualities, as to let multiple significances emerge to view; the metaphor of 'translucence' suggests less power, perhaps, but on the other hand achieves greater objectivity by suggesting less distortion from the interposition of the poet between sense image and the energetic reason.

The new importance of this mediatory role of the imagination becomes clearer when we see it translated into religious terms. Coleridge is discussing faith as the complement and basis of all knowledge. The two ideas of reason are oneness and allness, but the understanding constantly represents totality with some kind of limit, either the infinite without unity (atheism) or unity without the infinite (anthropomorphic monotheism). Religion balances the two tendencies, since it contemplates the particular, the individual (products of the understanding), but as this exists and has its being in the universal (and so is one with pure reason) (*Ibid.*, Appendix, v). Thus, the task of imagination is parallel to the role of religious faith as mediatory between two partial abstractions the mind is prone to, the phenomenal knowledge of the understanding and the universal laws of the reason. What faith produces in the sphere of religion, imagination does in the realm of creative knowledge: it reveals the 'hidden mystery in every, the minutest, form of existence', 'the actual immanence of All in Each' (*Ibid.*, 62–3).

The ground of this analogous relationship of each thing's being to every other's is God's own being. 'The fact, therefore, that the mind of man in its own primary and constitutent forms represents the laws of nature, is a mystery which of itself should suffice to make us religious: for it is a problem of which God is the only solution, God, the one before all, and of all, and through all!' (*Ibid.*, Appendix, xviii) Coleridge elsewhere resorts to the mysterious figure of the footprint on the snow, to illustrate how both subject and object are rooted in the divine ground: everything we know is shaped by the structure of the mind, perceived through 'a frame-work which the human imagination forms by its own limits, as the foot measures itself on the snow; and the soul truth of which we must again refer to the divine imagination, in virtue of its omniformity' (*Friend*, I, 520). So by giving the imagination a more modest place in the hierarchy of the mind's faculties—less universal than reason, but less captive to phenomena than understanding— and by developing the description of its product, the symbol, as the vehicle for the translucence of the universal in the concrete and the eternal in the temporal, Coleridge is able to give a clearer and more coherent theory of imagination than he had earlier provided. And this view of imagination, by reason of its analogous resemblance to the fundamental role of faith as the ground of the most profound religious experience, is no less grand than the vision which the Schellingian theory supported, with the important difference that this explanation does not lead to a pantheistic conclusion the way the earlier one did.

X

The mediatory function of the imagination seems to be the dominant idea that survives from these diverse speculations. It is the leading thought of the thirteenth lecture of the series given in 1818–19 (the last substantial evidence of Coleridge's concern for literary theorizing), called 'On Poesy or Art', where art is 'the mediatress between, and reconciler of, nature and man' (*Biog. Lit.*, II, 253). This lecture Coleridge took in great part from Schelling, but its central proposition is the familiar one of the artist as the interpreter of the language of nature. He does not copy the outside, the *natura naturata*, but masters the essence, the *natura naturans*, 'which presupposes a bond between nature in the higher sense and the soul of man'. He 'must imitate that which is in the thing, that which is active through form and figure, and discourses to us by symbols'. Art, finally, is 'the abridgement of nature' (*Biog. Lit.*, II, 257, 259, 262).

Coleridge's speculations end where they begin, with on the one hand the poet reading with devout wonder the signs of the divine presence in the world around him and, on the other hand, the philosopher explaining a theory of the mental faculties which will account for the oneness we long for and in some sense experience amid the multiplicity of phenomena. Berkeley and Hartley are far behind, but idealist metaphysics and empirical psychology are still the two poles around which Coleridge's thought moves. Only the focus of the problem shifts. Earlier it was the difficulty of accounting for the effect of certain kinds of poetry; later it was the ambitious project of explaining the unity of all knowledge; finally, it became the question of how to relate the human to the divine ground of being. The imagination served differently to answer each of these questions, perhaps most satisfactorily—from our point of view—only when the third problem re-ordered the earlier formulations about its role. But it was characteristic of Coleridge that his questions kept changing, and that he finally gave no satisfying explanation of his literary theories pure and simple. The student who goes with him on his way will find himself, like Hazlitt, ambling from one side of the path to the other, and may, like Hazlitt, be annoyed at his vagaries. What he will gain, though, is the experience of a mind at work, on questions that deeply concerned him, trying to find answers he could live by.

XI

Response to Coleridge has varied with awareness of the importance of the problem he was trying to resolve and sympathy with the direction his solutions took. One way of dismissing his whole point of view has been simply to see him as a figure by-passed by the age. Carlyle's picture of him, in his *Life of John Sterling* (1851), as a metaphysical dreamer escaped from life's battle, is not so very different in conclusion from Pater's view in *Appreciations* (1889), where Coleridge is a type of the romantic *ennuyé*, whose quest for the absolute has been rendered irrelevant by empirical and relative philosophy of the modern age.

Those who shared Coleridge's sense of disparateness and lack of relation and the need to find an integrating principle took him more seriously. Mill's respect grew out of a concern for a common problem: how to give to ideas a philosophical ground broad enough to include past values as well as present utility—Coleridge was the explicator of the one, Bentham of the other. Mill's sympathy was perhaps closely connected with the circumstance that both he and Coleridge approached the problem as an epistemological one, a point of view not taken very seriously by later English literary critics until relatively recently. In this sense Mill might have been speaking of the whole of the nineteenth century when he wrote in his *Westminster Review* essay: 'the class of thinkers has scarcely yet arisen by which he is to be judged'.

In the twentieth century the pioneering work on Coleridge was John Livingston Lowes's *The Road to Xanadu* (1928). That documentation of the complex interconnectedness of the reading that went into *Kubla Khan* and *The Ancient Mariner* demonstrated the seriousness with which Coleridge had to be taken by literary scholars and also raised a number of questions about the psychology of imaginative creation. Two attitudes to Lowes's questions are exemplified by Irving Babbitt and I. A. Richards. Babbitt, in *The 19th Century and After* (1929), is anti-romantic, really anti-modern, suspicious of the subjective and the spontaneous, hearkens back to a classical theory of imitation, and sees Coleridge's theory of imagination as suffering from too much transcendental mist. On the other hand, Richards's book, *Coleridge on Imagination* (1934), takes the theory of imagination seriously as anticipating the kind of explanation of poetic creativity which modern empirical psychology recognizes.

When post-World War I literary criticism set out to discredit the moralizing of the late Victorian poetry and the sonorous inconsequentiality of so much pre-war verse, it found this alliance with psychology useful. The purification of poetry from rhetoric and triviality led to an interest in the formal aspects of works of literature, led in fact to the New Criticism. Analyses of metaphor, symbol, diction, structure, and so forth, became the means by which a new and tighter critical vocabulary was developed. A fundamental assumption was the autonomy of the poem and of the poetic process. This point of view called into existence as a correlative theory a psychology of the creative imagination, and in this way Coleridge's ideas were taken up by the dominant school of literary criticism in the universities and journals over the past forty years.

Numerous recent studies testify to the continuing interest in Coleridge's literary theory, an interest that is not likely to abate so long as new material from the notebooks and manuscripts is being published. Whether Coleridge's ideas will remain so intriguing to literary critics of the next generation is difficult to say. There is, on the one hand, evidence of a growing movement to transcend formal criticism. Still, it is difficult to imagine that we have not a great deal to learn before we can give an adequate account of the creative imagination, and Coleridge will always be interesting for his work in this area. Nor does it seem that we have yet in prospect an adequate overall view of the development of that enormous shift in thought between the eighteenth and twentieth centuries of which romanticism in literature is one of the clearest phenomena and of which Coleridge was for the English speaking world one of the major interpreters. That problem alone seems likely to be capable of keeping Coleridge's ideas alive for some time to come.

5: *Coleridge and Criticism:*
II. Critical Practice

R. H. FOGLE

COLERIDGE'S PRACTICAL criticism, however fragmentary, is entirely consistent with his general principles. In assessing its value one needs to consider, too, the less ponderable matter of his vast experience and tact in dealing with imaginative literature. To commence with his principles, Coleridge intends to be broadly traditional and synoptic. His inclusiveness, however, has its special emphasis; in his own terms, his 'individuation', although it participates in the universal, has yet its particular bent. His thought is not wholly Platonic nor Aristotelian, but he is more Platonic than Aristotelian. His first concern is Oneness, and he speaks often of 'principles', sometimes of 'fixed principles' and deductive reasoning, but his solicitude for particulars is remarkable.

Thus he says that the poem is 'discriminated by proposing to itself such delight from the whole as is compatible with a distinct gratification from each component part', and in its scrupulous balance of partness and wholeness this is his definition of the ideal aesthetic object, or of Beauty itself. In a more elaborate formulation he adds a characteristic emphasis: the poetic imagination, 'while it blends and harmonizes the natural and the artificial, still subordinates art to nature; the manner to the matter; and our admiration of the poet to our sympathy with the poetry'.[1] Thus he is at once traditional and Romantic in his preferences, just as he sees Shakespeare as universal through his Romanticism.

Correspondingly, Shakespeare is Coleridge's norm of literary value, the One to whom he always implicitly refers. At the opposite extreme, however, he estimates the individual work in its own terms by criteria

---

[1] *Biog. Lit.*, II, 12.

that are strictly and exclusively applicable to itself. He speaks frequently of *classes*, too, which are middle points between the One of the
ideal and universal (Shakespeare) and the Many (the individual work
or, at times, writer). These classes derive most frequently from the
mental faculties of Reason, Imagination, Fancy, and Understanding.
For example, 'the great and prevailing character of Spenser's mind is
fancy under the conditions of imagination, as an ever present but not
always active power. He has an imaginative fancy, but he has not
imagination, in kind or degree, as Shakespeare and Milton have. . . .'[1]

Pepys, like his age, represents the predominance of Understanding.
In him 'the understanding is *hyper-trophied* to the necrosis or marasmus
of the Reason and Imagination. . . . He was a *Pollard* man without
the *top* (*i.e.*, the Reason as the source—of *Ideas*, or immediate yet not
sensuous Truths, having their evidence in themselves; and the Imagination, or idealising Power, of symbols mediating between the Reason and
Understanding).' Historical periods themselves become classes, insofar
as particular mental faculties dominate them. Thus, as with Pepys, the
Restoration and the early eighteenth century are commercial and
materialistic, and the low faculty of Understanding is in the ascendent.
Dryden and Pope, whatever their virtues, never rise to the poetic
imagination. 'Cowley *was* a Poet, which, with all my unfeigned
admiration of his vigorous sense, his agile logical wit, and his high
excellences of diction and metre, is more than (in the *strict* use of the
term, Poet) I can conscientiously say of D RY D E N. Only if Pope was a
Poet as Lord Byron swears, then Dryden, I admit, was a very *great*
Poet.'[2]

Shakespeare, however, is beyond periodicity, the greatest poet of all
time, in whom ideal and actual are one, who attained the consummate
fusion of nature and art, of judgement and genius. Coleridge, applying
his principles 'to purposes of practical criticism', examines Shakespeare's
early poetry in an endeavour 'to discover what the qualities in a poem
are, which may be deemed promises and specific symptoms of poetic
power, as distinguished from general talent. . . .'[3] The endeavour is

[1] *Miscellaneous Criticism*, 38.
[2] *Miscellaneous Criticism*, 284–5.
[3] *Biog. Lit.*, II, 13.

characteristic. An organicist, Coleridge continually employs the antitheses organic-mechanical, genius-talent, imagination-fancy, and the
like, and he is particularly interested in beginnings, as the vital germs or
seeds (or ideas) at the source of creation. Thus he gives special attention
to the early scenes of Shakespeare's plays, as here to early poems. The
virtues he finds are organic, genial—*poeta nascitur non fit.*

First, in *Venus and Adonis*, is 'the perfect sweetness of the versification', with the reflection that 'the sense of musical delight, with the
power of producing it, is a gift of imagination'. This sweetness is inseparable from 'propriety', and as a total effect it amounts to 'harmony',
a central term for Coleridge. Unity, originality, vitality, propriety,
fervour, continuity are present, all endowments of genius and imagination, along with the objectivity that is Shakespeare's unique attribute.
It is unnecessary to speak at length of this famous critique, but two
passages are especially indicative of Coleridge's critical sensibility and
method. The first concerns organic continuity: 'I think I should have
conjectured from these poems, that even then the great instinct, which
impelled the poet to the drama, was secretly working in him, prompting
him—by a series and never broken chain of imagery, always vivid and,
because unbroken, often minute. . . .' This is the continuity of nature,
of organic life, and Shakespeare consummately embodies it.

The second passage belongs to the peroration.

> What then shall we say? even this; that Shakespeare, no mere
> child of nature; no *automaton* of genius; no passive vehicle of
> inspiration, possessed by the spirit, not possessing it; first studied
> patiently, meditated deeply, understood minutely, till knowledge,
> become habitual and intuitive, wedded itself to his habitual
> feelings, and at length gave birth to that stupendous power, by
> which he stands alone, with no equal or second in his own class;
> to that power which seated him on one of the two glory-smitten
> summits of the poetic mountain, with Milton as his compeer,
> not rival.

The implications of this are anterior to practical criticism, but illuminate
Coleridge's practice. First, a point so large that we tend to look beyond
it to particulars, is the nature of his dialectic. 'In order to obtain adequate
notions of any truth, we must intellectually separate its distinguishable

parts: and this is the technical process of philosophy. But having so done, we must then restore them in our conceptions to the unity, in which they actually co-exist; and this is the result of philosophy.'[1] Shakespeare's genius and his judgement are separate only in analysis, and not in reality; and the conscious and unconscious are one. The process is both 'critical' and 'transcendental', for Coleridge is re-appraising the traditional antitheses of aesthetics and criticism, and resolving them by raising his discourse to a higher plane.

A further point involves the comparison of Shakespeare and Milton as representatives of different classes. 'While the former darts himself forth, and passes into all the forms of human character and passion, the one Proteus of the fire and the flood; the other attracts all forms and things to himself, into the unity of his own ideal.'[2] Ultimately Coleridge gives supremacy to Shakespeare. The relations of the classes must be established, and they point to the One, which governs all. Meanwhile, however, each must receive the fullest attention in itself.

The great poet is self-conscious, though his creative genius wells from the unconscious. Shakespeare is at once within and outside his plays, projecting himself yet always preserving his identity. Early, in *Venus and Adonis*,

It is throughout as if a superior spirit more intuitive, more inti-mately conscious, even than the characters themselves, not only of every outward look and act, but of the flux and reflux of the mind in all its subtlest thoughts and feelings, were placing the whole before our view; himself meanwhile unparticipating in the passions, and actuated only by that pleasurable excitement, which had resulted from the pleasurable fervour of his own spirit in so vividly exhibiting what it had so accurately and pro-foundly contemplated.

Shakespeare never falls into 'accidentality'; maintaining self-possession, he never sacrifices his own intellect and imagination in portraying a lower state of being. He is marvellously accurate in the Nurse and Mistress Quickly, those prodigies of inconsequence. Yet he does not fall into inconsequence himself in picturing it.

[1] *Biog. Lit.*, II, 8.
[2] *Biog. Lit.*, II, 20.

A Shakespeare play is a living organism, a growing plant evolved from the seed of an idea. Its unity is the vital unity of an harmonious natural scene, a banyan tree with its surrounding seedlings.[1] It is a complex, a growing set of relationships, in continuous motion with continual subtle shiftings in direction. In it are perpetual slight modulations, in contrast, gradation, tempo, and intensity, the whole a complex synthesis, unified and yet fully developed in particulars. Coleridge's critical methods correspond with his idea of Shakespearean unity:

> Each scene of each play I read, as if it were the whole of Shakespeare's Works—the sole thing extant. I ask myself what are the characteristics—the Diction, the Cadences, and Metre, the character, the passion, the moral or metaphysical Inherences, and fitness for theatrical effect, and in what sort of Theatres—all these I write down with great care and precision of Thought and Language—and when I have gone thro' the whole, I shall then collect my papers, and observe, how often such and such Expressions recur and thus shall not only know what the Characteristics of Shakespeare's Plays are, but likewise what proportion they bear to each other.[2]

His terminology makes frequent reference to *passion*. Though it is most evident in Coleridge's treatment of Shakespeare, it might well be said that all his literary criticism is an attempt to explain the language of passion, or 'the logic of passion,' and its relations with and differences from the language of ordinary logic and exposition. Among critics of our time, John Crowe Ransom is comparable to him, despite great differences in vocabulary, in Ransom's sustained effort to establish the 'ontology' of poetry through its language. Thus his critiques of Shakespeare's plays discourse on passion in Roderigo, in Cleopatra, in Cressida; the passions of nature in the storm scenes of *King Lear*; passions as a cause and justification of word-plays (rather a sore point with Coleridge), and as a justification of breaches of conventional grammar and word-order; passion as a cause of poetic language; passion and the English language; and, as a whole, the relation of passion to figurative language, and the considerations of naturalness,

[1] See *Sh. Crit.*, I, 5, 216, *passim*.
[2] CL, II, 1054.

probability, appropriateness, and propriety that arise from the relationship.[1] In this entire matter I myself find Coleridge extremely Longinian,
though I am forced to note his lack of enthusiasm for Longinus.[2]

As has been noticed above, Coleridge gives disproportionate
attention to Shakespeare's opening scenes, in which he anticipates and
prepares. An organicist, Coleridge is interested in the creative process,
the vital beginnings of things—thus the peculiar weight of the word
genial in his criticism. Furthermore, he has much to say of 'dramatic
illusion',[3] and it is at the beginning that the illusion has to be established. Noteworthy among his discussions of 'preparation' are the
opening scene and the apothecary scene of *Romeo and Juliet*; the opening of *Hamlet*, in relation to other Shakespeare plays; the first act of
Othello, and the element of preparation throughout; the beginning and
the use of the fool in *Lear*; and the function of the Weird Sisters in
Macbeth.[4]

Coleridge's sense of gradation, contrast, and progression is closely
related to his interest in beginnings. He speaks of the 'gradual rise into
tragedy'; of an 'exquisitely natural transit into the narrative retrospective'; of transition in the passions; of the relationship of gradation
to artistic illusion; of alternation and transition; of the infinite number
of gradations between identity and contrariety, and of gradual growth.
His comments on shift of tempo and change of intensity are most often
to be found in connection with opening scenes, or 'lyric movements'
such as the parting of Polonius and Laertes. In general his vocabulary
emphasizes the subtle modulations that constitute organic movement
and connection, reminding us of the imagination that 'fuses and blends
each into each'.[5]

What Coleridge says of his own preparation—'Each scene of each

---

[1] For references to passion see *Sh. Crit.*, I, 9, 15, 40–41, 44, 56, 60, 77,
99, 110–11, 135, 143–4; II, 72–4, 88, 96–98, 102, 106–8, 109, 144–5.
[2] See *Miscellaneous Criticism*, 320.
[3] On dramatic illusion see R. H. Fogle, *The Idea of Coleridge's Criticism*,
Berkeley and Los Angeles, 1962, 115–124, 181n.
[4] See *Sh. Crit.*, I, 5, 11, 18–20, 37–40, 45–46, 49–53, 56, 60–64, *passim*.
[5] *Sh. Crit.*, I, 18, 19, 25, 36–37, 39, 60, 72, 116–17, 140, 181–2; II, 79,
108–9, 131–2, 135.

play I read, as if it were the whole of Shakespeare's Works'—is fully borne out in his critiques. And one might hark back to his notion of the poem, which proposes to itself 'such delight from the whole as is compatible with a distinct gratification from each component part'. This reconciliation is to my eye omnipresent in Coleridge's criticism, but perhaps drawn originally from his reading of Shakespeare, in whom parts are both means and ends, appropriate and at the same time intrinsically charming. So too his attention to Shakespeare's metre is directed both toward its separate identity as end and to its functionality as means, and he characteristically asserts that 'Wherever regular metre can be rendered truly imitative of character, passion, or personal rank, Shakespeare seldom, if ever, neglects it.'[1] Verse, even dramatic verse, is never merely functional and expressive for Coleridge.

Milton is Shakespeare's equal and counterpart as the supreme poet of another class, though like the protocol of Kai Lung's mandarins it would seem to be a matter of 'equal but appreciably lower', as has already been suggested. As to class itself,

> speaking generally, it is far, far better to distinguish poetry into different classes; and, instead of fault-finding, to say this belongs to such or such a class—thus noting inferiority in the *sort* rather than censure on the particular poem or poet. We may *outgrow* certain *sorts* of poetry (Young's *Night-Thoughts*, for instance) without arraigning their excellence *proprio generi*. In short, the wise is the genial; and the genial judgement is to distinguish accurately the character and characteristics of each poem, praising them according to their force and vivacity in their own kind— and to reserve reprehension for such as have no *character*—tho' the wisest reprehension would be not to speak of them at all.[2]

This might be called the organicist's credo, but it differs, let us say, from the Henry James dictum in 'The Art of Fiction' by adding the concept of class itself to the individual object, as an intermediary between part and whole, to present Coleridge's unique interpretation of organicism.

Milton owes more to his period, or rather periods, than does

[1] *Sh. Crit.*, I, 12, 21–22, 141–2, 223.
[2] *Miscellaneous Criticism*, 70.

Shakespeare. The 'stars of the Parliament' must yield in lustre to 'the constellation at the court of Elizabeth'. 'But then, on the other hand, there was a vehemence of will, and enthusiasm of principle, a depth and earnestness of spirit, . . . an aspiration after reality, permanence, and general good,—in short, a moral grandeur in the latter period, with which the low intrigues, Machiavelic maxims, and selfish and servile ambition of the former, stand in painful contrast.' Milton belongs to both, and yet a third period, the Restoration. 'In the close of the former period, and during the bloom of the latter, the poet Milton was educated and formed; and he survived the latter, and all the fond hopes and aspirations which had been its life; and so in evil days, standing as the representative of the combined excellence of both periods, he produced the Paradise Lost as by an after-throe of nature.' Milton possessed a goodness above his times, and almost above fallen human nature: 'it is better to have no wound than to experience the most sovereign balsam, which, if it work a cure, yet usually leaves a scar behind'. He was, 'as every truly great poet has ever been, a good man'. Coleridge approaches *Paradise Lost* by 'impressing on your minds the conditions under which such a work was in fact producible at all, the original genius having been assumed as the immediate agent and efficient cause; and these conditions I find in the character of the times and his own character'. One defect, 'a characteristic controversial spirit', comes from the poet's time. 'And, so far as Pope's censure of our poet,—that he makes God the Father a school divine—is just, we must attribute it to the character of his age, from which the men of genius, who escaped, escaped by a worse disease, the licentious indifference of a Frenchified court.'[1]

Dealing with an epic, Coleridge commences with 'the plan and ordonnance of the Poem'. *Paradise Lost* is the greatest of all epics, in possessing the fullest inevitability and totality. 'Consider the exquisite simplicity of the Paradise Lost. It and it alone really possesses a beginning, a middle and an end; it has the totality of the poem as distinguished from the *ab ovo* birth and parentage, or straight line, of history.' Coleridge now turns to the subject. Compared to the *Iliad*, 'The superiority of the Paradise Lost is obvious in this respect, that the interest transcends the limits of a nation.' The subject is the Fall of

[1] *Miscellaneous Criticism*, 158-9.

Man, and Milton treats it with propriety. 'Nothing is touched . . . but what is of general interest in religion; anything else would have been improper.' Klopstock fell into wilfulness in his treatment of the theme, and violated the canons of poetic illusion. 'I admit the prerogative of poetic feeling, and poetic faith; but I cannot suspend the judgement even for a moment. . . . The feigned speeches and events in the Messiah shock us like falsehoods; but nothing of that sort is felt in the Paradise Lost, in which no particulars, at least very few indeed, are touched which can come into collision or juxtaposition with recorded matter.' Milton has likewise 'exhibited marvellous skill' in keeping most of the 'insuperable difficulties' of his subject out of sight, particularly the antinomy of Satan's war against God. 'The statement of a being of high intellect, warring against the supreme Being, seems to contradict the idea of a supreme Being.' Milton, however, manages as well as possible 'by keeping the peculiar attributes of divinity less in sight, making them to a certain extent allegorical only'.

The pre-eminence of *Paradise Lost* appears most strongly in its language and versification, which are uniquely organic both in themselves and in their inter-relationship. They are 'peculiar in being so much more necessarily correspondent to each than those in any other poem or poet. The connection of the sentences and the position of the words are exquisitely artificial; but the position is rather according to the logic of passion or universal logic, than to the logic of grammar.' Thus Coleridge remarks in *Biographia Literaria* 'that it would be scarcely more difficult to push a stone out from the pyramids with the bare hand, than to alter a word, or the position of a word, in Milton or Shakespeare (in their most important works at least) without making the author say something else, or something worse, than he does say'.

To Coleridge *Paradise Lost* is predominantly a subjective poem. He reasons in part that 'In all modern poetry in Christendom there is an under consciousness of a sinful nature, a fleeting away of external things, the mind or subject greater than the object, the reflective character predominant.' Further, there is his hypothesis of Milton himself: 'John Milton himself is in every line of the Paradise Lost. . . . There is a subjectivity of the poet, as of Milton, who is himself before

himself in everything he writes; and there is a subjectivity of the
persona, or dramatic character, as in all Shakespeare's great creations,
Hamlet, Lear, &c.' Adopting this point of view, he has no difficulty
with such passages as the Hymn to Light at the beginning of *Paradise
Lost*, Book iii. To Dr. Johnson this apostrophe was one of those name-
less graces which no art, nor rational criticism, could reach; he could
only ask tolerantly, 'Superfluities so beautiful, who would take away ?'
For Coleridge there was no problem: 'The apostrophe to light . . . is
particularly beautiful as an intermediate link between Hell and Heaven;
and observe, how the second and third book support the subjective
character of the poem.' He concludes that 'In the Paradise Lost the
sublimest parts are the revelations of Milton's own mind, producing
itself and evolving its own greatness. . . .'[1] Johnson was of course a
great master of antithesis, which goes a long way towards explaining
the reconciler Coleridge's extreme distaste for all his works.

With Shakespeare and Milton, Wordsworth completes Coleridge's
central triad of great poets. Shakespeare is the poetic genius of all
times, Milton the great poet of the spirit and the representative of
Coleridge's favourite period of English history. Wordsworth is the great
modern poet, the example of poetic imagination and, Coleridge hoped,
the greatest philosophical poet in history. (Hoped, because he did not
finally measure up to the critic's *idea* of the poet.) Whereas, it may be
said, in Shakespeare idea and actuality were one and Shakespeare
approached complete self-awareness, Wordsworth was imperfect in
self-knowledge. Unlike Shakespeare, his judgement was unequal to his
genius, his fancy lagged behind his imagination. The result, as Coleridge details it in *Biographia Literaria* XXII, is 'accidentality', or lack
of universality, though Wordsworth's occasional lapses are tiny beside
his poetic virtues.[2]

A modern poet, Wordsworth conquers time by his greatness. In a
letter to Thomas Poole, who as a friend and partisan of Coleridge was
irritated by his praise of Wordsworth, the critic writes,

[1] Citations on Milton are drawn from *Miscellaneous Criticism*, 157ff.
On Milton see also R. F. Brinkley, *Coleridge on the Seventeenth Century*,
Durham, North Carolina, 1955.
[2] See Fogle, *Idea of Coleridge's Criticism*, 79ff.

You charge me with prostration in regard to Wordsworth. Have I affirmed anything miraculous of W.? Is it impossible that a greater poet than any since Milton may appear in our days? . . . What if you should meet in the letters of any then living man, expressions concerning the young Milton *totidem verbis* the same as mine of Wordsworth, would it not convey to you a most delicious sensation? Would it not be an assurance to you that your admiration of the *Paradise Lost* was no superstition, no shadow of flesh and bloodless abstraction, but that the *Man* was even so, that the greatness was incarnate and personal.[1]

In 'To William Wordsworth' Coleridge achieves a brilliant flash of insight, aided by critical faith:

> *O great Bard!*
> *Ere yet that last strain dying awed the air,*
> *With stedfast eye I viewed thee in the choir*
> *Of ever-enduring men. The truly great*
> *Have all one age, and from one visible space*
> *Shed influence! They, both in power and act,*
> *Are permanent, and Time is not with them,*
> *Save as it worketh for them, they in it.*
> *Nor less a sacred Roll, than those of old,*
> *And, to be placed, as they, with gradual fame*
> *Among the archives of mankind, thy work*
> *Makes audible a linked lay of Truth,*
> *Of Truth profound a sweet continuous lay,*
> *Not learnt, but native, her own natural notes!*

This poem, written on hearing Wordsworth recite *The Prelude* in 1807, is a superb piece of interpretative criticism, in which Coleridge outlines 'the growth of the poet's mind' with wonderful conciseness.

> *Of the foundations and the building up*
> *Of a Human Spirit thou hast dared to tell*
> *What may be told, to the understanding mind*
> *Revealable; and what within the mind*
> *By vital breathings secret as the soul*

[1] CL, I, 584.

> *Of vernal growth, often quickens in the heart*
> *Thoughts all too deep for words!*

Coleridge's figures present organic life, growth, and continuity, as with the 'linked lay' of the lines earlier quoted, the 'sweet continuous lay,/ Not learnt, but native, her own natural notes!' And it is interesting to consider that the contrast which gives the poem its structure, between Wordsworth's fruition and his own blighted career, is presented in terms of flowering:

> *And all which I had culled in wood-walks wild,*
> *And all which patient toil had reared, and all,*
> *Commune with thee had opened out—but flowers*
> *Strewed on my corse, and borne upon my bier*
> *In the same coffin, for the self-same grave!*

Coleridge had already set forth his hopes for Wordsworth, in a letter to William Sharp in 1804:

Wordsworth is a Poet, a most original Poet—he no more resembles Milton than Milton resembles Shakespeare—no more resembles Shakespeare than Shakespeare resembles Milton—he is himself; and I dare affirm that he will hereafter be admitted as the first and greatest philosophical Poet—the only man who has effected a compleat and constant synthesis of Thought and Feeling and combined them with Poetic Forms, with the music of pleasurable passion and with Imagination or the modifying Power in that highest sense of the word in which I have ventured to oppose it to Fancy, or the *aggregating* power—in that sense in which it is a dim Analogue of Creation, not all that we can *believe* but all that we *conceive* of creation. Wordsworth is a Poet, and I feel myself a better Poet, in knowing how to honour *him*, than in all my own poetic Compositions, all I have done or hope to do—and I prophesy immortality to his *Recluse*, as the first and finest philosophical Poem, if only it be (as it undoubtedly will be) a Faithful Transcript of his own most august and innocent Life, of his own habitual Feelings and Modes of seeing and hearing.[1]

[1] CL, II, 1033-4.

Wordsworth, then, bids fair to become the greatest poet in a new class, the philosophical. One notes in this passage a considerable number of Coleridge's familiar preoccupations: the synthesis of thought and feeling; the music of passion; imagination and fancy; and imagination as analogue of Creation. With such hopes for *The Recluse*, Coleridge was vastly disappointed with *The Excursion* when it appeared, and explained his disappointment in much detail. One cannot refrain, incidentally, from sympathizing with Wordsworth, so roundly scolded for failing to do what he presumably had never intended to do. To have an admirer like Coleridge was a very complex privilege.

Briefly, to Coleridge *The Excursion* was inorganic. Turning to external manners and moral codes, Wordsworth fails to recreate by imagination, but accepts an objective and static world—and we remember that to Coleridge 'all objects (*as* objects) are essentially fixed and dead'.[1] He noted in the poem the accidentality that was Wordsworth's chief defect, in a letter to Lady Beaumont:

> I have sometimes fancied that, having by the conjoint operation of his own experiences, feelings, and reason, *himself* convinced *himself* of truths, which the generality of persons have either taken for granted from their infancy, or, at least, adopted early in life, he has attached all their own depth and weight to doctrines and words, which come almost as truisms or commonplaces to others.[2]

To Wordsworth he wrote, 'It is for the biographer, not the poet, to give the *accidents* of *individual* life. Whatever is not representative, generic, may be indeed most poetically expressed, but is not poetry.' He continued,

> I must recall to your mind what my *expectations* were [based on *The Prelude*]: and, as these again were founded on the supposition that (in whatever order it might be published) the poem on the growth of your mind was as the ground plot and the roots, out of which 'The Recluse' was to have sprung up as the tree, as far as [there was] the same sap in both, I expected them, doubtless,

[1] *Biog. Lit.*, I, 202.
[2] CL, IV, 564.

to have formed one complete whole; but in matter, form, and product to be different, each not only a distinct but a different work.

The Excursion was inorganic, then, simply in breaking the growth and vital continuity of *The Recluse*. It is to be remarked, however, that Coleridge shows his usual solicitude for the interests of the particular. *The Recluse* is to be 'one complete whole', but made up of parts that are 'each not only a distinct but a different work'.

He goes on to explain his 'expectations' further. As 'the *first* and *only* true philosophical poem in existence' *The Recluse* was to have reconciled the opposition of philosophy and poetry, so that the philosophy would not merely have harmonized with but actually aided 'the unity (beginning, middle, and end) of a poem'. Consequently 'whatever the length of the work might be, still it was *determinate* length; of the subjects announced, each would have its own appointed place, and, excluding repetitions, each would relieve and rise in interest above the other'. *The Recluse*, in fact, was to have been a totality, unified by organic relationships, its form the embodiment of its inner life and growing from its meaning ('determinate length'); an upward progression ('rise in interest'); and a connection of the parts to the whole and to each other, while each is a whole in itself ('each would have its own appointed place'). These relationships would involve contrast, harmony, and gradation ('each would relieve and rise in interest above the other').[1]

For Coleridge this break was perhaps crucial. *The Excursion* proved that the enormous promise of Wordsworth's earlier poetry was not to be fulfilled. But Wordsworth as an idea and a vital germ remained: the great modern poet, the interpreter of the spirit of his age.

Shakespeare, Milton, and Wordsworth were the supreme English poets of imagination, the great seminal forces of poetic tradition. For Coleridge, John Donne was definitely not in the main stream of this tradition. He is one of 'Our faulty elder poets', who 'sacrificed the passion and passionate flow of poetry, to the subtleties of intellect, and to the starts of wit', who 'sacrificed the heart to the head'.[2] He is

[1] CL, IV, 572f.
[2] *Biog. Lit.*, I, 15.

therefore not a poet of the imagination, not a 'totality'. He lacks passion, and out of wilfulness and pride he expends his great powers upon trivial topics; in general, his poems are *tours de force*, displays of virtuosity, motivated by 'the desire of exciting wonderment at his powers'. His chief characteristic is wit. Despite these disabilities, Coleridge admires him greatly.

> *With Donne, whose muse on dromedary trots,*
> *Wreathe iron pokers into true-love knots;*
> *Rhyme's sturdy cripple, fancy's maze and clue,*
> *Wit's forge and fire-blast, meaning's press and screw.*

'Wonder-exciting vigour, intenseness and peculiarity of thought, using at will the almost boundless stores of a capacious memory, and exercised on subjects, where we have no right to expect it—this is the wit of Donne!' He is unique, yet akin to Shakespeare. 'After all, there is but one Donne! and now tell me yet, wherein, *in his own kind*, he differs from the similar power in Shakespeare? Shakespeare was all men, potentially, except Milton; and they differ from him by negation, or privation, or both. This power of dissolving orient pearls, worth a kingdom, in a health to a whore! this absolute right of dominion over all thoughts, that dukes are bid to clean his shoes, and are yet honoured by it!' It is a 'lordliness of opulence, in which *the* positive of Donne agrees with *a* positive of Shakespeare', yet their powers are not identical. Coleridge is talking of a wit so great as to be irresistible, but its 'lordly opulence' suggests the 'aggregative' power of fancy, and not the modifying power of imagination. And Donne's whole gift is only one to Shakespeare's many.

With these limitations set, Coleridge's admiration for Donne is whole-hearted, and his attention close. 'The Good Morrow' is 'Too good for mere wit.' 'The Canonization' is 'One of my favourite poems', and it evokes the interesting remark that 'As late as ten years ago, I used to seek and find out grand lines and fine stanzas; but my delight has been far greater' since it has 'consisted more in tracing the leading thought thro'out the whole. The former is too much like coveting your neighbour's goods; in the latter, you merge yourself in the author, you *become He*.' 'A Valediction Forbidding Mourning' is 'An admirable poem which none but Donne could have written. Nothing was ever more admirably made out than the figure of the Compass.' And finally, Coleridge says of 'The Extacy' that 'I should never find fault with metaphysical poems, were they all like this, or but half as excellent.'

As he invariably does with poets, Coleridge pays close heed to Donne's metre and versification, and with notable results in examining the 'muse that on dromedary trots'. 'To read Dryden, Pope, &c., you need only count syllables; but to read Donne you measure *time*, and discover the time of each word by the sense of passion.' His scansion of Donne's lines is unerring[1] and his generalization on the problem thoroughly judicious: '*all* Donne's poems are equally *metrical* . . . though smoothness (*i.e.*, the metre necessitating the proper reading) be deemed inappropriate to songs; but in poems where the writer thinks, and expects the reader to do so, the sense must be understood in order to ascertain the metre.' One might hesitate over the implications of this dictum, but concede that with Donne at least it is appropriate and very helpful. Coleridge as always has tried to get at the life-principle of his subject.

To Coleridge Donne is a fine but eccentric poet, outside the genuine imaginative tradition. His distinction between imagination and fancy leaves Donne on the wrong side of the fence. He is *facile princeps* in his class, no doubt, but the class itself is inferior. Unlike the poet 'in ideal perfection', he does not fuse feeling with thought, art with nature, nor is he able to subordinate 'our admiration of the poet to our sympathy with the poetry'. 'Our genuine admiration of a great poet is a continuous *undercurrent* of feeling; it is everywhere present, but seldom anywhere as a separate excitement', according to *Biographia Literaria* I.

Here Coleridge represents a standard Romantic view, though he doubtless helped to form it as well. Keats expresses it still more memorably: 'I think Poetry should surprise by a fine excess and not by Singularity—it should strike the Reader as a wording of his own highest thoughts, and appear almost a Remembrance . . . Its touches of Beauty should never be half way thereby making the reader breathless instead of content. . . .' Time, Grierson, and T. S. Eliot have, as we know, reversed this pattern. It is Donne and the metaphysicals who

[1] See *Miscellaneous Criticism*, 134.

fuse thought and feeling, and the Romantics who divide them. The distinction of imagination-fancy has fallen, to be replaced by 'serious wit'. But Coleridge reared his judgements on a firm foundation. Time may have more than one turning, and a Coleridgean Parliament overset again a king now fifty years in power.

As Wordsworth was the great modern poet, for Coleridge Sir Walter Scott was the great modern novelist. But whereas Wordsworth was above his age, and indeed above the influences of time, Scott's great popular success was the result of his timeliness; his work was well-adapted to the weaknesses of his public. In Wordsworth imagination predominated; Scott is almost wholly confined to the fancy. This being so, Coleridge's marginalia on Scott's novels are largely devoted to Scott's failures in harmony, appropriateness, organic unity, and above all essential probability, which must stem from imagination. In one vital respect, however, Scott rises above his limitations: his principal theme is timeless and universal.

In a long letter to Thomas Allsop Coleridge outlines the short-comings of his age and Scott's relations to it. His purpose is

> To bring proofs of the energetic or inenergetic state of the minds of men, induced by the excess and unintermitted action of stimulating events and circumstances,—revolutions, battles, *newspapers*, mobs, sedition, and treason trials, public harangues, meetings, dinners; the necessity in every individual of ever increasing activity and anxiety in the improvement of his estate, trade, &c., in proportion to the decrease of the actual value of money, to the multiplication of competitors, and to the almost compulsory expedience of expense, and prominence, even as the means of obtaining or retaining competence: the consequent craving after amusement as proper *relaxation*, as *rest* freed from the tedium of vacancy; and, again, after such knowledge and such acquirements as are *ready coin*, that will pass *at once*, unweighed and unassayed. . . .[1]

[1] *Cf.* Wordsworth, Preface to the second edition of *Lyrical Ballads:* 'A multitude of causes, unknown to former times, are now acting with a combined force to blunt the discriminating powers of the mind, and, unfitting it for all voluntary exertion, to reduce it to a state of almost savage torpor'.

Of this state of mind Scott furnishes the ideal example.

> I chose an example in literature, as more in point for the subject
> of my particular remarks, and because every man of genius, who
> is born for his age, and capable of acting *immediately* and widely
> on that age, must of necessity *reflect* the age in the first instance,
> though as far as he is a man of genius, he will doubtless be him-
> self reflected by it reciprocally. Now I selected Scott for the very
> reason, that I do hold him for a man of very extraordinary
> powers. . . .

Coleridge explains Scott's peculiar fitness for his time a little more fully
elsewhere, however: 'The great felicity of Sir Walter Scott is that his
own intellect supplies the place of all intellect and character in his
heroes and heroines, and *representing* the intellect of his readers, super-
sedes all motive for its exertion, whether as above or below.' A further
explanation occurs in the letter to Allsop: Scott never approaches the
genius of Fielding, Smollett, Sterne, and Richardson in portraying
individual characters, but 'still the number of characters *so good*
produced by one man, and in so rapid a succession, must ever remain an
illustrious phenomenon in literature, after all the subtractions for those
borrowed from English sources, or compounded by blending two or
three of the old drama into one'.

This praise is obviously carefully apportioned, and Coleridge's
marginalia to the novels tend to emphasize defects and inharmonies,
all stemming from Scott's lack of imagination, and almost all amounting
to failures in essential verisimilitude. Thus *Waverley* causes Coleridge's
mind to run on the problem of superstition and the supernatural, and
Scott is on the whole found wanting. On the one hand, he achieves
credibility by questionable means. 'Sir Walter Scott, an orthodox
cosmolater, is always half and half on these subjects. The appearances
are so stated as to be readily solved on the simplest principles of
pathology: while the precise coincidence of the event so marvellously
exceeds the ordinary run of chances, as to preserve the full effect of
superstition for the *reader* and yet the credit of unbelief for the writer.'
It is hard to say if this is praise or blame, but it would seem to be tinged
with contempt. There can be no doubt about a reference to *The Abbot*:
'Sir Walter Scott should never have meddled with the supernatural, for

he cannot blend it with the natural. Imagine the supposed experiences of Halbert in *The Monastery*—and you feel how impossible these in themselves justly delineated natural feelings became. The *supernaturalist's* must be a transitory character, never *carried* on. He must exist only in and for the supernatural tale.'

Confined as he is to the fancy, Scott cannot achieve organic relationships, or genuine probability. It is 'Scott's great defect' that 'Nothing is evolved out of the character or passions of the agent; but all is accident *ab extra*.' Thus his dialogue is seldom dramatically appropriate; it has charm, and yet an 'utterly impersonal and undramatic stuff and texture.' A conversation in *The Heart of Midlothian* is '*wit, head*-work, a falsetto imitation of Shakespeare's Dame Quickly', and *Guy Mannering*, which Coleridge praises, is marred by 'the *falsetto* of Meg Merrilies'. A chapter in *The Monastery* 'might be chosen by a philosophic critic to point out and exemplify the differences of fancy and imagination'. Here is 'abundance of the former with the blank-absence of the latter. Hence the '"*incredulus odi*" which it leaves on the mind—the imperious sense of the absurdity of the arbitrary *fiction*.' And Scott has sorely erred (in *Peveril of the Peak*) in modelling his Fenella on Goethe's *Mignon*. He has thus 'placed himself in rivalry with Goethe in, probably, the only point in which he had no possible chance of suceeding—*i.e.*, in the imaginative, as contra-distinguished from the fanciful'. Coleridge concludes that 'Unworthy of Sir Walter Scott as was this pilfering imitation of Goethe's *Mignon*, it was still more *unwise*. For it flashes upon us the difference in kind between the cabinetwork of talent, and the offspring of genius!'

Yet it would seem that Scott *does* rise to genius in his principal theme, 'the struggle between the Stuarts and the Presbyterians and sectaries'. This topic

> can never be obsolete, for it is the contest between the two great moving principles of social humanity: religious adherence to the past and the ancient, the desire and the admiration of permanence, on the one hand; and the passion for increase of knowledge, for truth, as the offspring of reason—in short, the mighty instructs of *progression* and *free agency* on the other. In all subjects of deep and lasting interest, you will detect a struggle between two

opposites, two polar forces, both of which are alike necessary to our human well-being, and necessary each to the continued existence of the other. Well, therefore, may we contemplate with intense feelings those whirlwinds which are for free agents the appointed means, and the only possible condition of that equilibrium in which our moral Being subsists, while the disturbance of the same constitutes our sense of life. Thus in the ancient Tragedy, the lofty struggle between irresistible fate and unconquerable free will, which finds its equilibrium in the Providence and the future retribution of Christianity.[1]

This is an instance of Coleridge's archetypal reconciliation of opposites, mutually subsisting and supporting each other, which constitute the unity of reality, although for the comprehension of the understanding they are two; and thus it exemplifies the structure of his dialectic, underlying his practical criticism as it underlies all his discourse and thought.

[1] Citations on Scott are drawn from *Miscellaneous Criticism*, 321–42.

6: Coleridge and Wordsworth

R. L. BRETT

IT IS significant, perhaps, that the title of this chapter reverses the order in which the names of the two men are generally associated. In the history of English poetry Wordsworth is rightly seen, of course, as a major figure, but sometimes this has been accompanied by a view of Coleridge as a poet who produced a handful of brilliant poems during the years when the two men were intimately related, but who faded into obscurity when this brief, creative period ended. On this view Wordsworth's poetic career was spread over a life-time and his achievement was a cumulative one which reached its summit with the publication of his greatest poem, *The Prelude*, in the year of his death, 1850; Coleridge, on the other hand, was a poet *manqué* who dissipated his energies in metaphysical speculation, journalism and the giving of public lectures. At times a moral judgement has crept into this assessment. Wordsworth was the embodiment of duty, a family man for whom domestic ties and obligations, above all, were paramount; Coleridge was a failure as a husband and a father, and his career ruined by broken resolutions and addiction to opium. Oversimplified and even distorted as this picture might be, it is to be preferred to that of some earlier critics who regarded both men as betrayers of their own principles, as youthful revolutionaries who became middle-aged Tories and in the process lost their poetic powers as well as their revolutionary zeal.

In the last decade or so, however, there has been a growing realization that the later of these views is almost as unsatisfactory as the earlier one. Coleridge has come to be increasingly recognized as a prophetic thinker. His understanding of the intellectual and spiritual forces at work in his own day is now seen to be more profound than that of his contemporaries and to anticipate in a remarkable way the shape these forces would take. We recognize that he laid the foundations on which religious faith could be built in an age of increasing agnosticism and that his writings anticipated the development of existentialism and depth-psychology. All this we acknowledge, but it is doubtful even now if we recognize fully the relationship between Coleridge's philosophy and literary interests, or comprehend his real achievement as a thinker and a man of letters. Indeed, such language reveals how difficult it is to find a single term which does justice to Coleridge; words like 'poet', 'philosopher', 'sage', and 'man of letters', all seem inadequate of themselves as descriptions of what he contributed to the movement of thought and sensibility in his own day and beyond. What we are beginning to see more clearly, as his Notebooks and other writings become available in modern editions, is that Coleridge's thought, more than that of most men, shows a continuous development, and that the years of his most intimate association with Wordsworth were not an interlude given to poetry in a life mainly devoted to other things, but rather the formative period of his life.

This is not to say that Wordsworth was the teacher and Coleridge merely the pupil; nor even that Wordsworth was always the dominant figure in the partnership. The relationship between them was more complex than that. But undoubtedly in the early years of their acquaintance Coleridge felt that Wordsworth was the greatest man he had ever known. Writing to Thomas Poole about Wordsworth he said, '. . . since Milton, no one has *manifested* himself equal to him' (C L, I, 582). Indeed his friends sometimes felt that Coleridge's admiration for Wordsworth was excessive and Lamb, for instance, explained Coleridge's removal of his household to Keswick as the need to be near 'his god Wordsworth'. And yet, as we look at the relationship between these two gifted men it becomes clear that Wordsworth's debt to Coleridge was as great, if not greater, than Coleridge's to him and that Coleridge was a decisive influence in his life and work.

Coleridge's admiration for Wordsworth's poetry had started in 1793 at a meeting of a literary society in Exeter where Wordsworth's poems were read aloud. But it was not until two years later in Bristol that the

two men first met. Wordsworth had gone to Bristol from London to
stay with his friends the Pinneys, a family of sugar merchants in the city;
Coleridge had gone there to discuss with Southey their plans to set up a
Pantisocratic community on the banks of the Susquehannah. Both men
were about to achieve a more domestic way of life than had been possible for either of them over the previous years and were to do so in
circumstances that would make it easier for them to develop a greater
intimacy. Coleridge was about to marry Sara Fricker, Mrs. Southey's
sister, and was soon to settle at Nether Stowey, while Wordsworth was
soon to be established with his sister Dorothy at the Pinneys' country
house at Racedown in Dorset.

Naturally their interest in poetry was a major factor which turned
acquaintance into friendship. In April, 1796, Coleridge, in a note to his
Poems on Various Subjects, wrote of

> Mr. Wordsworth, a Poet whose versification is occasionally
> harsh and his diction too frequently obscure; but whom I deem
> unrivalled among the writers of the present day in manly senti-
> ment, novel imagery, and vivid colouring.

Coleridge must have presented Wordsworth with a copy of this volume
as soon as it appeared, for in a letter to John Thelwall, an atheist and a
republican, who had disapproved of *Religious Musings* (one of the
poems in the collection), he declared,

> A very dear friend of mine, who is, in my opinion, the best poet
> of the age . . . thinks that the lines from 364 to 375 and from 403
> to 428 the best in the Volume,—indeed worth all the rest—And
> this man is a Republican, and at least a *Semi*-atheist. (C L, I, 215–16)

These references indicate an admiration for each other's writings and
suggest either discussions or correspondence about poetry. But the
letter suggests another interest in common, politics.

Wordsworth and Coleridge had both been associated with revolutionary circles on coming down from Cambridge. Wordsworth, indeed,
had been in France and had taken sides in the struggle there. Coleridge
was active in politics when he and Wordsworth met and, in 1795, was
delivering lectures in Bristol against the government and the war with

France. In the spring of the next year he founded *The Watchman*, a journal which disseminated his political ideas to a wider public. Although Coleridge had supported the Revolution, by this time his republican principles rejected violence or bloodshed. His plan for Pantisocracy envisaged a self-supporting community, having all things in common ownership, and this, rather than the overthrow of society, was the main-spring of his revolutionary creed. When the Pantisocracy scheme fell through he was seeking a way of life which would embody these principles. In *Reflections on Having Left a Place of Retirement* he writes of leaving Clevedon, where he spent his honeymoon, and of the struggle ahead:

> *I therefore go, and join head, heart, and hand,*
> *Active and firm, to fight the bloodless fight*
> *Of Science, Freedom, and the Truth in Christ.*

(PW, I, 108)

The programme he adopted for himself was not that of violent change. He hoped to propagate his opinions while maintaining himself and his family by working in the garden of the cottage found for him at Nether Stowey by Thomas Poole. '*My Farm*', he writes to Thelwall,

> will be a garden of one acre and an half; in which I mean to raise vegetables and corn for myself and Wife, and feed a couple of snouted and grunting Cousins from the refuse. My evenings I shall devote to Literature; and, by Reviews, the Magazine [i.e. *The Monthly Magazine*], and the other shilling-scavenger Employments shall probably gain 40£ a year—which Economy and Self-Denial, Gold-beaters, shall hammer till it cover my annual Expences.   (CL, I, 277)

Lamb, who knew Coleridge well, was dubious about his capacities as a farmer and his scepticism was well founded, for Coleridge's enthusiasm soon faded. But it is likely that Coleridge's plan had its attractions for Wordsworth. Wordsworth's republican sympathies remained unaltered, but his revolutionary views had received some hard blows in the period which followed his return from France. When he learned of the Terror and the excess of the Jacobins his mind was thrown into turmoil at what he felt was a betrayal of the high hopes with which the Revolution had started. Coleridge's intention of working for a new society, not by revolution but by living on the land and supporting himself by his own labours, must have appealed to Wordsworth with his memory of the independent like of the dalesmen whom he had known as a boy. Both men had read with enthusiasm Godwin's *Political Justice* which had appeared in 1793, and though both of them were soon to become disenchanted with its main doctrines, they were at one with Godwin in rejecting revolution as an instrument of political change.

With an identity of interest in poetry and politics, then, it is no wonder that Coleridge and Wordsworth were attracted to each other. But this in itself would not have created the special bond which held them together. Indeed, it was more than a year after their first meeting that their friendship became an intimate one. Wordsworth and his sister Dorothy had settled at Racedown in September 1795; the Coleridges moved to Nether Stowey on the last day of 1796. There had been correspondence between them since their first meeting, and Wordsworth had visited Nether Stowey in March 1797, but it was not until June 1797, when Coleridge returned this visit at Racedown, that they felt the special nature of their relationship. Wordsworth, recollecting this momentous occasion some forty years later, said that he and his sister 'both have a distinct remembrance of his arrival. He did not keep to the high road, but leaped over a gate and bounded down a pathless field by which he cut off an angle.'[1] Coleridge stayed with the Wordsworths for three weeks and was soon back with a chaise to transport them to Nether Stowey. A fortnight later the Wordsworths moved to Alfoxden and they and Coleridge became neighbours. The period of collaboration had begun.

What was it during this summer of 1797 which set the seal upon their friendship? We have seen that the two men shared similar interests in poetry and politics, but it was something more personal, something related to their characters and emotional needs which made them wish to be near each other. Temperamentally they were very different. Wordsworth was a reserved and taciturn North-Countryman, who did not make contact with people easily, but whose friendships, once established, were firm and constant; prudent and independent in

[1] WL, *The Later Years*, III, 1263.

money-matters, with a resolute will. Coleridge, on the other hand, was voluble in speech, quickly at home in any social gathering, mercurial in spirits but easily discouraged, completely unpractical with money, but, like Wordsworth, a man who valued his friends. In some ways, of course, they complemented each other; Wordsworth was attracted by Coleridge's spirits and capacity for emotional sympathy, while Coleridge admired the strength and stability of Wordsworth's character. Each of them recognized the genius that resided in the other, but it was more than this which brought them together; it was the support and encouragement they gave each other which was, perhaps, paramount. This becomes clearer when we realize that both men at this time were looking for new bearings.

When Wordsworth took up residence at Racedown he was on the verge of an emotional breakdown. The previous three years had been for him ones of tremendous strain and divided loyalties. He had been caught up in the Revolution, had fallen in love with Annette Vallon and had fathered her child. Forced to leave France by lack of money, he had had to face the disapproval of his family and was unable to return because his own country was at war with France. Then the promise of the Revolution itself had been thwarted by the Jacobins and his early hopes had turned to disappointment and profound scepticism. *Tintern Abbey* looks back over the previous five years to the time when, in 1793, six months after his return from France, he had visited the Wye. His divided feelings can be gauged from his description of himself as

> *more like a man*
> *Flying from something that he dreads than one*
> *Who sought the thing he loved.*

On his way to the Wye, Wordsworth had crossed Salisbury Plain on foot, and the poem *Salisbury Plain*, which has its origins in this journey, is full of forebodings and melancholy. Nor was Wordsworth's mood a transitory one. The first months at Racedown were occupied with revising *Salisbury Plain* (which was later given the title of *Guilt and Sorrow*), and then, after nearly a year, he composed his blank-verse tragedy *The Borderers*. This, too, is a work concerned with guilt and the psychology of evil. Neither the play itself nor the prefatory essay is purely autobiographical, but both show a preoccupation with the questions of what makes a man a criminal and on what does moral health depend, and it is difficult to avoid the conclusion that they are intimately related to Wordsworth's state of mind at this time.

Nearly all critics have rightly connected *The Borderers* with Wordsworth's reading of Godwin's *Political Justice*, though some have seen it as an expression and others as a repudiation of Godwin's theories. Wordsworth probably read Godwin's essay in 1794, during his disillusionment with the way things were going in France. His revulsion at the excesses of the Jacobins led him to welcome an argument for reform based upon an appeal to reason and the control of the passions. Godwin saw education rather than revolution as the agent of social change, for he believed that men's wills were moved by the mere demonstration of a rationally valid argument. Wordsworth was to describe in Book XI of *The Prelude* the attraction such a notion had for him at this time:

> *This was the time, when, all things tending fast*
> *To depravation, speculative schemes—*
> *That promised to abstract the hopes of Man*
> *Out of his feelings, to be fixed thenceforth*
> *For ever in a purer element—*
> *Found ready welcome. Tempting region that*
> *For Zeal to enter and refresh herself,*
> *Where passions had the privilege to work,*
> *And never hear the sound of their own names.*
> *But, speaking more in charity, the dream*
> *Flattered the young, pleased with extremes, nor least*
> *With that which makes our Reason's naked self*
> *The object of its fervour.* (223–235)

But Godwin's theories had a more personal appeal. At the time when he came under Godwin's influence Wordsworth was suffering from a state of depression in which his guilt concerning Annette and the ambivalence of his feelings towards France had assumed morbid proportions. Godwin's theories must have promised him a way out of this neurotic state, by suggesting that the force of his feelings could be checked by the exercise of rational control. Moreover, Godwin had condemned marriage as an institution which could not be defended on rational grounds and this might have moderated his sense of guilt about Annette. Even more than this, Godwin's doctrine of necessity suggested that guilt was a meaningless concept; blame-worthiness and culpability are irrational feelings, according to Godwin, because in the end the human will is not free. It may be socially expedient to punish a wrong-doer, but Godwin admits this with some reluctance and with the proviso that it does not reflect upon the guilt or otherwise of the person punished. Such notions must have seemed attractive at first sight to Wordsworth, but a neurotic state is not cured by an attempt at rational control; indeed, it is likely to grow worse. So, although *The Borderers* can be viewed as an exploration of this territory, the poem as a whole indicates Wordsworth's growing conviction that Godwin does not provide the key to human behaviour.

At the time when he wrote *The Borderers* Wordsworth had come to realize that the feelings cannot be denied; that it is no use turning one's back upon remorse for the past, as Godwin had counselled, but rather that one must accept oneself and one's responsibility for past actions. This recognition was slow in coming but it appeared as a gleam of light across the desolate moorland which Wordsworth used in the poetry of this time to symbolize his despair. The image occurs in the fragment entitled *Incipient Madness,* and it is on the edge of a moor that Marmaduke in *The Borderers* utters words that could have been spoken by Wordsworth himself:[1]

> *Deep, deep and vast, vast beyond human thought,*
> *Yet calm—I could believe that there was here*
> *The only quiet heart on earth. In terror,*
> *Remembered terror, there is peace and rest.*

It was through what Wordsworth later described as a 'wise passiveness' that the process of healing began, aided by the beneficent effect of nature and the companionship of his sister Dorothy. But to these was soon to be added the influence of Coleridge. In Book X of the 1805 version of

---

[1] See M. Moorman, *William Wordsworth. The Early Years, 1770–1803,* 1957, 306.

The Prelude, Wordsworth describes how, in an attempt to secure relief from his feelings, he had turned to mathematics, that most rational of activities and one which Godwin no doubt would have approved. It was at this time that Coleridge came as a counsellor and friend.

> *I . . . for my future studies, as the sole*
> *Employment of the enquiring faculty,*
> *Turned towards Mathematics, and their clear*
> *And solid evidence—Ah! then it was*
> *That thou, most precious Friend! about this time*
> *First known to me, didst lend a living help*
> *To regulate my soul.*   (902–16)

Coleridge himself was no stranger to mental depression. Certainly before moving to Nether Stowey he seems to have passed through one of those periods compounded of anxiety, depression and psycho-somatic illness which were to plague him for so much of his life. Writing to Thomas Poole he gives the kind of vivid and detailed account of his illness which we find so often in his letters:

> On Wednesday night I was seized with an intolerable pain from my right temple to the tip of my right shoulder, including my right eye, cheek, jaw, and that side of the throat—I was nearly frantic—and ran about the House naked, endeavouring by every means to excite sensations in different parts of my body, and so to weaken the enemy by creating a division. It continued from one in the morning till half past 5, and left me pale and fainty . . . I have suffered this day more bodily pain than I had before a conception of . . . My medical attendant decides it to be altogether nervous, and that it originates either in severe application, or excessive anxiety.—My beloved Poole! in excessive anxiety, I believe, it might originate! —I have a blister under my right-ear, and I take 25 drops of Laudanum every five hours.   (CL, I, 249–50)

The anxiety Coleridge refers to was partly concerning the move to Nether Stowey. The desire to be near Poole, whom he admired so much, had become imperative and he urges Poole to lose no time in finding a suitable house. But even when the move had been accomplished Coleridge was still subject to fits of depression. In a letter to Cottle he describes how Wordsworth's first visit to Nether Stowey found him in 'a depression too dreadful to be described', and how Wordsworth's 'conversation, etc. roused me somewhat' (CL, I, 319).

No doubt constitution and early upbringing were contributory factors in Coleridge's depression, but, like Wordsworth, he, too, was at a critical period of his life. Pantisocracy had come and gone, but in the process he had acquired a wife and was now faced with the need to support her and the baby Hartley. Like Wordsworth, he had held firm to his political principles, but no longer believed in revolutionary methods. Writing to his brother George, he explains his change of mind:

> I therefore consent to be deemed a Democrat and a Seditionist . . . but I have snapped my squeaking baby-trumpet of Sedition and the fragments lie scattered in the lumber-room of Penitence.

What he needs, he explains, is a period of quiet and reflection, in which he can take stock of himself and his beliefs.

> And feeling this, my Brother! I have for some time past withdrawn myself almost totally from the consideration of *immediate* causes, which are infinitely complex and uncertain, to muse on fundamental and general causes—'the causae causarum'.
>   (CL, I, 397)

This letter was written in March 1798, when Coleridge and Wordsworth had been living as neighbours in the Quantocks for eight months and it shows both how close the two men had grown together in their interests and attitudes, and the kind of help Coleridge was able to give Wordsworth. Coleridge continues,

> I devote myself to such works as encroach not on the antisocial passions—in poetry, to elevate the imagination and set the affections in right tune by the beauty of the inanimate impregnated, as with a living soul, by the presence of Life—in prose, to the seeking with patience and a slow, very slow mind 'Quid sumus, et quidnam victuri gigimur [']—What our faculties are and what they are capable of becoming.—I love fields and woods and mounta[ins] with almost a visionary fondness—and because I have found benevolence and quietness growing within me as that fondness [has] increased, therefore I should wish to be the means of implanting it in others—and to destroy the bad passions not by combating them, but by keeping them in inaction.

At the time of the Pantisocratic scheme Coleridge had been a disciple of Godwin; he had read *Political Justice* and had met Godwin in London. But his disenchantment with Godwin's theories began earlier than Wordsworth's and as his disagreement grew, he planned to write an answer to *Political Justice*. He described this in some detail in a letter to Thelwall, but, like so many of his projects, it remained an idea only. The grounds of his disagreement were many, but the letter to his brother indicates that he considered Godwin mistaken in thinking that the feelings should be repressed by the reason. Even the evil passions, he explains, are best dealt with not by repression, but by recognizing them and yet not acting upon them. Coleridge believed in a fruitful union between the faculties of the mind, for he wrote to Thelwall, 'I feel strongly and I think strongly, but I seldom feel without thinking, or think without feeling.' (C L, I, 279) It was Coleridge's constant endeavour, which he later expressed in *Biographia Literaria,* 'to keep alive the heart in the head'. It was his belief that Hartley's philosophy acknowledged this unity which so attracted him and led him to transfer his intellectual allegiance from Godwin to Hartley.

What Coleridge offered Wordsworth, then, was a sympathetic understanding of the depression which weighed upon his mind and a deliverance from the moral and intellectual anarchy into which Godwin's theories had led him; an anarchy which was both a cause and a product of this depression. Coleridge was already deeply concerned with the workings of the human mind and could give Wordsworth a new psychological self-awareness, but, coupled with this, the visionary side of his nature was leading him to believe that all things are parts of a living whole and that a recognition of this will bring spiritual harmony and mental peace. The combination of the two was the secret of the healing power Coleridge brought to Wordsworth. It was Coleridge's conviction that a 'visionary fondness' for 'fields and woods and mountains' would set 'the affections in right tune' and give rise to benevolence, which became the mainspring of Wordsworth's poetry and fostered his belief that love of nature leads to love of man. Wordsworth expressed this in its simplest form in *The Tables Turned,* written in 1798:

> *One impulse from a vernal wood*
> *May teach you more of man;*
> *Of moral evil and of good,*
> *Than all the sages can.*

In the companion piece, *Expostulation and Reply*, he combines it with the Hartleian notion that our mental states depend upon environment rather than innate ideas or capacities. In the *Advertisement* to *Lyrical Ballads* he explains that the poem arose 'out of conversation with a friend who was somewhat unreasonably attached to modern books of moral philosophy'. The friend was William Hazlitt, who visited Alfoxden in May and June, 1798. Hazlitt was a disciple of Godwin and was writing an *Essay on the Principles of Human Action*. Wordsworth reminds his friend that reason is not the only, nor even the main, principle of human conduct.

> *Nor less I deem that there are powers,*
> *Which of themselves our minds impress,*
> *That we can feed this mind of ours,*
> *In a wise passiveness.*

Coleridge's help in restoring Wordsworth's emotional equilibrium contributed to a process that had already been started by the quiet of country life and the companionship of Dorothy. But what he was able to do more than either of these was to stimulate Wordsworth's poetic genius; to encourage him to make his feelings the subject of his poetry rather than to suppress them, and to give him a *rationale* for the poetic experiments he had in mind. Coleridge recognised that Wordsworth's genius consisted, above all, in 'the union of deep feeling with profound thought; the fine balance of truth in observing; with the imaginative faculty in modifying, the objects observed'. Wordsworth was to create poetry in which his observation of ordinary life became a means of expressing this union of deep feeling and profound thought; a union by which he was able to penetrate mere appearances and see into the life of things. This was, continues Coleridge, Wordsworth's

. . . original gift of spreading the tone, the atmosphere, and with it the depth and height of the ideal world around forms, incidents and situations, of which for the common view, custom had bedimmed all the lustre, had dried up the sparkle and the dew drops.

(Biog. Lit., I, 59)

The impetus given to Wordsworth's poetry by the liberation of his emotions is seen not only in the *Lyrical Ballads* themselves, but in the Preface he added to the 1800 edition, in which he describes the purpose of his experiments. 'Their principal object', he tells us, was to trace 'the primary laws of our nature: chiefly as far as regards the manner in which we associate ideas in a state of excitement'. Behind the Hartleian terminology with which Coleridge had familiarized him, it is evident that Wordsworth is concerned not with thought and feeling as separate elements in the human mind, but with their interaction; with ideas connected not by logic but under the influence of strong feeling. Ideas which are brought together in this way cease to be merely ideas and become images and symbols. 'Low and rustic life' was chosen because here the intellect and the feelings are more likely to be united than amongst educated people whose ideas are ordered largely by convention. For Wordsworth it was not their artistic form or the story the poems told that was important. What made them different from contemporary poetry was that 'the feeling therein developed gives importance to the action and situation and not the action and situation to the feeling'. Nevertheless, their appeal is not simply an emotional one; they are meant to engage our deepest thoughts as well as our deepest feelings. Indeed, it is impossible to do the one without the other. 'For all good poetry', declares Wordsworth,

> is the spontaneous overflow of powerful feeling; but though this be true, Poems to which any value can be attached, were never produced on any variety of subjects but by a man who being possessed of more than usual organic sensibility had also thought long and deeply.

For his part, Wordsworth gave Coleridge true friendship grounded in depth and strength of character. Coleridge found in Wordsworth the kind of support he had received from Thomas Poole, but allied to a poetic sensitivity which stimulated his own writing. Coleridge's personality was one that responded with great loyalty when his admiration and affection had been evoked. Certainly the help he afforded

Wordsworth was offered gladly to one he felt his superior. Indeed, his friends thought Coleridge's admiration for Wordsworth overdone and something which showed emotional dependence. There may be some truth in this, for Coleridge, in a characteristic reference, told Cottle,

> I speak with heart-felt sincerity and (I think) unblinded judge-ment, when I tell you, that I feel myself a *little man by his side*.
>
> (CL, I, 325)

Nevertheless, as he witnessed the growth and expression of Words-worth's poetic powers, he achieved a greater self-knowledge and insight about the course his own poetry should take.

In Chapter IV of *Biographia Literaria* Coleridge looks back on this period when he and Wordsworth collaborated in *Lyrical Ballads* and assesses the qualities in Wordsworth's genius which made such an appeal to him. He notes the union of deep feeling and profound thought, the ability to observe the familiar and to invest it with new life, and he then proceeds, after the passage we have already quoted, to analyse this 'original gift'.

> To find no contradiction in the union of old and new; to con-template the ANCIENT of days and all his works with feelings as fresh, as if all had then sprang forth at the first creative fiat; characterizes the mind that feels the riddle of the world, and may help to unravel it. To carry on the feelings of childhood into the powers of manhood; to combine the child's sense of wonder and novelty with the appearances, which every day for perhaps forty years had rendered familiar:
>
> . . . this is the character and privilege of genius.
>
> (*Biog. Lit.*, I, 59)

This reads remarkably like Arnold's later tribute to Wordsworth's genius in *Memorial Verses*, written on the occasion of Wordsworth's death in 1850.

> *He laid us as we lay at birth*
> *On the cool flowery lap of earth,*
> *Smiles broke from us and we had ease;*
> *The hills were round us, and the breeze*
> *Went o'er the sun-lit fields again;*
> *Our foreheads felt the wind and rain.*

> *Our youth return'd; for there was shed*
> *On spirits that had long been dead,*
> *Spirits dried up and closely furl'd,*
> *The freshness of the early world.*

Wordsworth had recovered a lost innocence; he had passed through a period of guilt and depression, a dark night of the soul, and was now able to celebrate this new vision in his poetry. Putting it in the phraseology of Blake, he had grown from innocence, through experience, to a new and more mature innocence. Coleridge had not suffered the same emotional crisis as Wordsworth, but he knew what depression was and his sensitive spirit was always keenly aware of personal guilt and the need for forgiveness. His letters and the Notebooks reveal in many places his consciousness of sin; his whole life, indeed, can be seen as a spiritual struggle in which he sought to crucify the natural and sinful man and to achieve the freedom of a new life in Christ. He differed from Wordsworth in being *animae naturaliter Christianae*, but, nevertheless, their personal needs brought them together in a common concern with the subject of guilt and expiation. This is seen in their abortive collaboration in a poem about Cain, which Coleridge describes in the Prefatory Note to his prose fragment, *The Wanderings of Cain*, where he tells us, 'the Ancient Mariner was written instead'.[1] To Coleridge, who had struggled to express his search for truth in the rather turgid verse of *Religious Musings*, and who was now endeavouring to square Hartley's doctrines with his reading of the mystics, Wordsworth's new found ability to express his emotional recovery in poetry that was fresh and immediate came almost as a revelation. He himself, of course, had been an agent of that recovery, but the healing power he had given Wordsworth, although a deeply personal thing, had been bound up with his intellectual enquiries and speculation. Not only had Wordsworth been delivered from the depression and guilt which weighed upon him, but he was able to communicate the wisdom he had acquired in simple

---

[1] No doubt the psycho-analytical critic would link the subject of Cain to the childhood incident (CL, I, 353–4), in which Coleridge attacked his brother with a knife and then ran away from home. The incident may have been traumatic and related to Coleridge's sense of guilt as an adult.

language and living images and this gave inspiration and a new strength to Coleridge's own poetry.

Although they are different in form and style, *The Ancient Mariner* and *Tintern Abbey* are both about this central experience which Coleridge and Wordsworth shared. It is fitting that they should be the first and last poems in the 1798 edition of *Lyrical Ballads*, which was the product of their close friendship and collaboration. Both poems are about a man who leaves home, who endures great suffering and carries with him a burden of guilt and fear, but who finally achieves peace of mind. Both men are sadder and wiser as a result of their experiences. Wordsworth, as he stands on the bank of the Wye, looks back across the intervening years; 'five summers with the length of five long winters' had passed since he had first stood there. It had been a period, as he was to tell us in *The Prelude*, haunted by nightmares of the Revolution and Terror, of guilt concerning Annette, and of fear for his own sanity. But *The Prelude* takes us further back than this, to Wordsworth's childhood of which he wrote,

> *Fair seed-time had my soul, and I grew up*
> *Fostered alike by beauty and by fear.*

The bare moorland and mountain crags of his boyhood home were emblems of fear and desolation before they became a source of strength and consolation to Wordsworth. The five years between 1793 and 1798 had not only witnessed his emotional recovery, but had taught him that nature can minister to us even through fear. And so he assures his sister at the conclusion of *Tintern Abbey*

> *that Nature never did betray*
> *The heart that loved her.*

Coleridge's Ancient Mariner went through a more dramatic experience, but the pattern is the same. The strange voyage he made was a spiritual journey in which the mist and snow symbolize confusion of mind; the icebergs the threat of mental shipwreck; and the calm and drought, spiritual dryness and desolation. His shooting of the albatross brings alienation from his fellows and finally complete isolation when the mariner finds himself entirely alone on the open sea,

> *And Christ would take no pity on*
> *My soul in agony.*

Then the beauty of the water-snakes moves his spirit and there begins the process of regeneration. The rain falls upon his dryness like the grace of God, the wind comes as the breath of God and he returns after great tribulation to the safety of harbour.

Both poems show the same pattern of a lost innocence and the recovery of an innocence that is more mature and reflective because of suffering. But there are differences between the two poems. Wordsworth's poem is directly autobiographical and its style is not that of the ballads he had been writing but of what was to become his greatest poetry, a style Keats characterized as the 'egotistical sublime'. Coleridge, too, played his part here in shaping Wordsworth's poetic gift, for he had experimented in poems such as *Frost at Midnight* and *Fears in Solitude* with the style he had found in Cowper and (as Humphry House showed)[1] developed from it a medium ideally suited to introspection and mental soliloquizing. But, more than this, in *Tintern Abbey* Wordsworth had discovered himself. The poem is a microcosm of *The Prelude*, the work which was meant to be the prolegomenon to his great philosophical poem, but which in fact became his greatest achievement. By the time he came to write *Tintern Abbey* Wordsworth had started to lay the foundations of his future life as a man and as a poet.

The Ancient Mariner, on the other hand, is not directly autobiographical, but Coleridge nevertheless came increasingly to see himself in terms of his own creation and it is perhaps significant that its central character finds no resting place at the end of the poem but is doomed to endless wandering.[2] For Coleridge, unlike Wordsworth, was not at a period of consolidation, nor was he to achieve the settled home life that awaited Wordsworth; his enquiring spirit and troubled personality were to give him little rest before he reached the sanctuary of Highgate, and this was not to be for many years.

[1] H. House, *Coleridge: The Clark Lectures*, 1953, 71ff.
[2] Many years later when he wrote his epitaph he included the prayer, 'That he who many a year with toil of breath/ Found death in life, may here find life in death'. See George Whalley, 'The Mariner and the Albatross', UTQ XVI, 1946–7, and John Beer's chapter, p. 83 above.

Another great difference between the two poems is that Wordsworth's concern is with man's mind (what he was to describe as 'the main haunt and region of my song'), and with the relationship between the mind and nature. His poem is not religious, still less is it Christian in any real sense. The same is true of *Peter Bell,* which Wordsworth wrote in 1798 and which can also be seen as a companion piece to *The Ancient Mariner.* Peter's redemption from sin is brought about through the 'ministry of fear' which nature alone exercises and it does not require any supernatural agency. Coleridge's poem, on the other hand, is set in a Christian framework; guilt and expiation are dealt with not simply as states of mind, or psychological experiences, but as features of the spiritual life which demand a religious explanation. Unlike Wordsworth who believed only what he felt directly from his own experience and who was ready to base his life upon this experienced truth, Coleridge, although he could not believe anything he did not *feel* to be true, was not content unless he could justify his beliefs by the intellect, by a philosophy of religion. This difference between them was to lead to a divergence of interests, for Coleridge was to become absorbed in philosophy and theology, subjects which had little attraction for Wordsworth. But more than this, it was a difference of personality in the two men which was to become divisive in its effects.

When *Lyrical Ballads* was in the press, Coleridge went to Germany accompanied by William and Dorothy Wordsworth. One of their purposes was to learn enough German to enable them to earn money by translating German works into English, but for Coleridge it also meant an opportunity to acquaint himself with German philosophy and especially the writings of Kant. For Coleridge the visit was a success. He studied at the University of Göttingen, where he attended lectures, borrowed books from the library and was made much of by the professors. Here he acquired the kind of education which Cambridge had failed to provide and worked in a more disciplined way than ever before. For the Wordsworths, however, their stay in Germany was almost a failure. They left Coleridge and stayed for most of the time at Goslar, a small town in the Hartz mountains, cut off by what Wordsworth described as the worst winter of the century. They learned little German and were never accepted by polite society because it was thought that Dorothy was Wordsworth's mistress. Wordsworth wrote poetry, recollecting in tranquility the emotions associated with the countryside where he had spent his childhood, and completing a good deal of what was to become the first two books of *The Prelude*. His homesickness was expressed in the last of the 'Lucy' poems, which he wrote on his return to England:

> *I travelled among unknown men*
> *In lands beyond the sea;*
> *Nor, England! did I know till then*
> *What love I bore to thee.*

Nor was it homesickness simply for England; Wordsworth's nostalgia strengthened his resolve to return to the North and to settle in the Lakes. The Wordsworths, who returned from Germany before him, called on Coleridge at Göttingen on their journey home. Coleridge gave some account of their meeting in a letter to Poole:

> Wordsworth and his Sister passed thro' here, as I have informed you—I walked on with them 5 english miles, and spent a day with them. They were melancholy and hypped—W. was affected to tears at the thought of not being near me, wished me, of course, to live in the North of England . . . Finally I told him plainly that *you* had been the man in whom *first* and in whom alone, I had felt an *anchor*! With all my other Connections I felt a dim sense of insecurity and uncertainty, terribly uncomfortable—W. was affected to tears.   (CL, I, 490–91)

It is possible, though unlikely, that if it had been a straight conflict between the emotional forces which linked him to Wordsworth and Poole, Coleridge might have remained in the West of England. But there was a further force which, even if its strength was not consciously recognized, was to draw him to the North; this was Sara Hutchinson.

Wordsworth and Dorothy spent the first seven months after their return to England at Sockburn-on-Tees, the home of their friends the Hutchinsons. Here Wordsworth renewed an acquaintance with Mary Hutchinson, which was to develop into love and lead to their marriage, and it was here on a visit in October 1799, that Coleridge first met and fell in love with Mary's sister Sara. In December of the same year the

Wordsworths moved to Grasmere and in the following summer the Coleridges were installed in Greta Hall, Keswick. At first the arrangement worked well; Coleridge and the Wordsworths visited each other as frequently as they had done in the Quantocks and found pleasure in each other's company. But for Coleridge it contained the seeds of tragedy. Mrs. Coleridge had resented the move to the North and was jealous of her husband's absences at Grasmere, and their marriage was disturbed by recrimination and strife. Coleridge was sadly aware of the contrast between his own household and the domestic peace of the Wordsworth family circle where Sara Hutchinson was a frequent visitor. His health was bad and the wet climate brought on attacks of rheumatism. Anxiety, depression, guilt and pain all did their work and led to his seeking relief in opium.

It was on 4 April 1802, less than two years after his move to Keswick, that Coleridge wrote his verse-letter to Sara Hutchinson, which was published in October in a shorter and revised version in the *Morning Post*, as *Dejection: An Ode*. The fact that it was published on Wordsworth's wedding day suggests that the poem was more than a cry of despair on Coleridge's part, more even than a selfless celebration of the happiness which Sara had achieved with the Wordsworths, in spite of the pain he had brought both her and himself,—an interpretation advanced by Humphry House;[1] it suggests that Wordsworth himself was connected with its subject-matter. Mary Moorman[2] in her biography of Wordsworth gives the details of the composition of *Dejection*. Coleridge wrote the original version in the course of one evening, while Wordsworth and Dorothy were staying with him at Keswick. On 27 March William had written the first four stanzas of his *Ode: Intimations of Immortality from Recollections of Early Childhood*. It was not for another two years that the Ode was completed, but meanwhile he took the four stanzas to Keswick and Coleridge must have seen them before writing *Dejection*, for in his own poem Coleridge answers the question which Wordsworth had left unanswered at the end of the stanzas he had written:

[1] H. House, *Coleridge*, 1953, 137–8.
[2] M. Moorman, *William Wordsworth. The Early Years: 1770–1803*, 1957, 527–30.

> *Whither is fled the visionary gleam?*
> *Where is it now, the glory and the dream?*

Several critics have noted the relationship between these two Odes and their connection with Coleridge's earlier poem *The Mad Monk*. This earlier poem, which was published in the *Morning Post* in October 1800, contains these lines:

> *There was a time when earth, and sea, and skies,*
> *The bright green vale, and forest's dark recess,*
> *With all things, lay before mine eyes*
> *   In steady loveliness:*
> *But now I feel, on earth's uneasy scene,*
> *   Such sorrows as will never cease;—*
> *   I only ask for peace;*
> *If I must live to know that such a time has been!*
>
> (PW, I, 348)

Wordsworth must have had these lines in mind when he composed the opening lines of his *Immortality* Ode:

> *There was a time when meadow, grove, and stream,*
> *The earth, and every common sight,*
> *   To me did seem*
> *Apparelled in celestial light,*
> *The glory and the freshness of a dream.*
> *It is not now as it has been of yore:—*
> *   Turn whereso'er I may,*
> *   By night or day,*
> *The things which I have seen I now can see no more.*

Then in *Dejection* Coleridge takes up the theme again and attempts to explain the decline of his poetic powers and his depression;

> *A Grief without a pang, void dark and drear,*
> *A stifling, drowsy, unimpassion'd Grief*
> *That finds no natural outlet, no Relief*
> *In word, or sigh, or tear—*
> *This, Sara! well thou knows't,*

> *Is that sore Evil, which I dread the most,*
> *And oft'nest suffer!*[1]

A few years previously Coleridge had believed that nature's healing power would deliver one from such a state, that it would 'set the affections in right tune' and nourish the imagination. But now he knows that this is not so for him. He looks at the beautiful forms of nature and has to confess,

> *—I see them all, so excellently fair!*
> *I see, not feel, how beautiful they are.*

Nature can, in fact, betray the heart that loves her if that heart itself is dried up.

> *O Sara! we receive but what we give,*
> *And in* our *life alone does Nature live*
> *Our's is her Wedding Garment, our's her Shroud—*
>
> *Ah! from the Soul itself must issue forth*
> *A Light, a Glory and a luminous Cloud*
> *Enveloping the Earth!*

This light, he tells Sara, is Joy.

> *Joy, Sara! is the Spirit and the Power,*
> *That wedding Nature to us gives in Dower*
> *A new Earth and new Heaven,*
> *Undreamt of by the Sensual and the Proud!*

Even in his own misery Coleridge can rejoice that Sara will possess this joy in the happy household of William, Mary and Dorothy. The poem is addressed in the first place to Sara, but it is also offered to William whose marriage will unite the Wordsworth and Hutchinson families.

We know that Coleridge's unhappiness was a cause of great concern to Wordsworth and his sister. No doubt the two men discussed Coleridge's sad plight and Wordsworth when he wrote his *Immortality* Ode must have had his friend in mind. It is conceivable that the 'I' of

---

[1] This and the following quotations are from the earliest version of the poem as published in E. de Selincourt, *Wordsworthian and Other Studies*, 1947, 67–76, and reprinted in Appendix I of H. House, *Coleridge*, 1953.

the first four stanzas refers to Coleridge as much as himself and the incorporation of what amounts to a paraphrase of the lines from *The Mad Monk* supports this view. It is difficult to interpret Wordsworth's four stanzas as autobiographical for there is no evidence that he himself was unhappy, or conscious of any failure of the imagination when he wrote it; indeed, as his marriage approached, Wordsworth seemed a contented man, happy as the fulfilment of his cherished plans drew near. But what could Wordsworth do for his friend? The specific which had brought him relief in the dark days at Racedown was power-less, it seemed, to assist Coleridge. This was why he left his poem with an unanswered question.

Coleridge's intellectual convictions corroborated what his personal experience had led him to believe. This two-way traffic between his intellect and his experience was always a feature of Coleridge's mind; he could never believe something that was not hammered out on the anvil of his own life. While still at Nether Stowey he had come to distrust Hartley's emphasis on environment as the determining factor in the development of the personality, and could no longer believe Hartley's account of the mind as a passive receptacle of sense impres-sions. He expressed his doubts to Thomas Poole in a letter dated March 1801:

> If the mind be not *passive*, if it be indeed made in God's Image, and that too in the sublimest sense—the Image of the *Creator*—there is ground for suspicion, that any system built on the passive-ness of the mind must be false, as a system. (C L, II, 709)

Wordsworth, on the other hand, remained a disciple of Hartley and the Preface he added to the second edition of *Lyrical Ballads* in 1800 used Hartley's psychology to explain the processes of poetic composi-tion. In *Biographia Literaria*, written much later, Coleridge was to state his disagreement with this:

> With many parts of this preface in the sense attributed to them, and which the words undoubtedly seem to authorize, I never concurred; but on the contrary objected to them as erroneous in principle. (II, 7–8)

But already in 1802, a few months after writing *Dejection*, he indicated in a letter to his friend Sotheby, his dissatisfaction with Wordsworth's Preface, '. . . we begin to suspect, that there is, somewhere or other, a *radical* Difference [in our] opinions' (C L, II, 812). Coleridge of course, was not content to leave matters like this. He regarded Wordsworth as a philosopher as well as a poet and was constantly urging him to carry on with the writing of his great philosophical poem *The Recluse*. No doubt he tried to communicate to Wordsworth his growing enthusiasm for Platonism, whether found in the Socratic dialogues, the seventeenth-century divines or the later works of Berkeley, and for the new German philosophy of Kant. He had told Poole in March 1801, that he had proved the reputation of Locke, Hobbes and Hume 'wholly unmerited' and had done so 'entirely to Wordsworth's satisfaction'. In some measure his attempt to educate Wordsworth philosophically met with success; Wordsworth added to the 1802 version of the Preface to *Lyrical Ballads* a long passage on 'What is a Poet?', which approximated more to Coleridge's views, and when he completed the *Immortality* Ode he drew upon the Platonic doctrines of pre-existence and innate knowledge. But fundamentally Wordsworth's attitudes and opinions were fixed; they rested upon the vision of truth vouchsafed him when he emerged from the purgatory of fear at Alfoxden and knew that he was destined to be a poet.

Wordsworth seems to have become convinced of this at the beginning of 1804, when he found that the 'poem on his earlier life' could not be ended with his undergraduate days at Cambridge, but had to be continued into the momentous events of the French Revolution and his own personal crisis. By this time Coleridge was broken in health and in despair about his unhappy marriage, and was suffering from a deep depression for which opium was the only palliative. He came to stay with the Wordsworths in December 1803, before setting out for Malta, and was desperately ill for most of the three weeks of his visit. On 14 January 1804, he left them and it was to be three years before they would meet again. But Coleridge's influence remained. His sad situation and their disagreement left Wordsworth with the task of trying to accommodate Coleridge's opinions to his own poetic vision and to write something that would speak to his friend's condition. That Wordsworth regarded this as of the greatest importance can be seen from the letter he wrote to Coleridge on 6 March 1804. Coleridge was now in London waiting for a passage to Malta and Wordsworth tells him of the progress of *The Prelude*:

> I finished five or six days ago another Book of my Poem . . .
> I am positively arrived at the subject I spoke of in my last.
> When this next book is done which I shall begin in two or three
> days time, I shall consider the work as finish'd.[1]

We know that the subject Wordsworth spoke of was the imagination[2] (something that had become central to Coleridge's thought), and it is clear that he now considered this the great theme with which his poem should end. Imagination is the power by which the human mind and nature are related and it was on this subject that their views seemed to diverge.

The passage Wordsworth wrote finally found its way into the last book of *The Prelude* as it was eventually published. Here Wordsworth holds to his belief that nature's influence is such

> *That men, least sensitive, see, hear, perceive,*
> *And cannot choose but feel.* (XIV, 85–6)

But he is ready to acknowledge that this power

> *is the express*
> *Resemblance of that glorious faculty*
> *That higher minds bear with them as their own.*
> (XIV, 88–90)

No doubt he counted Coleridge as one of these 'higher minds' and he continues with an assurance that the power is the source of joy and of that moral stability which will keep a man upright even in the worst vicissitudes. He is ready now to include the wisdom afforded by books as an auxiliary to the power of nature, and one can sense throughout this fifth book of the first version of *The Prelude* Wordsworth's endeavour to convince Coleridge that there are grounds for hope and that he

[1] WL, I (1967), 452.
[2] See M. Moorman. *William Wordsworth: The Later Years: 1803–1850*, 1965, 9–10.

will overcome his afflictions. Wordsworth worked hard at the poem and managed to complete the five books so that a MS copy of them reached Coleridge before he sailed for Malta.

But Wordsworth was not entirely successful in his purpose. Indeed, the wonderful years were over when the two men could think as with a single mind. When Coleridge returned to England he seemed worse rather than better and his friends were shocked at his appearance. Brandy and opium were to make him a difficult companion and put an intolerable strain upon those who tried to help him; the quarrel that finally separated him and Wordsworth was the culmination of a process of deterioration rather than a sudden break in their friendship. Nevertheless, we should bear in mind Lamb's injunction not to pity Coleridge in any patronizing way and should concentrate on the real issues that divided these great men rather than on the decline in their personal relationship.

As we know from Chapter XXII of *Biographia Literaria*, Coleridge was critical of the *Immortality* Ode and thought it contained what he called 'mental bombast';[1] more important, he was dissatisfied with Wordsworth's account of the imagination. But in spite of his disagreement and of the quarrel between them, he still felt that in Wordsworth he had known a man of genius and this conviction never left him. It was his attempt to explain the nature of this genius which led him to regard the imagination as the central and unifying faculty of the human mind. 'The poet', he was to write in *Biographia Literaria*,

> described in *ideal* perfection, brings the whole soul of man into activity, with the subordination of its faculties to each other, according to their relative worth and dignity. He diffuses a tone and spirit of unity, that blends, and (as it were) *fuses*, each into each, by that synthetic and magical power, to which we have exclusively appropriated the name of imagination.   (II, 12)

[1] In *The Friend*, however, Coleridge describes it as 'this sublime ode' and praises especially its idealist philosophy: the individual's 'sensation, which he is alike unable to resist or to comprehend, which compels him to contemplate as without and independent of himself what yet he would not contemplate at all, were it not a modification of his own being' (*Friend*, I, 509).

Wordsworth had demonstrated this power of the imagination in his poetry, even if he could not account for it in intellectual terms.

If his theory of the imagination was to be the cornerstone, the foundations of his philosophy were laid in the depths of Coleridge's personality; in his search for what would unify that personality and bring it fulfilment. Though Wordsworth may have failed to satisfy all the demands of Coleridge's mind and personality—only religion could do that—his life, his poetry and his friendship had spoken to those depths. So it was that in January 1807, a few months after his return from Malta, he listened with deep emotion to Wordsworth's reading of the now enlarged version of *The Prelude*—the poem known in the Wordsworths' family-circle as 'The Poem to Coleridge'—and felt moved to write his lines *To W. Wordsworth,* which began

> *O Friend! O Teacher! God's great gift to me!*[1]

Coleridge recognized in *The Prelude* Wordsworth's endeavours to grapple with the mysteries of the human personality; mysteries that were not simply a matter of philosophical or psychological speculation, but something that concerned the happiness of Coleridge and, through Coleridge, of Wordsworth himself. Whether this happiness was the result

> *Of tides obedient to external force,*
> *And currents self-determined, as might seem,*
> *Or by some inner Power; of moments awful,*
> *Now in thy inner life, and now abroad,*
> *When power streamed from thee, and thy soul received*
> *The light reflected, as a light bestowed—*

might still remain a mystery. But Coleridge in his own misery could admire Wordsworth's account of how he had conquered despair and preserved his hopes through all vicissitudes. And so he ended his own

---

[1] In the shortened and published form this was changed to 'Friend of the wise! and Teacher of the Good!', no doubt a reflection of the coolness that came into their relationship. The full version of the poem is printed in Appendix H of J. D. Campbell's edition of *The Poetical Works*, London, 1893.

lines with gratitude to Wordsworth for the example and the help he had
given him and with a prayer that he might make this example his own:

> *And when—O Friend! my comforter, and guide!*
> *Strong in thyself, and powerful to give strength!—*
> *Thy long sustainèd song finally closed,*
> *And thy deep voice had ceased—yet thou thyself*
> *Wert still before mine eyes, and round us both*
> *That happy vision of belovèd faces—*
> *Scarce conscious, and yet conscious of its close*
> *I sate, my being blended in one thought*
> *(Thought was it? or aspiration? or resolve?)*
> *Absorbed, yet hanging still upon the sound—*
> *And when I rose, I found myself in prayer.*

(PW, I, 408)

7: Coleridge and Philosophy

DOROTHY EMMET

T HE NAME 'Philosopher' covers a wide spectrum. A few philosophers—very few and those the greatest, Plato, Aristotle, Kant—
become founders of new ways of thinking and types of philosophy
which bear their name—Platonism, Aristotelianism, Kantianism. Others,
less original but not mere camp followers, may broadly accept the outlook and method of a founder, and be justly called Platonists, Aristotel-
ians, Kantians. But a school of philosophy is not a sect, and these, if
they are worth their salt as philosophers, will not just repeat the dicta
of the master; they will interpret and develop his ideas and find new
applications. Others, and these perhaps the majority of those professionally called philosophers, are neither originators nor close adherents
of a school. They will no doubt be adopting and adapting a particular
method, but they will mainly be trying to make close critical examina-
tions of some special problem or group of problems. Technical rigour
and concentrated mutual criticism will tend to set them apart from the
more general, looser discussions of ideas which go on among a wider
public. To the wider public and popularly, a 'philosopher' may be
anyone who looks or sounds wise—from Wordsworth's six years'
darling, 'thou best philosopher', to those who pronounce on life out of
native wit.

There are others who fall into none of these categories. They are not
founders of new ways of thought, nor close adherents of any one such;
they do not go on struggling, as technical philosophers do, in efforts to
get some limited problem or problems clearer, exposing themselves
deliberately to their own criticism and that of their peers. But they do
not just produce aphorisms, pontificate, or (more sympathetically) give

wise counsel. They are genuinely and seriously interested in thought; they have convictions which they want to express; and they read widely among the philosophers of the past, trying to find ways of thinking and terminologies to help them to say what they want to say.

One such was Coleridge, and it is as such that we should judge his philosophy. He was not the founder of a school, nor was he a close adherent of any one school. Attempts to put a label on him, and call him a 'Platonist', a 'Kantian', a 'traditional Idealist', or (more fashionably) an 'Existentialist' can only disguise his real originality, or produce the kind of criticism which raps him over the knuckles for deviationism, for instance for using a Kantian terminology in a sense different from that intended by Kant. It can also lead to preoccupation with the 'sources' of his thought—did he get the distinction between Fancy and Imagination from Schelling, or from Kant, or even further back, from the Cambridge Platonist Cudworth? It can make us divide his life up into periods, when he was a 'Hartleian' a 'Berkeleian', a 'Kantian', and finally perhaps some kind of Platonic-cum-Christian theologian.

Nor was he a philosopher in the professional sense. This is not meant as a patronizing remark; few professional philosophers have seen as far as Coleridge into the powers of the human mind. This is not just a way of saying that he did not earn his living by teaching philosophy, a trivial criterion. He did indeed advertise the Philosophical Lectures at 5*s* per lecture (with some reduction on serial tickets and on double tickets for the course of thirteen)—a fair sum at 1818 prices. They were not financially a success. To say he was not a professional is not meant as withholding a snob label or a financial one; it is the question of what we should look for in characterizing his thinking, and the terms in which it should be judged.

It is when he is trying to be most 'professional' as he understood this requirement that he is least readable; for instance, in the synopses of his *opus maximum*, his projected grand system. These perhaps lessen our regret that it was never completed. When Richards says[1] 'Coleridge was not, I suppose, a good Philosopher; he made too many mistakes *of the wrong kind*', one can see what he means. There are what our contemporaries call 'category mistakes'—different types of abstraction put

[1] *Coleridge on Imagination*, 10.

together where they do not logically cohere, metaphors unowned as such, and above all, the lack of close argument.

He is most illuminating in the occasional apparently throwaway remark, though with Coleridge we cannot be sure that anything was thrown away; it may be something that had been working in his mind and now comes out in a new unexpected context. Above all, he had certain things to say, which progressively became, if not altogether clearer, at any rate more insistently important to him. We shall try to see what these central intellectual convictions were, and how at different times and stages in his reading he sought the help of various philosophers in expressing them: his *reading* of philosophers rather than his discussion with them. Coleridge talked endlessly, and to all and sundry. But there do not seem to have been philosophers as such among his circle of friends and correspondents. Medical men and scientists— these were important—but not philosophers. One suspects that the philosophers he met in Germany discoursed to him rather than with him. The relevant period (1795–1825), was a thin generation for British philosophy, though more was going on in Scotland than in England. There were indeed the Benthamites, but they moved in a different circle, and when J. S. Mill speaks of Bentham and Coleridge as the two seminal minds of their generation, there is no evidence that they met in person, though they were to meet to great profit in the minds of Mill himself and of I. A. Richards. (Richards, while claiming to be writing as a Benthamite, gives one of the most perceptive interpretations we have of 'Coleridge on Imagination'.)

'Metaphysics and poetry and "facts of mind"—(i.e. accounts of all the strange phantasms that ever possessed your philosophy— dreamers from Thoth the Egyptian to Taylor the English pagan) are my darling studies', Coleridge wrote to Thelwall in 1796 (CL, I, 156). Metaphysics is often taken to mean purely speculative thinking, un-verifiable in experience, and unassimilable in science. Coleridge was to see it rather as a reaching out of the powers of the mind in responsive unity with powers in nature to which they are akin—'connatural', he says, adapting as he so often does an older term. But first he needs to understand these powers of the mind. 'All metaphysical philosophy indeed is at last but an examination of our powers of knowledge—and the different systems are best distinguished by their different accounts of these powers.' (*Notebooks*, III)[1]

He attacks metaphysics estranged from experimental physics and experimental psychology (*Philosophical Lectures*, 318); 'preparatory to the great anti-babel of metaphysical Science all sorts of material, psychological and logical, must be brought together' (*Notebooks*, III, 3254). Indeed he spent so long assembling all sorts of material that he never got beyond prolegomena to what was to have been the great work on metaphysics. We need not regret this unduly; as I have said, the synopses of the *opus maximum* are not very promising, while the comments on the odd facts of mind he records and describes can be illuminating in the extreme. These 'facts of mind' included unusual states and fringe experiences—what would nowadays be called 'paranormal phenomena'. Here Coleridge was both fascinated, and kept his head. He wanted to find ways of studying these seriously. 'Wisdom', he remarked, 'may be gathered from the maddest flights of imagination, as medicines were stumbled upon in the wild processes of alchemy.' (CL, I, 39.) One such fringe study was 'Mesmerism', as it was then called (the forerunner of hypnotism). Without benefit of Freud or Jung, he was very aware of what he called 'that shadowy half-being, that state of nascent Existence in the twilight of Imagination, and just on the vestibule of consciousness' (CL, II, 445). The 'facts of mind'—dreams, phantasms, anxieties—were dark as well as light. The point was to understand them.

This is the context in which to place his early enthusiasm for Hartley. Hartley had been a former member of Coleridge's own Cambridge college, Jesus College. The philosophy in his *Observations of Man, His Frame, His Duty and His Expectations* was by no means just an aridly mechanical one, much less materialism. It was a pioneer attempt to formulate a neurophysiology of sensation, with a view of vibrations as passing along nerve fibres to the brain, and setting up oscillations in the white medulla, and he tried to correlate these neurophysiological events with reflex mechanisms in observable behaviour.

[1] Dr Kathleen Coburn has kindly let me see the galley proofs of the third volume of the edited Notebooks. I owe her a great deal besides this.

All this was much better than the old notions of 'animal spirits' running up hollow tubes in the nervous system.[1] Coleridge was clearly fascinated by this prospect of a scientific account of sensation; and in *Religious Musings*, 1794, he classes Hartley with Bacon and Newton;

> he of mortal kind
> *Wisest, he first who marked the ideal tribes*
> *Up the fine fibres through the sentient brain*

'Ideal tribes' are the neural currents conveying sensations from which 'ideas' were derived. It is when we come to *how* ideas are derived from these neuro-physiological events that the trouble begins for psychologists and mental philosophers then and now. Hartley had his hypothesis, following closely on Locke, that we become aware of these sensory events as impressions, and that 'ideas' are derived by noticing their likenesses and differences, naming them and the ways in which they are connected. Connections coming from the coincidence of our impressions with one another on some occasion will set up linkages, so that the occurrence of one impression calls up the memory of others with which it is 'associated'. That something like this indeed happens we all know from our own experience. A poet will be a person who can store and call up a wide range of 'associations'—impressions visualized as 'images', or vividly characterized in words—which can illustrate and recall each other by non-obvious resemblances; Professor J. L. Lowes has traced a vast phantasmagoria of images on which Coleridge himself drew. Coleridge knew how much depended on the 'streamy nature of association'. He may or may not have subscribed to Wordsworth's programmatic statement in the preface to the 1800 edition of *Lyrical Ballads*:

> The principal object then was to make the incidents of common life interesting by tracing in them truly though not ostentatiously, the primary laws of our nature: chiefly as far as regards the manner in which we associate ideas in a state of excitement.

[1] Professor R. C. and Lady Kathleen Oldfield, writing as psychologists, give an appreciative account of Hartley's work in 'Hartley's Observations on Man', *Annals of Science*, 7, 371–81.

He would probably have been prepared to say that this was true, but not the whole truth. For by 1800 he had become clearer about the inadequacy of Hartleian association as an account of the more creative kinds of mental activity. It is not easy to say just when this happened. A letter of February 1801 not extant but quoted by Leslie Stephen[1] suggests he was still then following Hartley; while in March 1801 he writes to Thomas Poole that he has now emancipated himself from Hartley's views on Time, Space and Association. I do not believe that he suffered some sudden conversion as a result of reading Kant; in particular I do not believe he was suddenly converted between February and March, 1801. To think of him as having a purely Hartleian or a post-Hartleian period goes along with the affixing of labels which I repudiated earlier. Coleridge was continually wanting to understand 'facts of mind'. We know that he was a reader of Plato and the Neo-Platonists when he was a young man; and Charles Lamb told how even the 'inspired charity boy' at Christ's hospital used to talk about Proclus and Iamblichus.

The Notebooks show that he was reading Plato and the Neo-Platonists, and indeed the English Cambridge Platonists, all through what is supposed to be his Hartleian period. (See *e.g.*, I, 200, 201, 204.) What was he getting from them? Partly no doubt the odd observations of the occult to which he refers in the 1796 letter to Thelwall. But more importantly, Platonism in all its forms has always stood for the possibility of an original power of the mind to grasp ideas which cannot simply be derived from impressions of the senses; a power of 'thought' as distinguished from 'thoughts'. 'A *Thought* and Thoughts are quite different words from *Thought*.' (*Notebooks*, I, 1077) He is after the active power of thinking, as distinct from the distinct products, each of which can be called 'a thought' and associated with other thoughts. Later, Kant was to reinforce the conviction that thinking must be seen as an active, synthesizing power, and not as the product of a collocation of associations. Kant himself put this in a formidable technical vocabulary concerning the 'original synthetic transcendental unity of apperception'. But, as Dr Lovejoy points out,[2] the English Platonists (indeed we

[1] *Letters*, ed. E. H. Coleridge, I, 351n.

[2] 'Kant and the English Platonists' in *Essays Philosophical and Psycho-*

could say all Platonists) had believed in *a priori* powers of the mind before Kant. There was nevertheless a difference; Kant gave a tough-minded critique of the functions and scope of these *a priori* notions—notions not derived from experience. These were either Categories of the Understanding, providing a conceptual framework by which experience is turned from a confused 'manifold' into an orderly world of interrelated objects, or Ideas of Reason providing ideals of intellectual satisfaction. But without the materials of experience to work upon, order and interpret, these *a priori* functions of the mind are for Kant purely formal, producing possible ways of thinking, but not *knowledge*. The Platonic view of the scope of Ideas was not thus limited. Ideas could be grasped in the first instance by noticing likenesses and differences in the world we experience through our senses; what it is that tables have in common which makes us think of them as tables, and so too with triangles, men, just acts. . . . But for Plato this is not only an exercise in definition; the definition when reached is thought of as having a validity independent of the perceived instances which are grouped under it. The Idea of the Triangle will have a necessary, unchanging existence, no matter what slight deviations there may be in all the triangles we can see; and so too, it was hoped, might the Idea of Justice or the Idea of the Perfect Man.

In all his stages, and whoever his philosophic mentors at each of them, Coleridge was always struggling with this high notion of Ideas. He makes successive attempts to say what he means by 'Ideas', taking over the word, *faute de mieux*, because it was the one philosophers had continually used, but he realized that it had been used in manifold

---

logical in honour of William James. But Coleridge saw that the English Platonists were 'pre-critical'. In commenting on the Cambridge Platonist John Smith's *Select Discourses*, Coleridge says 'What they all wanted was a pre-inquisition into the mind, as part origin, part constituent, of all knowledge, an examination of the scales, weights and measures themselves abstracted from the objects to be weighed and measured by them; in short a transcendental aesthetic, logic and noetic. The honour of establishing a complete προπαιδεία of philosophy was reserved for Immanuel Kant.' (*Literary Remains*, III, 416, probably written during Coleridge's Highgate period) senses. For instance, in the British empiricists, from Locke to Hartley, 'ideas' included sensory impressions from which intellectual abstractions could be derived. In both cases they were thought of as objects of attention, entertained by a mind. The word 'entertained' suggests guests who can be idle while the host does the work. It was the active, subjective, side of ideas, the entertaining not the object entertained, which Coleridge wanted to describe. He missed it in Locke; he missed it still more in Hartley. For a brief period he seems to have thought he could find it in Berkeley's subjective idealism. To Berkeley, as to the empiricists, an 'idea' is a sensory idea which is an object of attention, and its *esse* is *percipi*; it exists in being perceived. But Berkeley also allows, in a way which echoed Plato, 'mind, spirit, myself', an active spiritual power which perceives, and which in the end comes to read the ideas it perceives as a 'divine visual language', symbols through which it communicates with the Divine Mind. For a brief period Coleridge looked to Berkeley as guiding light, and he called his son, born in 1798, Berkeley. The child died within a year, and Coleridge's 'Berkeleian' period seems to have been almost as short lived. Again, we must beware of labels, and I doubt whether he was ever seriously a 'Berkeleian'. In the note on the projected 'Hymns to the Sun, Moon and the Elements' (*Notebooks*, I, 174 [1795–6]), he writes, 'In the last Hymn, a sublime enumeration of all the charms or Tremendities of Nature—then a bold avowal of Berkeley's System!!!!' The four exclamation marks suggest that Coleridge knows he is being slightly outrageous. In the *Philosophical Lectures* of 1818 (p. 371) he says he was fascinated in his youth by the idealist notion of *natura naturans*, (in Berkeley's language, God) producing the word as *natura naturata* in the finite minds on which it acts, and he wrote in *The Eolian Harp* (1795),

> *And what if all of animated nature*
> *Be but organic Harps diversely framed*
> *That tremble into thought, as o'er them sweeps*
> *Plastic and vast, one intellectual breeze*
> *At once the Soul of each and God of all.*

Whether or not he was shaken by his pensive Sara's disapproval of the pantheistic leanings in this, at any rate, it was no final resting place.

The objective realities of nature beyond our minds had to be given a stronger status. Berkeleian idealism could be applauded as a counter-blast to materialism. (In *Notebooks*, I, 203 [1795–6], there is a memo., 'In the essay on Berkley [*sic*] to speak of Sir Isaac Newton and other material theists'; but we do not have the essay, and in any case, by 1798 and the visit to Germany, Coleridge was moving on to other mentors.)

Again, I think it is a mistake to see him as turning from one allegiance to another, and to say that he came back from Germany a 'Kantian'. He read Kant eagerly, and that before Kant's work had begun to penetrate into philosophical England or Scotland; and we can believe him when he says (*Biographia Literaria*, Ch. IX) that 'the writings of the illustrious sage of Königsberg, the founder of the Critical Philosophy more than any other work, at once invigorated and disciplined my understanding'. He took over Kant's distinction of the Understanding and the Reason in name, but his use of it was far from Kantian. For Kant, the Understanding, though indeed an original function of the mind, supplies a limited set of fixed categories in terms by which the materials of sensation are ordered. It is original, *i.e.* not derived from experience, but it is not original as inventive of alternative ways of ordering the world. The Reason produces Ideas which remind us of the incompleteness of our knowledge of the empirical world, by holding before us ideals such as that of the world seen as an intelligible unity, or the Soul as the active unity behind the succession of states studied by empirical psychology. But for Kant these Ideas of the Reason are *regulative*; they hold out ideals of intellectual satisfaction, intellectual carrots, which cannot be grasped by the empirical methods through which alone knowledge (as distinct from speculation) is possible. They do not give us substantive truth. Coleridge did not accept this restriction. He speaks of 'Ideas of Reason', but in an older, Platonic vein; trying to present them as instruments of an intuitive knowledge, which can penetrate beyond the knowledge obtained through the Understanding's operation on data supplied by the senses.

In his dissatisfaction with the confines in which Kant encloses knowledge, Coleridge was not alone. The German post-Kantian idealists, who were his contemporaries, were also trying to find a way of breaking out into the heady uplands of metaphysical realities beyond sensory experience. Coleridge's attitude to these attempts is interestingly ambivalent. First there was Fichte, for whom, in spite of applauding him for beginning his philosophy from 'act' and not from 'thing', he had a healthy, and I think not altogether unjustified, contempt. Kant had seen the moral Self, prescribing an absolute categorical imperative to itself, as the point where we break through to noumenal reality beyond the phenomenal world of the senses in practical moral faith. But for Fichte, the world only exists through the moral imperative of the self. Coleridge calls this 'a crude egoismus, a boastful and hyperstoic hostility to Nature, as lifeless, godless and altogether unholy.' (*Biog. Lit.*, I, 101–2.)

Schelling was a more serious proposition, and the later Coleridge has been accused of simply plagiarizing him. Coleridge foresaw (or had heard) the charge himself. In *Biographia Literaria*, Ch. IX, saying, 'In Schelling's *Natur-Philosophie* and the *System des Transcendentalen Idealismus* I first found a genial coincidence with much that I had toiled out for myself, and a powerful assistance in what I had yet to do', he claims that this was the *support*, not the source of his convictions; and anyhow truth is a divine ventriloquist: 'I care not from whose mouth the sounds are supposed to proceed, if only the words are audible and intelligible.' (*Ibid.*, 105) This does not deter him from lifting passages from Schelling's *System des Transcendentalen Idealismus* and translating them to form the intimidating manifesto of his projected Dynamic Philosophy at the end of the first part of the *Biographia Literaria*. Professor McFarland[1] has given a detailed, scholarly account of Coleridge's alleged plagiarisms, and has shown where these accusations have substance, as in these translations from Schelling. His book is likely to be indispensable for anyone interested in this kind of sleuth work. Not that this is by any means all that McFarland has to say; he also has a distinct view, which I shall notice later, of what was at the heart of Coleridge's attempts at a philosophical system and why it was bound to fail. Meanwhile I return to the use of Schelling. To lift the jargon-ridden sections from the *Transcendental Idealism* and pass them off in translation was not altogether a happy thought. Not only

[1] *Coleridge and the Pantheist Tradition*, Oxford, 1969.

are they heavy reading, but Coleridge himself was to question later whether they really said what he wanted to say about the 'unity of subject and object'. Schelling was looking for an intuitive knowledge in which a subjective idea authenticated its own objective validity, and Coleridge was after this too. Kant had denied there could be such self-authenticating intuitive knowledge, at least of matters of fact. The practical reason—that rationality in action which Kant called 'the will' —could indeed prescribe laws to itself which needed no external evidence to validate them. But these were imperatives for moral action, not objective knowledge of things in themselves. Schelling had tried to extract intuitive self-authenticating knowledge from the idea of our own self-consciousness. It was not only Descartes who was haunted by there being something both *a priori* and existentially inescapable about the fact of self-consciousness, though Descartes gave it its classical expression in his *Cogito ergo sum*. Beyond Descartes stood St Augustine and indeed a whole Platonizing tradition of philosophy, which took its stand on the fact of self-consciousness. The question is where to go to next. Schelling thought that where one went was to the notion of a 'Ground' of one's being which was not just one's personal self. The 'I am' from which thinking starts is inescapable, but it is not self-supporting or self-explanatory. So we turn to a kind of theism which owes as much to the mystics as to the philosophers; and indeed behind Schelling, as Coleridge well knew, stood Jacob Boehme, the Silesian cobbler of the end of the sixteenth and early seventeenth century. Coleridge had been a reader of Boehme even at Christ's Hospital, and the mixture of speculative cosmology and imaginative symbolism was after his own heart. Indeed he pays Boehme and his translator William Law and also George Fox—mystical enthusiasts all—the tribute of saying that what they did for him in an arid time was 'to keep alive the heart in the head' and prevent him being imprisoned in any dogmatic system. Nevertheless, in referring to them, and to Boehme in particular, he keeps his head. He suspects the imagery behind his cosmology may well have come from dream material. 'There is meaning, important meaning in both' (*i.e.* in both Boehme and dream material, both the exponents are almost accidental—such infinity of synonimes [*sic*] exist in the language of vision' (*Notebooks*, III, 3692). He saw that

Schelling was trying to make a coherent system out of the phantasmagoria of Boehme's dream world—'What Schelling identifies, J.
Behmen *jumbles*.' But in the end, for all his borrowings from Schelling,
it is perhaps Boehme, touching his imagination, rather than Schelling,
who is the deeper influence. He suspected that Schelling and indeed
even the greater Spinoza were trying to get reality out of abstractions.

So we come back from these borrowings to what Coleridge himself
was trying to say. That he put it into the terminology of a succession of
philosophers makes it the more difficult to disentangle. He was, as he
said, a 'library cormorant', but he was not a magpie, lining his nest with
scrapings from the history of philosophy. McFarland's verdict on this is,
I think, just. His borrowings 'though skirting and sometimes crossing
the boundary of propriety were not the thefts of a poverty-stricken
mind, but the mosaic materials of a neurotic technique of composition'.[1]
Coleridge himself put his own case:

> Those only who feel no originality, no consciousness of having
> received their Thoughts and opinions from immediate Inspiration
> are anxious to be thought originals—the certainty and feeling is
> enough for the other, and he rejoices to find his opinions plumed
> and winged with the authority of venerable Forefathers.
>
> (*Notebooks*, I, 1695)

His opinions may have been plumed in borrowings from venerable
forefathers. They are winged when they take off from the ground in the
images and phrases of his own genius. Here the very feature which
critics jump on as a defect in his philosophy may also have been its
strength; the influence of the heart on the head.[2] Coleridge knew him-

[1] *Coleridge and the Pantheist Tradition*, 32.
[2] See *e.g.* R. Wellek, *Immanuel Kant in England* Princeton, 1931,
Chapter III, 'S. T. Coleridge and Kant'. Wellek considers the study of
Coleridge's philosophy 'futile' because of the jumble of different kinds of
thinking, and because he uses Kantian terminology in a non-Kantian
sense.

H. N. Fairchild (*Religious Trends in English Poetry*) has a somewhat
patronizing attack especially on the weaknesses he sees in Coleridge's
theological views. He thinks Coleridge failed to find objective controls
over his subjective faith. On the other hand J. H. Muirhead, in his

self that this was how it was. 'My philosophical opinions are blended with, or deduced from, my feelings, and this, I think, peculiarizes my style of writing.' (C L, I, 164.) This catches him out in the prospectuses for his *opus maximum*, where he is discoursing on logic, and where he needs a clear cool look at what the argument really is and at the meanings of his terms.[1] But it is a strength when he tries to describe kinds of thinking in which the whole person—with his feelings, moral convictions, intuitions, imagination—is involved. Like most of his contemporaries, Coleridge sometimes used the terminology of the old faculty psychology, though he struggled against the notion that there were different faculties, as distinct from different powers of the one mind. He called it the 'faculty' of integrative thinking and the state of mind it represents 'Reason' as distinct from 'Understanding'. We can forget this dated demand for separate faculties and see how he describes the state of mind it represents. He uses the word 'Idea' though not without qualms as spanning both the mental activity and its products. 'Idea' had, of course, Platonic echoes.

Coleridge as a Philosopher gives a sustained and documented defence of him as a serious thinker. He sees him as a forerunner of a voluntaristic kind of idealism, where reality is found in the unity of the individual will with universal Will, though Muirhead thinks he still held too conservatively to Christian orthodoxy to enter fully into this kind of absolute idealism. Muirhead is here, I think, trying to impose more systematic unity on Coleridge than he will bear. Coleridge never achieved a 'system' in the idealist sense but rather a view of spiritual reality as experienced in creative will.

The images in which he expressed this owed more to his psychological and scientific interests than, I think, any of these writers allow, though Muirhead does indeed, call attention to the strength of his scientific interests (119–20).

[1] Alice D. Snyder in *Coleridge on Logic and Learning* (New Haven, 1929), gives an account of unpublished pieces of work, mostly in the form of manuscript notes, marginalia, unrevised mss. and manifestoes, which were to lead up to the *Opus Maximum*. In these Coleridge is presenting not so much a philosophical system as a philosophical cosmogony, a speculative view of the universe in terms of the polarization of Chaos and the Creative Logos, and the doctrines of the Fall and Redemption.

Plato adopted it as a technical term, and as the antithesis to εἴδωλα or sensuous images; the transcient and perishable emblems, or mental words, of ideas. The ideas themselves he considered as mysterious powers, living, seminal, formative and exempt from time.   (*Biog. Lit.*, I, 69n)

Again, in *The Friend* he writes,

A distinguishable power, self-affirmed, and seen in its unity with the Eternal Essence, is, according to Plato, an Idea; and the discipline by which the human mind is purified from its idols (εἰδῶλα)[1] and raised to the contemplation of Ideas and thence to the secure and ever progressive, though never ending, investigation of truth and reality by scientific method, comprehends what the same philosopher so highly extols under the title of Dialectic.
                                                   (*Friend*, I, 492)

A little later (p. 494 n) he says he would gladly find another term if he could, one 'less obnoxious to the anti-Platonic reader'. What he wants to secure is the notion of a mental *initiative* (an echo here of the use of 'initiative' in Bacon's *De augmentis scientiarum* vi. ch. 2).

Continually in the notebooks, he refers to the term, and groans at its ambiguities. What seems to emerge is that an 'Idea' is not just a word or phrase with semantic rules for its use, nor is it just a concept abstractly defined. It is something more dynamic. But I doubt whether Coleridge accepted the Platonic view (if it was this) that Ideas in themselves were living powers. When he speaks of them as such, he is thinking of them as activated in a person's mind, and as communicable in ways that kindle and excite the mind of another. In *The Statesman's Manual* (Appendix E), he writes:

A notion may be realised and becomes cognition; but that which is neither a sensation nor a perception, that which is neither individual (that is, a sensible intuition) nor general (that is, a conception), which neither refers to outward facts, nor yet is abstracted from the forms of perception contained in the under-

---

[1] Coleridge's Greek accents are as shaky as those of most of us who put them in from memory. When quoting I have reproduced them as given.

standing; but which is an educt of the imagination actuated by the pure reason, to which there neither is nor can be an adequate correspondent in the world of the senses—this and this alone is = an Idea. Whether ideas are regulative only, according to Aristotle and Kant; or likewise constitutive, and one with the power and life of nature, according to Plato and Plotinus (ἐν λόγῳ ζωὴ ἦν καὶ ἡ ζωὴ ἦν τὸ φῶς τῶν ἀνθρώπων) is the highest problem of philosophy, and not part of its nomenclature.

In a note on the Mode of Studying Kant (*Works*, Shedd, IV, 400) he says this distinction is of interest to the philosopher by profession alone; others may accept that even if the Ideas are only postulates of the Moral Reason, they are still practical guides to faith. Yet the philosopher in him could not be indifferent to their status. Ideas, he believes, give intuitive self-validating knowledge. What kind of knowledge? Coleridge is saying that the validity of Ideas does not consist in any relation of correspondence between them and external objects to which they refer. He is looking for a kind of thinking which produces its own objectivity, putting this in the terminology of the coincidence of Subject and Object. When we ask for examples, we get a quotation from Plotinus (*Biog. Lit.*, I, 173) beginning τὸ θεωροῦν μοῖ θεώρημα ποιεῖ ('with me the act of contemplation makes the thing contemplated'); and he goes on to instance the constructions of geometers. Mathematics is perhaps a dubious ally for Coleridge's purpose; it is indeed a kind of thinking whose validity is internal to itself, but this is because of its extreme formalism; the mathematician is operating symbols according to rules which he has himself set up.

The next example is our own existence, as involved in our self-consciousness; and in this case indeed the conditions which make it possible to enunciate the statement 'I am' are also the conditions of its validity ('if it were not true, I could not say it'). But the problem is what to say next.

Another clue is the autonomy of what Kant called the 'Practical Reason'. Man as a rational being prescribes a moral law to himself; and here again the condition of rational responsibility which makes it possible to prescribe the moral law also makes it obligatory to obey it. So this could be seen as a law validated by its own conditions, and indeed for Kant no external conditions are relevant to a categorical imperative. The subjective and objective could thus be said to coalesce but the categorical imperative is *prescriptive*, setting up a law which ought to be followed, not a description of reality.

The next clue to a kind of thinking which involves its own validity comes from some of the things Coleridge has to say about Imagination. He had many things to say about Imagination, and some of them have become classics in the theory of literary criticism. We are concerned with where he links Imagination to the Ideas of the Reason. In the *Statesman's Manual* passage, he speaks of an idea as 'an educt of the Imagination actuated by the pure reason, to which there neither is nor can be an adequate correspondent in the world of the senses'. Again, 'the rules of the Imagination are themselves the very powers of growth and production' (*Biog. Lit.*, II, 65).

Imagination does not just associate images as 'fixities and definites', thereby producing the possible banalities of Fancy. It produces from materials of imagery a new integral image which then seems to stand in its own right. Coleridge calls Imagination 'esemplastic power', saying he is coining the world from εἰς ἓν πλάττειν, to weave into one. To Kant, the Imagination is a faculty of forming an image for a concept. In the *Critique of Judgment* Kant described aesthetic experience as the harmonious free play of the Imagination and the Understanding, the enjoyment of images without having to ask whether they are faithful representations or afford truth of anything beyond themselves. Coleridge can link himself with this Kantian notion of the autonomy of the aesthetic judgement, but, again, makes it do more metaphysical work than Kant would have it do; its creations are not only the free play of our faculties, they are means of insight.

All these four kinds of example, where ideas claim their own validity, are recognizable kinds of rational functioning; the question is whether Coleridge and indeed the Platonists behind him are justified in thinking that they not only have logical, moral or aesthetic functions, but also cognitive ones. This brings us to how Coleridge sees metaphysics.

Clearly, not as a form of pure abstract argument. The abstract metaphysician, he says, should be sent to live in the airless condition of the Moon, when he will find his whole intellect annihilated. Coleridge was always fascinated by the Moon and imagery drawn from it.[1] Remarking that the Moon is 'at present uninhabited owing to its little or no atmosphere but may in time', he suggests 'An Atheistic Romance might be formed—a Theistic one too—Mem!' (*Notebooks*, I, 10) How excited he would have been by the recent landings on the moon! Moonlight also provides an analogy for metaphysical faith.

> Well, and of good right therefore, do we maintain with more zeal, than we should defend body or estate, a deep and inward convic-tion, which is as the moon to us; and like the moon with all its massy shadows and deceptive gleams, it yet lights us on our way, poor travellers as we are, and benighted pilgrims. With all its spots and ranges and temporary eclipses, with all its vain halos and bedimming vapors, it yet reflects the light that *is* to rise on us, which even now is *rising*, though intercepted from our immediate view by the mountains that enclose and frown over the vale of our mortal life.   (*Friend,* I, 97)

Metaphysical faith is our light in a moon-struck landscape. It is also a kind of thinking which is the opposite of what Whitehead has called 'the burden of inert ideas'. 'Metaphysics make all one's thoughts equally corrosive on the Body by the habit of making momently and common thought the subjects of uncommon interest and intellectual energy.' (*Notebooks,* I, 1313) Thus it calls for habits of alert, receptive con-centration. Among its enemies are the 'Preventive Substitutes of Occupation' of the 'Busy Indolent', who find ways of using their energies, while never seriously rousing themselves to think. It is likely to be effectively killed by the multitude of ways people find of

> Reconciling two contrary yet co-existent propensities of men, the Indulgence of Sloth with the Hatred of Vacancy; and which Class, besides Novels, contains in it *Gambling*, Swinging or Sway-ing on a chair, Spitting over a Bridge, Smoking, Quarrels after dinner between Husband and Wife when tête-a-tête, the reading word by word of all the advertisements of a Daily Advertiser in a Public House on a rainy Day.   (*Inquiring Spirit,* 173.)

[1] *Cf.* J. Livingston Lowes's chapter 'The Journeying Moon', in *The Road to Xanadu.*

Another enemy is what the medievals called *accidie*, deadness of feeling—the state of mind into which Coleridge saw so deeply in his *Dejection* Ode. Yet another enemy is *envy* (*cf. Philosophical Lectures*, 179) which can corrode a man's genius 'for all genius exists in a participation of a common spirit'. There is a sense too in which to love one's neighbour as oneself means *to love oneself.* 'Men are ungrateful to others only when they have ceased to look back on their former selves with joy and tenderness. They exist in fragments.' (*Friend*, I, 40)

All this might be said to concern the moral and psychological conditions for intellectual creativity rather than its cognitive validity. But for Coleridge anything we can say about reality must spring first and foremost from understanding of our own nature. 'When a system is stated, what says the Philosopher of London and Paris? Does he go into his own Nature, look at it steadfastly and observe whether or no it or the part of it then in question, corresponds with the Statement?' and he repeats the suggestion that this kind of philosopher should be sent to live in the thin atmosphere of the Moon (*Notebooks*, I, 1758). In metaphysics we seek to say something about reality through the ways we appropriate it into our own minds, the task is 'to make the external internal, the internal external' (*Biog. Lit.*, II, 258).

In exploring conditions of creative intellectual activity, involving conditions of feeling, moral conscience, concentrated awareness, Coleridge was exploring the workings of his own mind, when his 'shaping spirit of imagination' was living, and when (as more often) it was dead. He was coming to see that any account of the mind that did not bring out this distinction was a false one. Hence his final dissatisfaction with the Hartleian view of ideas as mechanically associated. As Richards says[1] he had to extricate himself from this Lockean form of empiricism 'not because it was "false", but because for himself at some hours, it was too painfully true. It was the intellectual equivalent of his uncreative moods'. The Platonic philosophy of Ideas, for all the 'dear gorgeous nonsense' he knew went along with it, and the Kantian philosophy of the synthetic *a priori*, for all the stern limitations it set on speculative knowledge, at any rate both centred on the initiative of the thinking Subject. The question is how far, in understanding the

[1] *Coleridge on Imagination*, 60.

workings of the mind, we can claim also to be understanding what lies beyond it.

One answer is that we do not need to do so, since what we call external reality is in the end the mind's own creation or a communication to our mind from an absolute mind. Coleridge may have come near to this extreme idealism in his brief Berkeleian period, and under the first impact of the post-Kantian idealists, the time when Wordsworth wrote his testimony in *The Prelude*:

> *Thou, my Friend! art one*
> *More deeply read in thy own thoughts; to thee*
> *Science appears but what in truth she is,*
> *Not as our glory and our absolute boast*
> *But as a succedaneum, and a prop*
> *To our infirmity. No officious slave*
> *Art thou of that false secondary power*
> *By which we multiply distinctions, then*
> *Dream that our puny boundaries are things*
> *That we perceive, and not that we have made.*
> *To thee, unblinded by these formal arts,*
> *The unity of all hath been revealed.*
> *And thou wilt doubt, with one less aptly skilled*
> *Than many are to range the faculties*
> *In scale and order, class the cabinet*
> *Of their sensations, and in voluble phrase*
> *Run through the history and the birth of each*
> *As of a single independent thing.*

(II, 209–27)

This was probably written in 1799; and Coleridge's short-lived little son Berkeley was born in 1798. So it may well have been his most 'idealist' period. But at all stages, in whatever 'voluble phrase' he is exploring the workings of the mind and the relations between mind and nature—how the 'external' becomes 'internal' and the internal external—he is also interested in *scientific* understanding. I doubt whether he would have been happy to call science 'that false secondary power by which we multiply distinctions'; indeed, in spite of a romantic interest in geometry, Wordsworth was an enemy to science as Coleridge never was. Coleridge was always interested in exact observations; not only exact observations of things in nature, noted and described in ways in which Wordsworth and Dorothy could join, but also in the kind of observation which needed experiment and laboratory conditions. He was fascinated as a schoolboy by his brother Luke's anatomical studies; he was close friend of a host of medical men; and above all he continually followed his friend Sir Humphrey Davy's chemical work. The note-books are full of examples of this interest. True, he was on the look-out for unifying principles behind distinct and apparently opposed appear-ances, and this may sound more like metaphysics than science. But here he had inklings of a more sophisticated view of science than the simple inductivism of his empiricist contemporaries.

There is a passage in *The Friend* which suggests that scientific explanation should not stop at hypotheses, but show them as deducible from wider theories. Moreover, hypotheses can have a pictorial aspect, which will have to be translated into mathematical terms to connect with the wider theory.[1]

> As little can a true scientific method be grounded on a hypothesis, unless where the hypothesis is an exponential image or picture-language of an *idea* which is contained in it more or less clearly; or the symbol of an undiscovered law, like the characters of unknown quantities in algebra for the purpose of submitting the phenomena to a scientific calculus. In all other instance, it is itself a real or supposed phenomenon, and therefore a part of the problem which it is to solve. It may be among the foundation stones of the edifice but can never be the *ground*.   (*Friend*, I, 477)

Thus Coleridge is struggling with the nature of theories as well as lower level hypotheses and observations. Hence perhaps his continual insistence that Bacon was to be seen as the 'English Plato'; both Bacon and Plato were looking for general principles in natural pheno-mena. 'The Logic of Plato consisted therefore in a perpetual investiga-tion of similitudes in things different and in differences in things similar

---

[1] On the pictorial element in a scientific hypotheses, *cf.* Margaret Masterman, 'Theism as a Scientific Hypothesis' III, in *Theoria to Theory*, vol. I, no. 3. The intuitable analogies used in wave and particle views in physics would be examples.

conducted by an Induction of Examples most frequently in the form of questions. . . .' Bacon carried this on not just intuitively, but as it could be applied to physics,—a third philosophy might end 'in deducing the Practice of Bacon from the Metaphysics of Plato'.[1] No doubt it would be an anachronism to read Bacon (or even Coleridge) as having fully grasped the character of the hypothetico-deductive method in science. But Bacon saw there must be intellectual initiative 'as the motive and guide of every philosophical experiment—the *"prudens quaestio"*, the forethoughtful query)' (*Friend*, I, 489), and Coleridge saw the need both for theory and for contact with experimental procedures.

He was thus no enemy to science; rather, he should be seen as in the succession of those from Plato onwards who have tried seriously to connect metaphysics and science. His approach is an instance of the kind of thinking which the Greeks and the Platonizing Greek Fathers of the Church (whom he read so eagerly) called 'Theoria', a kind of thinking which starts from science and reaches out to religious aspiration, with philosophy moving between the two. 'Philosophy', he says, (*Philosophical Lectures*, 55) 'is the middle state between science or knowledge and sophia or wisdom.' And there is the hope that the scientific and religious interests will fructify each other, and point to a common vision.

There is no doubt about the strength of Coleridge's religious concern at all stages of his life. Even when he was temporarily impressed by Hartley's associationism, this was because Hartley seemed to supply both a scientific and a religious account of the mind. His mechanistic view culminated in seeing a natural evolution of consciousness in which we should be conditioned to find our pleasure in 'theopathy', a happy harmony with God and His Laws.[2]

This insistent religious concern has led to the charge that 'the heart in the head', took possession and determined his outlook. There is certainly something in this, but again, we must try to see how the involvement of the heart could also be a strength. It shows itself in his view of Faith as involving an energy of the Will ('the Will' being, as he

[1] Snyder, *Coleridge on Logic and Learning*, 65–66, quoted from MSA.
[2] Richard Haven, 'Coleridge, Hartley and the Mystics', JHI, XX, 4, is convincing on the importance for Coleridge of this side of Hartley's thought.

says, an expression for the 'I', the active subject). This brings into action the whole person:

> Faith subsists in the *synthesis* of the reason and the individual will. By virtue of the latter therefore it must be an energy, and in as much as it relates to the whole moral man, it must be exerted in each and all of his constituents or incidents, faculties and tendencies;—it must be a total, not a partial, a continuous, not a desultory or occasional energy. And by virtue of the former, that is, reason, faith must be a light, a form of knowing a beholding truth.
>
> ('*Essay on Faith*', *Literary Remains*, IV, 438)

He then quotes freely from St. John's Gospel, ending with 'which light is at the same time the life of men.'

So we come back to his central conviction of a creative power at the centre of the personality, holding the person together and setting the imagination free to form an original vision, instead of drifting along with the streamy nature of association. He also knew very well that this power often failed him, and saw the failure as a moral one, a weakness of will. He has been accused of being obsessively concerned with his sins; but behind the moral language there is also a profound introspective analysis into states of mind in which his productive energy worked and those in which it failed to work[1]. The states in which he thought it worked seem to have fallen into two kinds. One was where the 'Will' —'Reason'—was most fully energizing, as in the state which he called 'Faith'. The other was where the mind blends into the world beyond in a state of recollectedness on the fringes of consciousness, where past associations and present perceptions fuse to form a new image. In a state like this, mind and body seem most nearly at one, and this, no less than the state in which Reason is most fully aware, is a state in which there is a felt 'unity of subject and object'. I suspect that he understood this kind of state better than he understood the harmony of Will and Reason, and it may be he had in mind both of these states when he said 'Metaphysics makes all one's thoughts equally corrosive on the body, by inducing a habit of making momently and common thought the subject

---

[1] There is a fuller discussion of this in my 'Coleridge on the Growth of the Mind', *Bulletin of the John Rylands Library*, vol. 34, no. 2, reprinted in K. Coburn, *Twentieth Century Views*.

of uncommon interest and intellectual energy.' (*Notebooks*, I, 1313) The capacity to experience this feeling was one which in the *Dejection* Ode he called 'Joy'. There is an entry in *Notebooks* I, 921 (February/March 1801), where he quotes from Wordsworth,

> *and the deep power of Joy*
> *We see into the Life of Things—*

(the roman type is his italics). He continues,

> *i.e.* by deep feeling we make our *Ideas dim*—and this is what we mean by our Life—ourselves. I think of the Wall[1]—it is before me, a distinct Image—here. I necessarily think of the *Idea* and the thinking I as two distinct and opposite Things. Now (let me) think of *myself*—of the thinking Being—the Idea becomes dim whatever it be—so dim that I know not what it is—but the Feeling is deep and steady—and this I call *I*—identifying the Percipient and the Perceived.

We come back to what, if anything, a knowledge of the 'facts of mind' can tell us about reality beyond us. Here Coleridge's more considered view seems to have been not the idealist one which sees nature as a product of our minds, but one of nature as a dynamic system with which the powers we find in ourselves are 'connatural' (his word; *cf.* *Biog. Lit.*, II, 243). If these powers in nature and ourselves are also seen as *divine,* is this a form of Pantheism? Pantheism indeed always had its pull for Coleridge, as did also Spinoza. Coleridge always spoke of Spinoza with deep appreciation, and testified that, if philosophy could be an 'It is' and not also an 'I am', Spinoza would have come nearest to the truth. The counter-pull to Spinozistic pantheism was not only the desire to come nearer to Christian orthodoxy (though no

[1] Professor Orsini in *Coleridge and German Idealism,* Southern Illinois University Press, 1969, has noted that the example of thinking of a wall and then of oneself as thinking of it was used by Fichte in his lectures and in a writing of 1797. There is no evidence that Coleridge had read this by 1801, but he may have heard of it indirectly. (Professor Orsini's book is a useful investigation into the extent of Coleridge's reading of Kant and the post-Kantian Idealists. His interpretation is however limited by his insistence on treating Coleridge's philosophy in complete separation from his work as a poet.)

doubt this weighed) but above all it was the insistent demand that philosophy should do justice to the 'I am'—subjective personal exist-ence. The struggle again Pantheism was above all a struggle against a view of the world as an impersonal deterministic system—Spinoza's 'pole of ice', as he saw it. But neither could he be satisfied with the notion of the Deity as a Supreme Being purely external to the world. Of this, he says (*Notebooks*, I, 1391), 'Mahometans, Brahmins, Christians worship the fainter image of their reason in a fountain or muddy river, as a divinity separate from itself.' This is 'anthropomorphitism', and (I, 922) 'as we recede from anthropomorphitism we must go either to the Trinity or to Pantheism—The Fathers who were Unitarians were Anthropomorphites' (an attack here on an earlier allegiance). The doctrine of the Trinity, as pointing both to a creative Logos in man and nature and to its oneness with Divine Life beyond them, he sees as more adequate to the mystery of Godhead. Writing in 1803, he refers appar-ently with approval to John Scotus Erigena's view that the Doctrine of the Trinity has to draw on language accommodated to our minds for we

> must *define* consequently and *personify* in order to understand and must have some phantom of Understanding in order to keep alive in the heart the substantial Faith. They are *Fuel* to the sacred Fire—in the Empyrean it may burn without Fuel and they who do so are Seraphs.   (*Notebooks*, I, 1382.)

Professor McFarland in *Coleridge and the Pantheist Tradition* has written of this struggle with Pantheism as the clue to Coleridge's philo-sophy, and has said that the impossibility of reconciling a philosophy of 'I am' and a philosophy of 'It is' was the real reason why he could never complete his system, since 'I am' breaks up any system into which it is introduced. Put less aphoristically, this is to say that a system must consist of elements impartially and impersonally interrelated, and cannot therefore include in itself the creative freedom of the human person. So we get a cleavage between the objective philosophies which talk about nature, and the subjective ones such as Existentialism which talk about personal values and personal decisions.

Coleridge would not, I think, have accepted this dilemma, and in any case 'systems' can be more and less rigorous. He struggled to include both nature and the creative self within the same view of reality, and did this by postulating a kinship between the dynamic powers in human nature and powers not yet conscious, but operative in all natural systems. Perhaps he owed something here to the view of 'plastic nature' in the Cambridge Platonists, and especially in Cudworth. But it is unlikely to have been a mere borrowing. Plato, Spinoza, Boehme, Schelling and many others had all fed this conviction of the central importance of spiritual power in Nature akin to the shaping spirit of Imagination. He sums it up in an entry in his notebooks (III, 4397), when he says the artist distinguishes himself from Nature in order to understand her.

> He absents himself from her only in his own Spirit which has the same ground with Nature, to learn her unspoken language, in its main radicals, before he approaches to her endless compositions of those radicals—. Not to acquire cold notions, lifeless technical Rules, but living and life-producing Ideas, which contain their own evidence and in the evidence the certainty that they are essentially one with the germinal causes in Nature, his Consciousness being the focus and mirror of both—for this does he for a time abandon the external *real*, in order to return to it with a full sympathy with its internal & actual—. Of all, we see, hear, or touch, the substance is and must be in ourselves—and therefore there is no alternative *in reason* between the dreary (and thank heaven! almost impossible) belief that every thing around us is but a phantom, or that the Life which is in us is in them likewise—and that to know is to *resemble*.

To *resemble*—not to copy. Coleridge was well aware of the difficulties in theories of 'representative ideas', producing mental replicas of external things. He was well aware that the creations of his imagination were not to be interpreted with any simple realism. They were ways in which sympathy with the outer reality re-created its character in symbolic form, making 'the external internal and the internal external'. For this, there must be active creative power, the shaping spirit. There must also be exact observation, images clearly realized, and there must be the almost sub-conscious free play of images. Coleridge has a charming analogy to illustrate the needed alternation between extreme concentration and relaxed receptivity.

Most of my readers will have observed a small water-insect on the surface of rivulets, which throws a cinque-spotted shadow fringed with prismatic colours on the sunny bottom of the brook; and will have noticed how the little animal *wins* its way up against the stream by alternative pulses of active and passive motion.　　　　　　　　　　　　　　　(*Biog. Lit.*, I, 85)

Out of all this the artist's 'esemplastic power' creates new unities, and Coleridge's faith is that in so doing he is in harmony with a wider power in Nature. Contemplating Nature 'I seem to myself to behold in the quiet objects, on which I am gazing, more than an arbitrary illustration, more than a mere *simile,* the work of my own fancy, I feel an awe, as if there were before my eyes the same power as that of the reason— the same power in a lower dignity, and therefore a symbol established in the truth of things, I feel it alike, whether I contemplate a single tree or flower, or meditate on vegetation throughout the world, as one of the great organs of the life of nature.' And he speaks of how a living thing 'with the same pulse effectuates its own secret growth . . . the plastic motion of the parts' (*Statesman's Manual*, Appendix B).

We come back to his continual struggle to say how an idea could be a living power, and not an abstract concept. The living 'Idea of Reason' in which the Subjective and Objective coalesce is seen as a power in the mind continuous with the process of growth in nature; this is his link between the 'I am' and the 'It is'. This coalescence could happen in the dream-like state representing the state of receptivity in the alternation of passive and active which he saw as necessary for the shaping spirit of Imagination. There was also the active state where the Will is in control, the Will which can also be called Reason, not meaning abstract thought, but the integrating creative power at the centre of the person as it comes into consciousness. The conditions for the operation of this power, Will-Reason-Imagination, Coleridge saw as moral as much as aesthetic. His moral faith was in the unity of our will with the divine power. His imaginative faith was in the continuity of our own creative powers with the unconscious processes of growth in nature. His metaphysics was an attempt to hold these two faiths together, not so much by clear abstract argument as by claims to insight in experiences where the inner and outer worlds met in symbolizing vision.

8: Coleridge and Religion

BASIL WILLEY

'A MAN'S religion,' said Carlyle, 'is the chief fact with regard to him'. This statement may seem absurd today, when many have no religion at all; but it was abundantly true of Coleridge, and in the sense intended by Carlyle. The quest for truth, and the vindication of the Christian faith as the only true philosophy, formed the master-current of his life, to which all his other myriad interests were but tributary rills. Thus any study of Coleridge in only one of his many guises—as literary critic, as poet, as political thinker, as metaphysician—is bound to be, in itself, incomplete. Coleridge was one to whom 'the unity of all hath been revealed', and no subject, for him, existed in isolation from the central theme—the 'ultimate concern'—or from all the others.

Coleridge set himself a stupendous life's task, no less than the overthrow of the most firmly-entrenched preconceptions of his time: the Locke tradition in philosophy, the associationism of Hartley, the Utilitarianism of Paley and Bentham, the necessitarianism of Priestly and Godwin, the Jacobinism of France, the pantheism of Spinoza and his followers, the deism and Socinianism of the eighteenth century. The task was all the heavier for him because in his youth he had himself undergone these influences, and the struggle to emancipate himself from them meant an enormous effort of self-knowledge and self-conquest. We all know that the results of it remained fragmentary and incomplete; but remembering how he was thwarted by ill-health, personal unhappiness, and self-reproach for his weakness of will, the wonder is that he achieved so much. He left us, far in advance of the time, all the essential 'blue-prints' for Christian apologetic in the nineteenth century and after; and he would not have been the great literary critic he is acknowledged to be if his theorizing—notably about the Imagination—had not been an inseparable part of his general philosophical campaign.

The pattern in the Coleridgean carpet is unbelievably complex, but I mean in this essay to try and follow the thread that leads from the Unitarianism of his Cambridge and Somerset days to the Christian orthodoxy of his mature years. First, then, how and why did he become a Unitarian? What was it like to be a Unitarian in the 1790s? And why did he finally come to reject Unitarianism?

In 1797, when he was in his twenty-fifth year, Coleridge began a series of autobiographical letters to Thomas Poole, and it is from these that we learn most of what is know about his childhood—that time when, as is now recognized, the shape of a man's mind and character is being moulded. His father, the Rev. John Coleridge, Vicar of Ottery St Mary in Devon, was the prime mover and influence. Every Coleridgean knows how he taught the boy about the starry heavens above, and how from earliest walks and talks with him

> my mind had been habituated *to the Vast*—and I never regarded *my senses* in any way as the criteria of my belief. I regulated all my creeds by my conceptions not by my sight—even at that age.
> (CL, I, 354)

Others, more 'rationally' educated, he adds, seem to 'contemplate nothing but parts . . . and the Universe to them is but a mass of *little things*'; whereas he had early acquired a love of 'the Great', and 'the Whole'. Here already are the deep-laid foundations of his philosophy and his religion: of his philosophy, in this sense of the Great and the Whole; and of his Christianity in the association of both with the faith and character of his father, with 'that venerable countenance and name which form my earliest recollections and *make them religious*'.[1]

At Christ's Hospital he became a 'playless day-dreamer, a *helluo librorum*'. Always apt, then as later, to take his intellectual colouring and enthusiasms from his current reading or his most admired associates, he was 'converted' to free thought at the age of fifteen by reading

[1] *Letters*, ed. E. H. Coleridge, II, CCXL, 19 May 1825.

Voltaire's *Dictionnaire Philosophique*. But, said Coleridge on the heights of Highgate years afterwards, 'my infidel vanity never touched my heart. With my heart I never did abandon the name of Christ.'[1] And just as, later, his head was with Spinoza while his heart was with Paul and John, so now, while he was excited by Voltaire, he was also feeding upon the Neoplatonists, and 'conjuring' over Boehme's *Aurora*[2] (in William Law's translation).

When Coleridge went up to Cambridge, in October 1791, it was with the general notion of becoming a parson—which was what his father, and his school, had always intended. But Jesus College was then in a ferment of 'left-wing' ideas and influences and Coleridge's impulse was always to associate himself ardently with whatever opinions seemed to him most stirring and most true. Later in life, when men thought him reactionary, he knew (and said) that this was only because he had got far ahead of them, and could see much farther; by then, for instance, he had been right through Unitarianism, seen through it, and 'come round to the other side'.[3] But for the time being Unitarianism, as represented in Cambridge by men like Gilbert Wakefield and William Frend, was as much one of the new, true 'causes' to which every advanced undergraduate should be 'committed', as any of those for which students 'demonstrate' today. To be a Unitarian at that time meant also, almost as a matter of course, to be, if not an avowed republican in politics, at least a warm sympathizer with the French Revolution, and a foe to 'aristocracy' and the Established Church. Radicalism in politics and rationalism in religion went hand in hand.

There is no need (and no space) to repeat here the story of the birth and growth of Unitarianism from Faustus Socinus (1539–1604)—or from Jesus himself, if we were to credit some Unitarian historians—to Joseph Priestley, whom Coleridge came to regard as the founder of modern Unitarianism. It was part of the great leftward drift in theology which began (as we may roughly say) in the sixteenth century, and culminated in the era of the French Revolution. During those centuries

---

[1] Gillman, *Life of S. T. Coleridge*, 1838, 23.
[2] See CL, IV, 751. And *cf.* Lamb's 'Christ's Hospital Five-and-Thirty years Ago'.
[3] *Table Talk*, 23 June 1834 (Oxford edn., 1917, 308).

the de-mythologizing of Christianity was proceeding steadily wherever thought was free; and mystery, miracle and finally the whole super- natural basis of the faith were being eliminated. Naturally, in England, it was among the Dissenters and radicals that this process went furthest; many of the Presbyterian and Independent congregations evolved during the eighteenth century into Unitarianism. But in that age, when the heavens seemed to declare the glory of God more persuasively than the Scriptures, a deistic turn of thought was very common even within the Established church. In such a climate the more mysterious of the orthodox tenets, such as the Incarnation, the Atone- ment and above all the Trinity, began to perish of cold. Most Anglican clergymen, indeed, managed to retain their Orders and benefices even if their views had veered, since ordination, towards Arianism, Socinian- ism or even pure deism. But there were some striking examples, of whom Theophilus Lindsey and William Frend are the best known, of resignation from Church livings by clergymen who had ceased to believe in the Trinity. If this seems to any present-day reader a strangely technical reason for courting martyrdom, one must remember that the point at issue was vital enough: it was whether or no Jesus of Nazareth was Almighty God in human form. The disinclination to credit any supernatural breaks in the chain of physical and historical causation had become so strong, in the eighteenth century, that many could only preserve their 'Christianity' by removing from it all that had hitherto distinguished it from 'natural' religion, and particularly by reducing Jesus to the level of 'a good man'—perhaps the best of men, but a human being and no more. Men like Frend took their beliefs so seriously that they felt obliged to break with a Church which accorded divine honours, and offered prayer, to one (though the noblest) of God's creatures.

It is not surprising that Coleridge as an undergraduate should have been caught up in this current of opinion. With a mind so fluid that it could hold Boehme and Voltaire in suspension with Synesius, and flow afterwards so rapidly into a succession of philosophic moulds— Priestley, Hartley, Godwin, Berkeley, Spinoza, Kant, Schelling—he naturally adopted at Jesus College the viewpoint of those he most admired, and whose convictions seemed to have the sharpest cutting-

edge. All Coleridge's biographers, beginning with Gillman, attribute to
William Frend the greatest influence over him at this time. But Unitarianism did not affect him through this contact alone, nor merely
through his living in the College which was then 'the hotbed of Cambridge radicalism'—the College in which R. Tyrwhitt had nourished a
group of 'young firebrands' including Wakefield, Frend and T.
Edwards.[1] It affected him as a prevailing wind of doctrine in a revolutionary era, and in this wider sense it can be seen penetrating his
thoughts until he was twenty-five (his own estimate, according to Gillman). In a negative sense it was there to the very end, since in later life
he never ceased to critize the creed of his youth and to explain, in detail
and in depth, why it no longer satisfied him.

When Coleridge was drafting *Religious Musings* in 1794, Hartley
and Priestley were his bright particular heroes. What attracted him
about both was the union in them of scientific enlightenment with a
confident, optimistic theism. In the France of the *philosophes* enlightenment was paired with infidelity: not so in England! Coleridge was
born with a believing temper and a questing intellect; and the tension
between these two elements within him (the heart and the head, as he
so often called them) determined the whole pattern of his life and
thought. He longed to find a clue to the mighty maze of things, and
tried system after system before his own self-knowledge taught him
that deep thinking without deep feeling, repentance, and faith, led only
to pantheism and spiritual pride. In his youth, as with most young men
of brilliant gifts, the intellect predominated, and he eagerly absorbed
any philosophy which seemed to explain the universe—particularly any
which, like Hartley's and Priestley's, confirmed his own innate sense of
an indwelling and omnipresent divine energy. In the thought of these
two writers, the blend of scientific precision with warmth of religious
conviction stirred him to hero-worship, and it was not until bitter
experience had revealed his own insufficiency that their essentially
limited and prosaic quality became manifest to him. Hartley taught
that life itself, through the beneficent workings of the Law of Association, automatically built up 'the being that we are', and led us on by
stages from the pleasures of sense to the love of God. How delightful,

[1] See B. R. Schneider, *Wordsworth's Cambridge Education*, 1957, 119.

and how reassuring!—especially to one who shrank from self-discipline and the demands of the active life. Priestley taught that 'Nature's vast ever-acting Energy'[1] was the energy of God himself, everywhere and always causing, impelling and sustaining. How glorious!—especially to one who longed to know all things and know that God was in them. Coleridge's characteristic phrase 'and what if—?' is a sign, when it occurs, that one such great thought has quickened his mind, and set the whole universe a-tremble with life and meaning:

> And what if all of animated nature
> Be but organic Harps diversely fram'd,
> That tremble into thought, as o'er them sweeps
> Plastic and vast, one intellectual breeze,
> At once the Soul of each, and God of all?[2]

This is pure Priestley, though that good man could not have expressed the thought so eloquently. But how much of Coleridge's after-development is foreshadowed in the lines that follow, where he assigns to Sara the role of the affable archangel in *Paradise Lost* checking Adam's inquisitiveness! Here Sara, in language full of Miltonic echoes, reproves Coleridge for his speculative flight:

> But thy more serious eye a mild reproof
> Darts, O beloved Woman! nor such thoughts
> Dim and unhallowed dost thou not reject,
> And biddest me walk humbly with my God.
> Meek daughter of the family of Christ!
> Well hast thou said and holily disprais'd
> These shapings of the unregenerate mind;
> Bubbles that glitter as they rise and break
> On vain Philosophy's aye-babbling spring.

It is typical that Coleridge, with his submissive temper and his tendency to look up to everybody else, should at this early stage transform Sara's very imperviousness to ideas into a sign of spiritual superiority. And, looking into the future, we may find tragic irony in his return to 'abstruse research' as a way of escape from domestic infelicity. The

---

[1] *The Destiny of Nations*, 461.
[2] *The Eolian Harp*, 44–48 (1795 and later).

Icarus-flight, the warmth and glow of the intellectual Sun!—then the melting wings, the return to earth; later, other flights horizontal or downward rather than heavenward, and painfully rather than rapturously sustained; finally, the long attempt to combine head and heart in a Christian philosophy adequate to the modern world—this is the outline of Coleridge's story, so early glimpsed in *The Eolian Harp*.

In *Religious Musings* he is very far from regarding the thoughts of Hartley and Priestley as 'dim and unhallowed'. Here is Hartley (on the soul):

> *From Hope and firmer Faith to perfect Love*
> *Attracted and absorbed: and centered there*
> *God only to behold, and know, and feel,*
> *Till by exclusive consciousness of God*
> *All self-annihilated it shall make*
> *God its Identity: God all in all!*
> *We and our Father one!*[1]

And Coleridge adds the footnote 'See this *demonstrated* by Hartley . . .'. Next, after salutes to Milton and Newton (both Arians, by the way) comes Priestley.

> *Pressing on his [Hartley's] steps*
> *Lo!* PRIESTLEY *there, Patriot, and Saint, and Sage.*

Priestley had indeed pressed on Hartley's steps; he had gone beyond him, abolishing the distinction between matter and spirit, and teaching a full necessitarianism. What appealed to Coleridge about Priestley's 'materialism' was that it made the best of both worlds; it offered all the attractions of materialism without the stigma. 'Matter' turned out to be a kind of energy (God's energy), and so, as Priestly said, it was as immaterial 'as any person could wish for', and 'the reproach of matter is wiped off'.

Such, then, were some of the influences which were shaping Coleridge's mind during his College years and immediately after—though one must never forget his Christian childhood and his schoolboy dippings into Neo-platonism and Boehme. During his four months' escapade in the 15th King's Light Dragoons, he wrote a series of letters

[1] *Religious Musings*, 39ff.

to his brother George, which reveal a good deal of his religious feeling at this time. We must, of course, in reading them, allow for the fact that George Coleridge was a parson, and for Coleridge's own chameleon-habit, which lasted for life, of adjusting his mental colour to that of his correspondents. In a mood of exaggerated self-abasement and repentance, he writes:

> I had too much Vanity to be altogether a Christian—too much tenderness of Nature to be utterly an Infidel. Fond of the dazzle of Wit, fond of subtlety of Argument, I could not read without some degree of pleasure the levities of Voltaire, or the reasonings of Helvetius—but tremblingly alive to the feelings of humanity, and susceptible of the charms of Truth, my Heart forced me to admire the beauty of Holiness in the Gospel, forced me to *love* the Jesus, whom my Reason (or perhaps my *reasonings*) would not permit me to *worship*. My faith therefore was made up of the Evangelists and the Deistic Philosophy—a kind of *religious Twilight*.   (C L, I, 78)

In writing to Southey, during the effervescence of the Pantisocracy scheme, his tone is very different; it is full of 'stern republican' sentiment and passion for social justice. He urges Southey 'for God's sake' not to enter the Church, avows fraternal love for 'Shad' (Southey's servant, who was to accompany the 'aspheterists' to the Susquehannah), and fears that the women in the party may corrupt the children. '*That* Mrs Fricker—we shall have her teaching the infants *Christianity*,—I mean—that mongrel whelp that goes under it's name . . .' (C L, I, 123)

At this time, and indeed for years to come, Coleridge was a quick-change artist, delighting to don one intellectual suit after another, and to speak and think in the appropriate dialect. To set ideas dancing and systems revolving, and to watch the outcome, was for him a self-justifying activity ('and what if—?'). Pantisocracy was itself a big 'what if—?' but, alas, it left him with an incompatible wife. Yet even at the height of his political phase, when he can avow himself 'a compleat Necessitarian' and a believer in the 'corporeality of *thought*—namely, that it is motion', and use all the current republican jargon about 'loath'd Aristocracy', he still figures as the champion of 'the Holy One of Nazareth'. In his political lectures at Bristol in 1795 (during which he was attacked by 'demonstrators' with placards and brickbats very much in the style of today, though for opposite reasons) he urges that the right approach to 'the poor' and the oppressed is to plead *for* them, not *to* them: 'Go preach the GOSPEL to the poor!', and, 'uniting the zeal of the methodist with the views of the philosopher', live and work personally among them. He invokes the doctrine of Necessity in its benigner aspect: vice is the inevitable result of 'circumstances', so don't blame the sinner, but alter the circumstances. Godwin had recently taught the same thing, but Coleridge, ever quick to see the further implications of any doctrine, is already on his guard against 'that proud philosophy which affects to inculcate philanthropy while it denounces every home-born feeling by which it is produced and nurtured'. Next year (1796) he will be condemning Godwinism still more roundly, especially for its atheism. He denounces the 'Establishment', political and religious, imputing to it all the miseries of bloodshed abroad and the police-state at home, but declares that the real enemy is 'not the religion of peace . . . of the meek and lowly Jesus, . . . but the religion of mitres and mysteries'.[1]

Gillman tells us that Coleridge considered himself to have been 'a Unitarian till twenty-five' (*i.e.* 1797). But the truth is that his mind was like quicksilver, and did not set, for the convenience of biographers, into rigid moulds of reason. Thus, as we know, he was still preaching Unitarian sermons as late as 1798, and early that year was on the point of entering the Unitarian ministry. But he had never ceased to draw nutriment from the deeper sources of Platonism and Christianity, and could never have shrunk into any sort of sectarian conformity. In his letters and notebooks one can watch his myriad-mindedness at work, bursting one barrier after another on the road to self-knowledge (or, as has been said, in the process of 'growledge'). In the *Biographia Literaria* (I, 114) he says of the time of *The Watchman* (1795–6) that he was 'at that time *and long after* [my italics], though a Trinitarian (*i.e.* ad normam Platonis) in philosophy, yet a zealous Unitarian in religion; more accurately I was a *psilanthropist*, one of those who believe Our Lord to have been a real son of Joseph, and who lay the main stress on the resurrection rather than on the crucifixion'. Gillman throws some

[1] See EOT I; *Conciones ad Populum.*

light on the 'ad normam Platonis' when he explains that Coleridge at this time 'could admit the Logos', while retaining doubts about the accepted doctrines of Incarnation and Atonement. He could accept that God from all eternity had ordained the existence of an emanation from Himself which, in the fullness of time, should be united with a human body; but he could not abide the idea of vicarious payment or expiation. He later came to believe, says Gillman, that the difference in his *metaphysical* notions from those of most Unitarians was what mainly led to his 'final reconversion to the whole truth in Christ'.[1]

No doubt this is so, but as we shall see, his 're-conversion' was far from being 'metaphysical' only.

On his 'Watchman' tour (early 1796) he met Dr Erasmus Darwin at Derby, and found him the most original and best-informed man in Europe; 'the everything', in fact, 'except the Christian'. He was amazed that so acute a mind should accept the atheistical platitudes that had startled him (S.T.C.) at fifteen, but at twenty had become ridiculous. Darwin would have accepted no scientific theory without the severest examination, yet 'all at once he makes up his mind on such important subjects as whether we be the outcasts of a blind idiot called Nature, or the children of an all-wise and infinitely good God'. (CL, I, 177)

How quickly Coleridge's mind was growing and taking shape appears from his changed attitude to Priestley and Godwin during the spring of 1796. In March he is asking the Rev. J. Edwards:

> How is it that Dr Priestley is not an atheist?—He asserts in three different places, that God not only *does*, but *is*, every thing.—But if God *be* every Thing, every Thing is God—: which is all, the Atheists assert. . . .   (CL, I, 192.)

Not quite 'all' perhaps; but Coleridge has already perceived how pantheism, so alluring to emancipated minds like his, and so congenial to the romantic imagination, merges paradoxically into atheism. If God 'is every thing', without remainder, there is nothing specially divine anywhere. All the atheist wants is to drop the 'if' clause and keep the conclusion.

[1] Gillman, *Life of S. T. Coleridge* (1838), 91ff., and 225.

The religious tone deepens in the autumn of 1796, and along with this comes a revulsion from revolutionary politics—indeed, from politics altogether. The pantisocratic dream has faded, to be replaced by a passionate desire for rural retirement and simplicity. Accordingly, 'I have snapped my squeaking baby-trumpet of sedition, and have hung up its fragments in the chamber of Penitences.'[1] In the autumn of this year (1796) it was to Thelwall, whose opposing views on almost everything put Coleridge on his mettle, that the best letters were written. Thelwall had been sneering at Christianity as a 'mean' religion, teaching 'Morals for the Magdalen and Botany Bay'. Coleridge replies by reducing Christian belief to two tenets: that there is a Father in Heaven, and that there is a future state of rewards and punishments. 'This is the Christian *Religion*' he declares, 'and all of the Christian *Religion*.' If this statement (especially its second half) causes any eyebrow to be raised, one must remember that Coleridge is writing to an embittered left-wing atheist and is therefore trying to be 'honest to God'. He scouts the imputation of meanness by illustrating the sublimity of the Biblical imagery, and by showing the all-inclusiveness and loftiness of Christian ethics.

From June 1797 onwards Coleridge's life and work were quickened and enriched by the friendship and companionship of the Wordsworths, William and Dorothy. During the spring of 1798 Wordsworth's close proximity, and the constant intercourse between Alfoxden and Nether Stowey, greatly influenced the colouring of Coleridge's mind and the tone of his feeling. Wordsworthian phrases are recurrent in his letters, and the Wordsworthian cast of mind and style of diction begin to predominate in his verse. The letter of 10 March 1798 (No. 238) to his brother George marks a crucial transition in Coleridge's thought—a transition, moreover, which accords with the Wanderer's advice for Correcting Despondency. First, he utterly abjures 'French metaphysics, French Politics, French Ethics and French Theology'. Governments have no 'talismanic influence'; we simply get the governments that our frailty, and our Original Sin, produce and deserve; all rulers are as bad as they dare to be. So,

[1] CL, I, 240. The 'baby-trumpet' reappears, p. 397 (March 1798).

> I have for some time past withdrawn myself almost totally from
> the consideration of *immediate* causes . . . to muse on funda-
> mental and general causes—the *causae causarum.*

He then paraphrases and finally quotes eighteen blank-verse lines from
the recluse-doctrine which the 'giant Wordsworth' had communicated
by reading to him from the MS:

> I devote myself to such works as encroach not on the anti-social
> passions—in poetry, to elevate the imagination and set the
> affections in right tune by the beauty of the inanimate impreg-
> nated, as with a living soul, by the presence of Life—in prose, to
> the seeking with patience . . . what our faculties are and what
> we are capable of becoming.—I love fields and woods and
> mountains with an almost visionary fondness—and because I have
> found benevolence and quietness growing within me as that
> fondness has increased, therefore I should wish to be the means
> of implanting it in others—and to destroy the bad passions, not by
> combating them, but by keeping them in inaction.

Then follow the lines: 'Nor useless do I deem' down to 'He seeks for
Good and finds the Good he seeks' (now to be found—*variatim*—in *The
Excursion* Book IV, 1207 ff.).

Now, too, he begins to reproach his own religion with being too
much an '*intellectual* passion', and therefore of little use 'in the hour of
temptation and calamity'. Writing to his Unitarian friend Estlin, he
regrets Wordsworth's lack of Christian faith (he had earlier called him
a 'semi-atheist'), and admits that he has to keep silent with him on this
theme—though Wordsworth, he declares, is a 'tried good man' as well
as a great one.

I shall pass over the visit to Germany (1798–9), though it was of
great importance in teaching him the language. The effective con-
frontation with Kant, Schelling, Fichte and others which so powerfully
influenced him later (and nineteenth-century English thought through
him) did not take place in Germany, but at Keswick in 1801 when he
opened his packing-cases of books and attacked their contents. But the
intellectual kinship he felt with Lessing, while in Germany, is very
significant, for in Lessing many of the lineaments of the mature Coleridge are already apparent. Like Coleridge, Lessing was in revolt against

the aridity of eighteenth-century thought, and pushing on towards a nineteenth-century standpoint—using *literary* perceptions and experience to fertilize his judgements of philosophical and religious systems. In particular, he laid down many of the positions about biblical interpretation which Coleridge later adopted in *Confessions of an Inquiring Spirit*.[1] He 'invented' the Coleridgean word 'bibliolatry';[2] he urged that Christianity existed before the New Testament; that the Bible 'contains' what belongs to religion but much else besides, and that no infallibility is to be ascribed to the 'much else'; that Christianity is not true *because* the evangelists and apostles taught it, but that they taught it *because* it was true; and that the authority of scripture rests, not upon any miraculous 'inspiration', but upon its own intrinsic truth—that in it which (as Coleridge afterwards said) 'finds us'. Coleridge certainly absorbed these views, and made them his own; and they entered so closely into his developing thought that much later, when he came to write the *Confessions*, he incorporated some material from his Lessing transcripts. The parallels are so close (sometimes almost verbal) that the pious J. H. Green, at the instigation of Coleridge's daughter Sara, wrote an Introduction in which these are set forth, and Coleridge's originality vindicated.[3]

After the return from Germany, Spinoza, the Great Alternative in all Coleridge's pre-Kantian and pre-Christian thought, still has him in thrall. On 30 September 1799, he tells Southey that in spite of domestic chaos he, 'sunk in Spinoza', remains 'as undisturbed as a Toad in a Rock'. Even when he had rejected all pantheisms as fatal to true religion and destructive of moral responsibility and freewill, Coleridge never ceased to revere Spinoza, both for his personal saintliness and for the intellectual grandeur of his system. And not only he, but the main body of romantic philosophers found inspiration in this once-despised and much-maligned thinker—formerly labelled 'atheist', but now 'the God-

[1] First published posthumously, in 1840, ed. H. N. Coleridge.
[2] Though, as the Rev. H. St J. Hart points out, Coleridge might have met the word in John Byrom (d. 1763), who uses it twice. See Hart's Introd. to his edn. of *Confessions*, 1956, 7.
[3] 1849, 2nd edn. See also James Martineau, *Essays, Reviews, and Addresses*, 1890, I, 'Lessing's Theology and Times'.

intoxicated man'. No wonder—at a time when not only Coleridge, but all speculative Europe, was smitten with a longing for the Great, the Whole and the Indivisible, hoping to find the One in the Many and the All, and feeling the presence of One Life, within us and without—no wonder then that Spinoza's majestic vision of One Substance, of which matter and mind are both modifications, proved irresistible. It was Lessing who said 'There is no other philosophy than the philosophy of Spinoza.' None, perhaps, if his premisses be granted. But Coleridge came to perceive that the Spinozistic alternative would not do for him; he must cling to Plato, Kant and Christianity, and his reasons for finally rejecting Spinoza were akin to his reasons for rejecting Unitarianism. Both substituted a cold impersonal abstraction—a 'ground of the Universe'—for the living God of Christianity.

> Socianism Moonlight—Methodism etc. A Stove! O for some Sun that shall unite Light and Warmth.

So Coleridge wrote twice in his *Notebooks* (1799 and 1802),[1] and who better fitted than he to unite them? To attempt it was his life's task: it was to have been the main theme of that *opus maximum* of which we begin to hear in 1799, and hear more constantly as the years go by.

The spring of 1801 was the most vital turning-point in Coleridge's thought. It was then that Kant took hold of him 'as with a giant's hands' and it was then that after intense self-corrosive thought (partly undertaken to escape from pain, domestic discord and self-reproach for his opium addiction) he finally extricated himself from the Locke tradition (the 'philosophy of death' as he called it later) and overthrew 'the doctrine of Association, as taught by Hartley, and with it all the irreligious metaphysics of modern Infidels—especially the doctrine of Necessity'.[2]

'My opinion is this', he says a week later,

> that deep thinking is attainable only by a man of deep Feeling, and that all Truth is a species of Revelation . . . I believe the Souls of 500 Sir Isaac Newtons would go to the making up of a Shakspere or a Milton . . . Newton was a mere materialist

[1] *Notebooks*, I, 467 and 1233.
[2] CLP II, 706 (To oole, 16 March 1801).

—*Mind* in his system is always passive—a lazy looker-on on an external world. If the mind be not *passive* [and Kant had shown him in what sense it was *active*], if it be indeed made in God's Image, and that too in the sublimest sense—the Image of the *Creator*—there is ground for suspicion, that any system built on the passiveness of the mind must be false.   (CL, II, 709.)

Kant would never have taken such possession, if Coleridge's own mind had not already long been gathering momentum for a total break with a (to him) sterile tradition, including his own past self and youthful enthusiasms. Let us briefly see which Kantian notions meant most to him.

First: the distinction between 'Reason' and 'Understanding'. Coleridge quickly saw the value of this for his defence of religious truth, and used the distinction freely in *The Friend, The Statesman's Manual* and *Aids to Reflection.* He gives meanings of his own to 'Reason' and 'Understanding' which are not those of everyday speech; I have elsewhere tried to explain them thus:

> Reason is the "organ of the super-sensuous"; Understanding the faculty by which we generalize and arrange the phenomena of perception . . . Reason seeks ultimate ends; Understanding studies means. Reason is the "source and substance of truths above sense"; Understanding the faculty which judges "according to sense"; Reason is the eye of the spirit, the faculty whereby spiritual reality is spiritually discerned; Understanding is the mind of the flesh.[1]

Religion and Ethics belong to the sphere of Reason, while Understanding works legitimately on the practical level, in science and all the affairs of mundane existence. Disaster occurs when either invades the other's province. In setting up Reason (*and* Imagination, its aesthetic counterpart) above the mind of the flesh,

> Coleridge was seeking to protect the region of spiritual experience against all attacks from the mere Understanding, that is, against the *Zeitgeist.*

If we allow the head disjoined from the heart, the 'mere reflective

[1] *Nineteenth Century Studies,* 29.

faculty', the 'unenlivened generalizing understanding' to invade the sphere of Reason, as happened pre-eminently in the eighteenth century, we get

> all the disastrous results seen in the previous century: material- ism, determinism, atheism, utilitarianism, the "godless revolu- tion", "moral science exploded as mystic jargon", "the mysteries of religion cut and squared for the comprehension of the under- standing", "imagination excluded from poesy".[1]

Secondly: 'Reality', the '*Ding an sich*', the noumenal world, is transcend- ent, and thus for ever inaccessible to the Understanding. This doctrine was in itself a safeguard against any pantheism which might tend (how- ever unintentionally) to identify or confuse 'God' with 'the World'. But, thirdly, this transcendent world *is* accessible to Reason through our moral experience, through the fact of *Conscience*. Coleridge leans his whole weight upon this doctrine, and builds religious faith firmly upon a moral foundation. According to Kant, Conscience, the category 'ought', obliges us with absolute authority to act only by the law we have ourselves evolved, the law of practical reason: that we must conduct ourselves always by maxims which are *universally* valid. Now this un- questioned authority of conscience, this 'categorical imperative'— what are the postulates necessary to validate it? They are God, Free- dom, Immortality: God the source and sanction of the moral law; Freedom, because without it there can be no moral choice or respon- sibility; Immortality to right the wrongs and the imbalances of this imperfect world. These ideas are not rationally demonstrable, but they are 'regulative' ideas, ideas which must be postulated, taken as real, to make sense of our moral experience. Conscience therefore, and not reasoning, bids us accept as real those ideas without which it would itself have no meaning and no authority. This is how Coleridge puts it:

> Conscience unconditionally *commands* us to attribute *Reality* and actual *Existence* to those Ideas, and those only, without which the conscience itself would be baseless and contradictory.
>
> (*Friend*, I, 112)

---

[1] The inset quotations are selected from *Nineteenth Century Studies*, 29–33. Most of the Coleridgean phrases are from *The Friend*.

The truths of religion, then, differ from those which the Understanding accepts, such as those of mathematics, in that the latter *must* be believed, while the former *may* be denied, but *will* be denied by no *good* man. In the *Biographia Literaria* he tells us that 'there had dawned upon me, even before I had met with the Critique of the Pure Reason, a certain guiding light':

> If the mere intellect could make no certain discovery of a holy and intelligent first cause, it might yet supply a demonstration, that no legitimate argument could be drawn from the intellect *against* its truth . . . I became convinced that religion, as both the cornerstone and the key-stone of morality, must have a *moral* origin; so far at least, that the evidence of its doctrine could not, like the truths of abstract science, be wholly independent of the will. It were therefore to be expected, that its *fundamental* truth would be such as MIGHT be denied; though only by the fool, and even by the fool from the madness of the heart alone! (*Biog. Lit.*, I, 134-5)

One of Coleridge's finest insights is to see that belief in God, if it *were* rationally demonstrable, would have no religious value. The existence of God, he says,

> could not be intellectually more evident without becoming morally less effective; without counteracting its own end by sacrificing the *life* of faith to the cold mechanism of a worthless because compulsory assent. (*Biog. Lit.*, I, 135-6)

The imagery of Life versus Death predominates in Coleridge's later thinking: Imagination is alive in its struggle to idealize and to unify, while Fancy deals only with objects which are fixed and dead; the Will asserts its life against the 'philosophy of death' which would bind it in chains of determinism; so here, Faith is a living, existential act, a deliberate decision, and not a dead, mechanical acceptance. He defines Faith as 'the personal realization of the reason by its union with the will'; 'it must be an energy . . .—a continuous, not a desultory or occasional—energy.'[1] God is the Great 'I am', the God of the living, not of the dead; and man claims kinship with the living God by echoing, however faintly, the same 'I am' in defiance of the philosophies of

[1] *Friend*, I, 432, and *Aids to Reflection*, 349 (Bohn edn.).

death. So too, in the culminating passage of *Aids to Reflection*, he tells
the beginner in the faith that 'Christianity is not a Theory, or a Speculation, but a *Life*; not a Philosophy of Life, but a Life and a living
Process'. Its proof lies in the trial: 'TRY IT!' (*Aids to Reflection*, 134)

But there was something else, which Coleridge did not find in Kant:
the 'fact' of Original Sin. This he found in his own experience, his ever-
present sense of weakness, failure and defeat; his need of redeeming
grace. By 'Original Sin' he did not mean 'man's first disobedience and
the fruit of that forbidden tree', but that radical imperfection in human
nature itself which led Paul to cry: 'The evil that I would not, that I
do.' Coleridge knew only too well that Kant's 'sense of duty' was not
enough; indeed he found it a positive hindrance, since to be obliged to
do anything was, for him, an almost certain guarantee that he would not,
could not, do it. In considering the stress he came to lay upon Will and
Redemption, then, one cannot forget his own weakness of will and his
tragic need for deliverance and renewal. None the less, we are all
(including St Paul) sinners, and Coleridge's special sins—from which
his acutely sensitive moral nature made him suffer a thousand times
more than most men—do not diminish the value and truth of his beliefs
on this matter. 'Conviction of sin' was, with him (as it is for all), a pre-
condition of the return to religion. One of the first clear statements of
his return is this, from a letter to George Coleridge (1 July 1802):

> I . . . have convinced myself, that the Socinian and Arian
> Hypotheses are utterly untenable . . . My Faith is simply this—
> that there is an original corruption in our nature, from which
> and from the consequences of which, we may be redeemed
> by Christ—not as the Socinians say, by his pure morals or excel-
> lent Example merely—but in a mysterious manner as an effect of
> his Crucifixion—and this I believe—not because I *understand* it;
> but because I *feel*, that it is not only suitable to, but needful for,
> my nature and because I find it clearly revealed.   (C L, II, 807)

The elements of his final faith are already present here, but for the first
formulation of a full Trinitarian position we must go to the Malta notebooks (1805). One can see what Miss Coburn means when she remarks
that 'Coleridge's return to orthodox Christianity is through the Logos,
not the Gospels, a metaphysical rather than a historical approach.'

(*Notebooks*, II, 2445n.) In 2445, for instance, he is still interpreting the persons of the Trinity *ad normam Platonis*, as 'Being', the 'Word' (or 'communicable Intelligibility') and 'Wisdom' (the 'Spirit of holy Action', 'proceeding at once from Life and Reason'). In 2448 the cold metaphysics are suffused with warmth from the heart and conscience. After calling Unitarianism 'the religion of a man whose Reason would make him an Atheist but whose Heart and Common Sense will not permit him to be so' he speaks of his 'necessary passage from Unitarianism . . . through Spinozism into Plato and St John', and of an 'awful Truth' which has just burst upon him: 'No Christ, No God!' This, he adds

> I now feel with all its needful evidence, of the Understanding: would to God, that my spirit were made conform [*sic*] thereto— that No Trinity, no God. . . . O that this Conviction may work upon me and in me and that my mind may be made up as to the character of Jesus, and of historical Christianity as clearly as it is of the Logos and intellectual or spiritual Christianity.

And later (2640), speaking of disbelief in the gospel miracles, he thus answers a supposed infidel:

> Well, Brother! but granting these miracles to have been false . . . yet still all the doctrines remain binding on thee? Still must thou repent, and be regenerated, and be crucified to the flesh, and this not by thy own mere being, but by a mysterious action of the Moral world on thee, of the *ordo ordinans*. Still will the Trinity, the Redemption, the assumption of Humanity by the Godhead remain Truth and still will the Faith in these Truths be the living fountain of all true virtue . . . Believe all these so as thy Faith be not merely *real* but *actual*.[1]

It was in the autumn of 1806 that Coleridge was making up his mind to be a full Trinitarian. A letter of 13 October to Thomas Clarkson (CL, II, 1193 ff.) gives as concise a summary as we need of his final position. God's Thoughts are more 'real' than what we call 'things'; he is a 'self-comprehending Being, *i.e.* he has an Idea of himself'. This Idea from all

[1] This passage re-appears somewhat elaborated in a letter (4 October 1806), to George Fricker. (CL, II, 1189–90)

eternity co-existed with God ('begotten' of him), and so is called God's 'Son'. He is the Image of God, in whom the Father beholds well-pleased his whole Being. But, lastly, the interaction of Love between Father and Son is 'intensely real' also, so real as to constitute a Third Person, proceeding 'co-eternally both from the Father and the Son—'

> and neither of these Three can be conceived *apart* nor *confusedly*, so that the Idea of God involves that of a Tri-Unity.

This, then, was how Coleridge arrived at 'No Trinity, no God'; there can be no adequate idea of God which has not this threefold structure. The Unitarian God is 'a mere power in darkness': 'no Sun, no Light with vivifying Warmth, but a cold and dull moonshine, or rather star-light, which shews itself but shews nothing else'.

In all this we certainly see Coleridge making his way to Trinitarian orthodoxy along the high metaphysical road. But the belief was far more to him than a matter of metaphysical speculation—though, being Coleridge, he had to think out the implications of his beliefs to their remotest limits and in their most abstract inter-relationships. The point is, *why* did he undertake this great journey, if intellectual curiosity was not the only reason? The answer—and Coleridge himself confirms it repeatedly—is, a deep yearning of his inmost soul for strength, support and forgiveness. He cried out for a Redeemer, and God had heard his cry. He had answered, by assuming humanity himself, and laying down his life for sinners. What did this mean, translated back into theological terms? It meant the doctrine of the Trinity.

Coleridge was too great a man ever to suppose that mere headwork could take the place of living faith; he knew the difference between the intellectually 'real' and the morally 'actual'. Even while he is expound-ing Trinitarian doctrine to George Fricker, he insists upon the 'vital head-and-heart FAITH in these truths'; they must be made true *for you* by living them out in daily life. Ten years before, in spite of his passion for metaphysics, he had known (and he never forgot) how flimsy a support they are in times of suffering:

> My philosophical refinements and metaphysical Theories lay by me in the hour of anguish, as toys by the bedside of a child deadly-sick. May God continue his visitations to my soul, bowing it

down, till the pride . . . of human Reason be utterly done away.
(CL, I, 267)

The final difficulty, that of reconciling historical Christianity with his already-accepted Logos-theology—that of accepting Jesus of Nazareth as the Logos incarnate—he overcame as soon as he had convinced himself that a historical break-through of redeeming love was a necessary climax to the whole scheme of divine administration. Thereafter, the unique fitness of Christianity to meet the spiritual needs of mortal men furnished the final proof of its truth.

In this essay I have mostly been following the chronological sequence, and basing the argument primarily upon Coleridge's Letters and Notebooks. I have done this for two reasons: first because I think it important to watch his mind in process of growth; and secondly, because his relevant published works (especially *The Friend*, the *Lay Sermons*, *Biographia Literaria*, *Aids to Reflection*, *Constitution of Church and State*, and *Confessions of an Inquiring Spirit*—or *Letters on the Inspiration of the Scriptures*) are much better known, and have already been widely discussed by many writers (myself included). At the point we have now reached, all these works, except *The Friend*, had yet to be written, but we have seen the materials for them forming in his mind. We have followed the 'pattern in the carpet' we set out to trace, and seen Coleridge passing through Unitarianism, going 'much further than the Unitarians', and so coming 'round to the other side'.[1]

Within the narrow limits of this essay, there is not much that can or need be added. Coleridge's later letters and notebooks (so far, that is, as they are as yet available to the general reader) are full of references to his projected *Opus Maximum*, which was to crown his life's work and unify his multitudinous thinking and reading in one vast synthesis. For instance, on 7 October 1815, he tells Daniel Stuart that its title will be 'Logosophia', and that it will comprise six treatises: (1) a history of Philosophy from Pythagoras to the present day; (2) a history of Logic; (3) 'The Science of Premisses', *i.e.* 'the examination of the Premisses which in ordinary and practical reasoning are taken for granted'; (4) a detailed Commentary on the Gospel of St John, intended to show that

[1] *Table Talk*, 23 June, 1834 (Oxford edn., 1917, 308.).

'Christianity is true Philosophy, and of course that all true Philosophy is Christianity'; (5) On the Mystics and Pantheists with the Lives of Bruno, Boehme, George Fox and Spinoza; (6) The causes and consequences of Unitarianism. We shall not properly know, until the existing portions of the *Opus* are published, how much more we shall have to learn about it. But we can see from the quoted tabulation that hints towards it are scattered everywhere throughout his writings, and indeed that all his books are fragments not yet built into the total structure.

Perhaps, in those fragments, we have enough, certainly enough to account for the great influence Coleridge exerted over some of the best minds of the nineteenth century. Everyone knows that J. S. Mill, a man of totally opposite views, called Coleridge one of 'the two great seminal minds of England [the other being Bentham] in their age', and added 'there is hardly to be found in England an individual of any importance . . . who did not first learn to think from one of these two'. Of those who did learn from Coleridge, it is enough to mention Sterling, Carlyle, J. S. Mill, J. C. Hare, Thomas Arnold, J. H. Newman, James Martineau, F. A. J. Hort, F. D. Maurice, Charles Kingsley and many others. A good deal has been written about Coleridge's influence upon the Broad Church movement (mainly through Maurice) and upon 'Christian Socialism'. But I think that if we live with him long enough, share his valiant struggles for faith against heavy odds, and watch his final attainment of it, we shall be inclined to see him rather as the prototype of those—like Kierkegaard perhaps, or the best of the Christian 'existentialists' of this century—who have sought to renovate the faith, not only by re-stating it intellectually but by living it out into reality themselves. *Aids to Reflection* is still a book which could speak straight to the condition of any well-disposed young pagan of today (if he would ever read it); and the *Confessions* (as I have already said) laid down, long before the Victorian 'Science and Religion' hubbub, nearly all the positions about biblical interpretation which are now taken for granted by everyone.

In his later years, Coleridge often regretted that he had not been a parson, and no doubt (once he had become orthodox) he would have been happier as such. Still more, perhaps, if he had been a College don, where he could have spellbound generations of the best young men, without having to worry about money matters or (in those days) the writing of books. But we must be thankful that he never took Orders, for his defence of the faith is incomparably more impressive as the work of a layman—of one, that is, who is not professionally committed to the defensive side, but has embraced the faith through intellectual conviction and imperious emotional need.

I conclude with two brief extracts from the as yet unpublished third volume of Coleridge's *Notebooks*.[1] The first is taken out of context, but serves as a motto for Coleridge's religious work:

> To make the intellectual Faith a fair analogon and unison of the Vital faith . . . [3278].

The second:

> But O! not what I understand, but what I *am*, must save or crush me! [3354].

---

[1] By permission of Miss K. Coburn, who has kindly allowed me to see the proofsheets.

For permission to quote these two extracts I am also indebted to the courtesy of Mr. A. H. B. Coleridge and of the Bollingen Series, Princeton University Press and Routledge & Kegan Paul (London).

9: Coleridge and Politics

JOHN COLMER

'IT IS very unpleasant to me to be often asked if Coleridge has changed his political sentiments—for I know not properly how to reply—pray furnish me.' We do not know how Mrs Coleridge's correspondent, the Somersetshire tanner Tom Poole, replied; but it would have been difficult to furnish a satisfactory answer in 1799, and it became increasingly so as the poet continued to modify his political ideas in the light of external events and in harmony with changes in his philosophical and religious thought. His political enemies, among them Hazlitt, solved this problem by interpreting his whole development as a cowardly turning from the brave ideals of the French Revolution to the 'unclean side' of high Toryism. Such crude misinterpretations have retained some currency, because they have permitted succeeding writers to align Coleridge with Wordsworth and Southey and to see all three as representative political renegades, deserters from the cause of freedom. But since R. J. White, F. M. Todd and Geoffrey Carnall have dispelled this myth in relation to Coleridge, Wordsworth and Southey respectively, there is nothing now left to support the traditional grouping of the three Romantic 'turn-coats'.[1] If we look at what each wrote, especially the early works, a different and more illuminating picture emerges.

In many ways the most interesting period of Coleridge's political writings was the first. Reading his Bristol Lectures of 1795 and the essays in *The Watchman*, we are immediately aware of the intense

[1] R. J. White, *The Political Thought of Samuel Taylor Coleridge*, London, 1938; F. M. Todd, *Politics and the Poet: A Study of Wordsworth*, London, 1957; Geoffrey Carnall, *Roberth Southey and his Age*, Oxford, 1960.

intellectual effort he made to come to terms with the various political theories brought into being by the French Revolution. And since that Revolution was itself the culmination of a whole century's thought, in grappling with the theories of Burke, Paine and Godwin, Coleridge was involved in a radical reassessment of his eighteenth-century heritage. Just as his achievement as a poet sprang partly from assimilating what was best in the eighteenth-century poetic tradition and partly from 'the magical and synthetic power of the imagination', so his political achievement sprang from a discriminating view of the past and his genius for producing a new and original synthesis. In *Edmund Burke*, Alfred Cobban sees Coleridge's political thought as part of a general Burkeian revolt against the eighteenth century, but in doing so he obscures Coleridge's actual debt to earlier thinkers. The doctrine of Necessity and the association of ideas, formulated most completely by David Hartley and explicated and reinforced by Joseph Priestley, dominated every branch of Coleridge's thought until his final rejection of Hartley in 1801. He was a child of as well as a critic of the eighteenth century.

A thorough immersion in politics was an almost inescapable fate for the young writers of Coleridge's generation. Whether we turn to Hazlitt's nostalgic evocation of the spirit of the age, to the impassioned optimism of Wordsworth's vision in *The Prelude*, when 'the whole Earth,/The beauty wore of promise', or to Blake's early prophetic poems, we are reminded of the formative influence that the French Revolution exerted on the minds of the young intellectuals in the 1790s.[1] But it was not outward events alone nor the need to earn money through political journalism that impelled Coleridge into radical politics. Two strands of thought, the one Christian and the other Platonic, lie behind Coleridge's life-long concern with politics. The 'system of Jesus', a phrase used in one of the Bristol Lectures on Revealed Religion to distinguish it from the Godless systems of Paine and Godwin, provided a perfect model for a life of humanitarian action founded on love. The elect are those who pursue the regeneration of society through imitation of Christ—

[1] The best brief account is M. H. Abrams 'English Romanticism: The Spirit of the Age', in *Romanticism Reconsidered*, ed. Northrop Frye, New York, 1963.

in whose sight
All things are pure, his strong controlling love
Alike from all educing perfect good

(*Religious Musings*, 56-58)

Coleridge's message in his early political lectures, 'Go, preach the
GOSPEL to the poor', his insistence to the radical orator John Thelwall
that Christianity was 'a religion for Democrats', that it 'certainly
teaches in the most explicit terms the Rights of Man', that 'it commands
it's disciples to go everywhere, and every where to preach these rights'
(CL, I, 282), his reference to the Bible as 'The Statesman's Manual' in
1816, and the argument of his last work *On the Constitution of the Church
and State* all point to the fact that his Christian commitment to politics
was fundamentally consistent throughout his life. And the same is true
of the second main strand, the Platonic,which underlies his recognition
that man can only reach fulfilment through society. Writing to the
Abolitionist Thomas Clarkson on 13 October 1806, and using a figure
that he was to repeat years later, Coleridge brings together the Platonic
and Christian elements in his thought

> A male and female Tyger is neither more or less whether you
> suppose them only existing in their appropriate wilderness, or
> whether you suppose a thousand Pairs. But Man is truly altered
> by the co-existence of other men; his faculties cannot be deve-
> loped in himself alone, and only by himself. Therefore the human
> race not by a bold metaphor, but in a sublime reality, approach
> to, and might become, one body whose Head is Christ (theLogos).
>
> (CL, II, 1197)

The little known lectures on politics and religion that Coleridge
delivered in Bristol in 1795 deserve more attention than they are
usually given. The political lectures were published as pamphlets in
1795 and subsequently made more generally available by Coleridge's
daughter Sara, in *Essays on his Own Times*, but the six *Lectures on
Revealed Religion* have remained unpublished for 175 years and will be
available to the general reader for the first time in the *Collected Coleridge*. Not only do these two sets of lectures prove how deeply Coleridge was involved in the radical protest against the war with France

and the Pitt/Grenville 'Gagging Bills'; they also illustrate his strenuous efforts to define his own position in relation to the contemporary ideological debate. They illustrate, too, the fundamental consistency between the preoccupations of his Jacobinical youth and those of his middle age.

A central figure in the contemporary ideological debate was William Godwin. There was much in Godwin's *Political Justice* (1793) that Coleridge was already predisposed to accept. David Hartley had made him a Necessitarian even before he read of the doctrine of Necessity in Godwin: 'I am a compleat Necessitarian—and understand the subject as well almost as Hartley himself—but I go farther than Hartley and believe the corporeality of *thought*—namely, that it is motion—.' (C L, I, 137) And he had met most of Godwin's central ideas in the writings of the scientific rationalist Joseph Priestley. Consequently, Godwin did not provide the blinding flash of illumination that he did for Wordsworth. Coleridge's understanding of the broader philosophical context of Godwin's writings enabled him to examine them with a more critical and discriminating eye. The point is well made by Peter Mann, in his Introduction to the *Lectures on Revealed Religion* in the first volume of the *Collected Coleridge*;[1] and the publication of the lectures makes clearer than ever before the religious grounds of Coleridge's rejection of Paine and Godwin and that, for all his connections with Unitarian radicalism, he had little sympathy for the narrow sectarian aims of English dissent.

The main elements that attracted him to *Political Justice* were Godwin's analysis of the corrupting effects of property, his faith in the communication of truth, his interpretation of all phenomena as part of a necessary process, his trust in non-violence, and his vision of the inevitable triumph of truth. What prevented him from accepting Godwin entire were Godwin's atheism and his false psychology. Coleridge's Christian sense of the reality of evil as distinct from error made it impossible for him to share Godwin's optimistic rationalism. And the idea of universal benevolence in *Political Justice* appeared to have no foundation in human psychology. It ignored the facts of individual

[1] I am grateful to the editors, Lewis Patton and Peter Mann, and to the general editor of the *Collected Coleridge*, Kathleen Coburn, for allowing me to consult proofs of this volume before publication.

growth as they had been scientifically explained by David Hartley and as the poet himself had experienced them. Whereas Godwin warns his readers of the dangers of the domestic affections, only modifying his views six years later in the Preface to *St. Leon*, Coleridge insists that the affections expand 'like the circles of a Lake—the Love of our Friends, parents, and neighbours lead[s] us to the love of our Country to the love of all Mankind. The intensity of private attachment encourages, not prevents, universal philanthropy.' These words in the third of the *Lectures on Revealed Religion* (1795) re-echo those in a letter to Southey a year earlier:

> The ardour of private Attachments makes Philanthropy a neces-
> sary *habit* of the Soul. I love my *Friend*—such as *he* is, all mankind
> are or *might be*. The deduction is evident—. Philanthropy (and
> indeed every other *Virtue*) is a thing of *Concretion*—Some home-
> born Feeling is the *center* of the Ball, that, rolling on thro' Life
> collects and assimilates every congenial Affection.   (CL, I, 86)

The movement of the Conversational Poems outwards from the love of one person to a love that encompasses God, Nature and Society embodies this deeply felt truth.

In the process of defining his own ideas in relation to those of others and in advising his Bristol audiences how a true friend of freedom should act, Coleridge touched on themes in 1795 that were to occupy a central place in his mature political thought: the freedom of the press, the communication of truth, the importance of desynonymizing key terms, the function of education in effecting social reform, the creation of an elect (an interesting anticipation of his later idea of the 'clerisy'), the analysis of the forces that cause a loss of national character, the relationship between private and public morality, and above all the importance of relating all political issues to 'fixed and determinate principles of action' (EOT, I, 24). Such a list of themes suggests that there was more justification than has often been allowed for Coleridge's claim that there was 'not a single political Opinion' which he held in youth which he did not continue to hold in later life (CL, IV, 719). A copy of *Conciones ad Populum* in the Houghton Library, Harvard, contains the following manuscript note pasted on the inside cover:

Except the two or three passages involving the doctrine of Phil. Necessity & Unitarianism I see little or nothing in these *outbursts* of my *youthful* zeal to *retract*, & with exception of some flame-colored Epithets applied to Persons, as Mr Pitt & others, or rather *Personifications* (for such they really were to *me*) as little to regret.[1]

Although Coleridge's various attempts to prove that he had never been a Jacobin involved some distortion of the truth, as when he omitted the most 'Jacobinical' passages of a Bristol lecture on reprinting it in *The Friend* (Section the First, Essay XVI), there is substantial truth in R. J. White's claim[2] that there is both a horizontal and a vertical unity in all Coleridge's thought. Horizontally, or temporally, his ideas were subject to a process of slow organic growth over the years rather than to any sudden change. And vertically his political opinions developed in harmony with his maturing philosophical and religious ideas. The abandonment of the doctrine of Philosophical Necessity, that 'labyrinth-Den of Sophistry' (CL, II, 1037), was accompanied by corresponding changes at the other levels, religious and political.

What is perhaps most surprising about the early political writings is Coleridge's capacity to educe general principles from a complex and inflammatory situation without any slackening of his grasp of the actual. He was certainly carried away by the excitement of the moment in Bristol, as he later admitted to Sir George Beaumont, allowing himself to choose sentences and sentiments simply because 'they were wild, and original, and vehement and fantastic' (CL, II, 1001). And he was duly reproved for this at the time by Tom Poole's brother Richard, who cautioned the young poet: 'The cause of truth and reason never wants violence or invective for its support; sober argument and rational investigation are alone necessary to convince the unprejudiced and disinterested.' In spite of the incongruity between the rhetorical style and the incisive analysis, the Bristol political lectures remain of permanent interest, since they contain the seeds of all Coleridge's later thought.

[1] Printed *variatim* in James Gillman, *The Life of Samuel Taylor Coleridge*, 1838, 73.
[2] See his Introduction to *The Political Thought of Samuel Taylor Coleridge*, 24.

Inevitably the two questions that most exercised the minds of his Bristol audiences in 1795 were: Was the war against Revolutionary France a just and necessary one? and, How should the friends of freedom act to best forward their cause? Coleridge's answer to the first was an uncompromising No—only after the Peace of Amiens did he come to recognize that the war was a just one. His answer to the second was that the friends of freedom should act as individuals, in the light of their Christian conscience. In the political lectures and in a public meeting convened to forward a loyal address, he pointed to the paradox that the war with France and Pitt's repressive measures against radical and reform associations, both of which policies were intended to prevent the growth of Jacobinism in Britain, were having precisely the opposite effect. His account of the influence of a system of spies and informers on the national spirit is a horrifying one, for which, however, there is ample documentation in the lecture itself, in the work of historians like P. A. Brown, and in the accounts of contemporaries, Thomas Holcroft, for example, who wrote:

> Men even of respectable characters and honest intentions now thought it an heroical act of duty, to watch the conduct of their intimate friends, excite them to utter violent or seditious expressions, and afterwards to turn informers against the intemperance they had provoked.

'Anonymous letters are employed to blast the peace and destroy the personal security of the best and worthiest members of the community', Thelwall complained in a lecture on 'The Moral Tendency of a System of Spies and Informers'. A few years later, Coleridge himself was to receive the unwelcome attentions of a government agent at Nether Stowey—the famous 'Spy-Nosey' episode, told in Chapter 10 of *Biographia Literaria*, and now substantiated by A. J. Eagleston.[1] But, in Bristol, he went unscathed. Later, he attributed this to a number of factors: that the Government treated Southey and himself as harmless boys; that it knew that they were unconnected with any club or Jacobin association; and that his own declamation against such clubs and societies, as an *imperium in imperio*, saved them from imprisonment. (CL,II, 1000–2)

[1] *Coleridge: Studies by Several Hands* ed. E. Blunden and E. L. Griggs, 71.

The principles that should be observed in the communication of truth and the dangerous role of political associations in the life of the State were matters that continued to exercise his mind until his death. It is worth examining these in some detail. Because freedom of speech had been challenged in 1795, Coleridge was more concerned to establish its importance than to define the responsibilities that should accompany it, though indeed even at this early stage he frequently asserts the correlative nature of rights and duties in response to the popular demand for the rights of man. In the lecture *On the Present War,* he recognized the duty of considering 'the character of those, to whom we address ourselves, their situations, and probable degree of knowledge', but this qualification was of less importance than the assertion that 'to promulge what we believe to be truth is indeed a law beyond law' (EOT, I, 60), and the thesis that the balance of the constitution depended on the freedom of the press, a freedom which gave the people 'an *influential* sovereignty' (EOT, I, 91). When nearly fifteen years later, he returned to this subject, in the essays 'On the Communication of the Truth' in *The Friend,* the treatment was more ample and philosophic, and the emphasis was now placed on the responsibility for considering the likely consequences of our communications. This was an expression of what was perhaps the most important change of all in Coleridge's thought, the change from a loose equation of religious and social morality to a formal distinction between the two. In religion we are concerned with the individual and his conscience; in politics with the citizen and the state. Although there is much ground common to both and although politics should, according to Coleridge, always be founded on moral principles, he makes a clear distinction between the communication of the religious truths of the Reformation to all and the communication of political truths, just as he makes a clear distinction elsewhere (*Table Talk,* 28 December 1831) between the 'only pure democracy', the church, which considers individuals as equal in the sight of God, and the state, which considers unequal classes and interests. In *The Friend,* he makes a similar and related distinction between Religion and Law, Religion which is concerned with the individual conscience and inner motive, and Law which is concerned with external action alone. To allow Law to dictate to the individual's conscience was to set up 'a busy and inquisitorial tyranny,' a point of view he summed up succinctly in a marginal note in a copy of the *Encyclopaedia Londinensis*:

> Not the practice of *virtue,* but the peace of Society and the Legality of the Individuals, are the objects of the Law; these secured, we may safely trust to Religion, Education, and Civilisation for the rest.

F. J. A. Hort believed that to apply the distinction between Law and Religion to 'all the changing conditions of human life', was the 'special problem of the nineteenth century'.[1] In many countries it remains unsolved, particularly in the area of literary censorship.

Behind the whole discussion of the communication of truth in *The Friend* there still lies Godwin's *Political Justice*.[2] Even Coleridge's ingenious distinction between 'verbal' and 'moral' truth may be traced back to Godwin, although the example of Blifil is Coleridge's own. But although much of the framework is derived from *Political Justice*, the actual argument demolishes Godwin's naïve faith in a rational populace and the inevitable conquest of error. To believe that truth by 'a natural gradation' would reach every level of society if everyone were free to communicate the truth as he saw it, was to ignore differences in intellectual capacity, the force of selfishness and greed, and the reality of evil. Far from advocating censorship or state restrictions of any kind, Coleridge argues in favour of a free press and an extension of education to combat ignorance. But it is clear that he had a very qualified faith in the ordinary citizen's capacity for statecraft. This is apparent from his references to the formative influence of recluses of genius, from his analysis of societies in terms of the philosophic ideas of the age, and from his practice of addressing his later works to the upper and middle classes.

The problems relating to the role of political associations in the state were also partly Godwinian in origin. In *Political Justice,* Godwin had argued that neither government nor any form of political association was necessary, since each man possessed the sovereign power of

[1] F. J. A. Hort, *Cambridge Essays,* 1856, 349.
[2] See Lucyle Werkmeister, *MP*, LV, 3, 1958, 170–7.

reason. And, in 1795, he had published a pamphlet, *Considerations on Lord Grenville's and Mr Pitt's Bills,* in which he condoned the Ministry's action against associations like the London Corresponding Society, and attacked the activities of the popular demagogue, John Thelwall. Godwin's failure to speak out against the two Bills appeared cowardly to Coleridge, although in fact it was perfectly in line with his academic quietism. But to speak out did not for Coleridge imply approval of political association as the best way to secure social justice. And there is no evidence that Coleridge was ever a member of any political club or association. His missionary solution to the problem of the poor called for individual action, one 'should be *personally* among the poor, and teach them their *duties* in order' to 'render them susceptible of their *rights*' (EOT, I, 22). And he was content that the power of the press and the right of petition gave the people sufficient influence over government. Although he may, as he claims, have seen the dangers of an *imperium in imperio* from the start, it was only when the character of the associations changed from being predominantly middle-class to working-class organizations that he attacked them as dangerous to the state. In doing so, he never seems to have realized that he might have been succumbing to that very 'panic of property' that he attributed to the Pitt Ministry in the 1790s. Nor was he prepared to recognize that, in fact, every society contains within itself a multiplicity of autonomous associations, all acting, in some degree, as pressure groups. The fear of 'secret' societies is probably ineradicable because irrational; it is reflected strongly in Conrad's *Under Western Eyes* and in James's *The Princess Casamassima,* and it has assumed hysterical and dangerous forms more recently in Europe and America. Coleridge's warnings of the dangers of 'club government' in *The Courier* 'Letters to Judge Fletcher' and in the *Lay Sermons* were not as hysterical as Wordsworth's and Southey's outbursts, but for all their high-minded philosophical tone and serious concern with national education, they were narrowly class-centred, the products of fear rather than sympathetic insight. This he saw himself many years later in 1832.

> But in truth and candor it should be said, that the Working Classes did not substitute Rights for Duties, and take the former into their guardianship, till the higher classes, their legitimate

protectors, had subordinate *Persons* to *Things*, and systematically perverted the former into the latter.[1]

In the middle period of his life, by the time he came to publish his periodical *The Friend*, founded in 1809 to 'aid in the formation of fixed principles in politics, morals, and religion', Coleridge had read most of the main works of European political philosophy, including neglected works like Harrington's *Oceana*, and had acquired an extraordinarily wide experience of practical politics. This experience included the planning of Pantisocracy, to which, he later claimed with some exaggeration, he owed his 'clearest insight into the nature of individual man' and his 'most comprehensive views of his social relations', 'the true uses of trade and commerce, and how far the *wealth* and relative *power* of nations promote or impede their *welfare* and inherent strength' (*Friend*, I, 224). The experience also included giving political lectures in Bristol and Bath; founding his own paper *The Watchman* 'That all may know the TRUTH; /And that the TRUTH may make us FREE!!'; writing highly influential articles in the national daily *The Morning Post* between 1799 and 1804; and acting as a high-ranking Public Servant in Malta, from which he believed he learnt: 'quickness in discovering men's characters . . . the *inside* character of many eminent living men' and to 'know by heart the awkward and wicked machinery, by which all our affairs *abroad* are carried on' (CL, II, 1178). Up until 1809 all his political writing had been occasional and reflected his genius for referring the issues of the day to 'fixed principles'; no opportunity had ocurred to discuss the main theories of government. *The Friend* gave him his first chance to expound these theories, to analyse the fallacy of founding the basis of government on fear (the system of Hobbes) or on pure reason (the system of Rousseau), and to argue for the necessity of founding government on expedience and consent (the system he himself adopted).

[1] Coleridge wrote this manuscript note on 20 January 1832 after re-reading the attack on 'club government' and Jacobinism that he had made in 1814 in the fourth 'Letter to Judge Fletcher' in *The Courier*. A notebook in the Berg Collection, New York, contains the six Letters in the hand of an unknown amanuensis, together with retrospective notes by Coleridge.

It comes as a surprise to most readers of Coleridge to find that he argues in favour of expedience. How then does he reconcile a belief in the prime importance of first principles with such a philosophy of political expedience ? In dealing with the three main theories of government in the essays 'On the Principles of Political Knowledge' in *The Friend*, he insists that each must be related to the theory of knowledge of which it was the natural and inevitable product. In the case of the philosophy he espoused, it sprang from the basic distinction between Reason (the legislative function of the human mind) and Understanding (which he refered to in one of the *Courier* essays as 'the calculating faculty, which is properly the executive branch of self-government'). From Reason we derive our guiding ideas and principles, but the task of embodying them in laws and institutions is the work of the Understanding. Coleridge thus takes up a position midway between the champions of pure Reason and of pure Expedience. On the one hand, he dismisses Rousseau with an argument reminiscent of Burke's idea of man's 'mixed nature', but altogether more philosophic:

> Man is something besides Reason; because his Reason never acts by itself, but must clothe itself in the substance of individual Understanding and specific Inclination, in order to become a reality and an object of consciousness and experience. (*Friend*, I, 201)

On the other hand, he launches a prolonged attack on Utilitarianism and Expedience, unilluminated by ideas derived from the Reason. Nevertheless, because he believed that 'the chief object for which men first formed themselves into a State was not the protection of their lives but of their property' and that a government could never recognize individuals but only classes and interests, the basis of this political theory, unlike his ethical theory, was utilitarian. To judge the rightness of our private actions solely by their consequences was the act of an unscrupulous villain; to judge the rightness of political actions by their likely consequences was the act of a wise statesman. F. D. Maurice described the essence of Coleridge's position in *The Friend* when he said that Coleridge

> has been convinced that society is a reality, that it would not become at all more real by being unmade and reconstructed, and

therefore he has begun to inquire what are the grounds of its reality, and how we may be preserved from making it into a fiction and a falsehood.[1]

The enquiry into the grounds of social reality was taken a stage further in the *Lay Sermons* 1816–7 and culminated in Coleridge's last published prose work, *On the Constitution of the Church and State*, in which he outlined his idea of the constitution in terms of a balance between the 'forces of permanence', which he identified with the landed interest, and the 'forces of progression', which he identified with the commercial interest, both dependent on a 'continuing and progressive civilisation' created by a third force, the National Church or Clerisy, without which there could be neither permanence nor progression. It is a work that has been ably summarized by many writers, including Basil Willey in his *Nineteenth Century Studies*, and therefore requires no further summary here. Of *Church and State* a recent critic, David Calleo, has written: 'It is difficult to point to many investigations of the modern constitutional State that are at once so comprehensive in scope and so rich and provocative in detail.'[2] Another critic, William Kennedy, has described it as 'a case study of the application of the ideas of reason to social and economic problems'.

Decidedly the two most important contributions that *Church and State* made to nineteenth-century political philosophy were Coleridge's idea of the 'clerisy' and his definition of the positive and negative ends of government. By the clerisy he meant a nationally endowed permanent class or order with the following duties:

> A certain smaller number were to remain at the fountain heads of the humanities, in cultivating and enlarging the knowledge already possessed, and in watching over the interests of physical and moral science; being, likewise, the instructors of such as constituted, or were to constitute, the remaining more numerous classes of the order. This latter and far more numerous body were to be distributed throughout the country, so as not to leave even the smallest integral part or division without a resident guide,

[1] 'Dedication' to *The Kingdom of Christ*, ed. A. R. Vidler, London, 1958, II, 352.
[2] *Coleridge and the Idea of the Modern State*, Yale Studies in Political Science 18, New Haven and London, 1966, 119.

guardian, and instructor; the objects and final intention of the whole order being these—to preserve the stores, to guard the treasures, of past civilization, and thus to bind the present with the past; to perfect and add to the same, and thus to connect the present with the future; but especially to diffuse through the whole community, and to every native entitled to its laws and rights, that quantity and quality of knowledge which was indispensable both for the understanding of those rights, and for the performance of the duties correspondent. Finally, to secure for the nation, if not a superiority over the neighbouring states, yet an equality at least, in that character of general civilisation, which equally with, or rather more than, fleets, armies, and revenue, forms the ground of its defensive and offensive power.

(*Church and State*, ch. V, 2nd ed. 1830, 49-50)

This idea of clerisy inspired both defenders and reformers of the English church, defenders like Blomfield, the Bishop of London, whose *Charge* of 1830 Coleridge enriched with annotations that demonstrate his grasp of the problems of translating the idea into practice[1] and reformers like Thomas Arnold for whom, as Basil Willey remarks, 'Coleridgean "Ideas" become a programme of action'. It also inspired the Utilitarian John Stuart Mill, who quoted the whole passage in his famous essay on Coleridge and who saw in the distinction between private property and the 'Nationalty', that is, the national wealth inalienably set aside for the support of learning, an argument from an

---

[1] In his marginal comments on Blomfield's *Charge,* Coleridge criticized 'the senseless waste of a clergyman's time' at ill-attended mid-week services and insisted that his attention to parochial schools was the 'most helpful part of his administrative exertions'. In general, he approved of Blomfield's views on the religious education of the poor, but criticized him for not distinguishing between the 'National Church' and the 'Church of Christ'. Whereas Thomas Arnold envisaged an army of non-commissioned officers revitalizing the Church, Coleridge described Blomfield's association of parochial assistants as a 'Scotch Eldership in disguise', and asked 'Why, an association ? to visit the poor parishioners *ex officio,* like the Window-light Man or Tax-Gatherer ?' The annotated copy is in the British Museum, C.61.c.9. For a general account of Blomfield's reforms, see Olive Brose, *Church and Parliament: The Reshaping of the Church of England, 1828-60*, Stanford, 1959, 67-97.

unexpected quarter for State endowed education. If the National Church or Clerisy fails to discharge its function, Mill argues, 'the State may withdraw the fund from its actual holders, for the better execution of its purposes. There is no sanctity attached to the means, but only to the ends.'[1] This is what Coleridge feared might happen, not what he intended. His tract is an urgent plea for the Church of England to assume its full educational responsibilities. Ten years later, in 1840, Julius Hare in a *Charge* to the clergy of Lewes, claimed that the very attempts that had 'been made to deprive the Church of the conduct of the education of the people' had 'awakened the Church to a clearer and livelier conviction that she, and she alone, can truly educate the people'. Using very Coleridgean phrasing, he said: 'She alone can train and cultivate all the faculties with which man is endowed in their rightful harmony and subordination'. Although Coleridge spoke of the connection between the Christian Church and the National Church or Clerisy as a 'blessed accident', his idea of the third order in the state was essentially Christian, not secular.

The second most valuable contribution to nineteenth-century political theory, the distinction between the positive and negative ends of government, was first sketched in *The Friend*, 1809, summarized in the second *Lay Sermon*, 1817, and fully integrated into his mature idea of the constitution in *Church and State*, 1830. Its influence was of crucial importance, since the main emphasis had been placed on the negative ends of government by earlier thinkers: its role in maintaining internal order and in defending its inhabitants from foreign invasion. Bentham and his followers certainly advocated a positive role for government through a system of enlightened legislation, but Bentham's felicific calculus offered a chilly, mechanistic approach to the task of creating a just society in which men could realize their full potential. Contrast what Coleridge called the 'bran *new style* of the catechistic Bentham' with his own more humane, Platonic account of the positive ends of government:

> 1st. to make the means of subsistence more easy to each individual: 2d. that in addition to the necessaries of life he should derive

---

[1] *Mill on Bentham and Coleridge*, ed. F. R. Leavis, London 1950, 145.

from the union and division of labour a share of the comforts and
conveniences which humanize and ennoble his nature; . . .
3dly. the hope of bettering his own condition and that of his
children. . . . Lastly, the development of those faculties which
are essential to his human nature by the knowledge of his moral
and religious duties, and the increase of his intellectual powers
in as great a degree as is compatible with the other ends of social
union, and does not involve a contradiction. (*Friend*, I, 252–3)[1]

Seen in its appropriate context of nineteenth-century *laissez-faire*
political theory, this is a remarkable and prophetic statement of the
positive ends of government. The idea of the harmonious development
of all man's powers became the central inspiration of Arnold's *Culture
and Anarchy*, and for Newman and many later writers on education it
became the hallmark of a liberal education as distinct from vocational
training.

In discussions of Coleridge's politics, as in discussions of his literary
criticism, a quite false distinction has often been made between his
theory and practice. If, however, on the analogy of de Saussure's
famous distinction between *la langue* (the language system) and *la
parole* (the individual's use of that system), we say that we need to know
Coleridge's critical 'system' before we can 'decode' his judgements on
Shakespeare and Wordsworth fully, we can also say that we need to
know his political 'system' before we can interpret his judgements on
Pitt and Napoleon, or his observations on parliamentary reform, the

[1] Sometime between 1823 and 1825 Coleridge wrote in a notebook: 'To
secure to each the greatest sphere of freedom compatible with the safety,
the security, & the unity of the whole, this, it has often been asserted,
is the proper aim & true object of a state & therefore contains the
definition of the word. This is very plausible, it says much and there
was a time, and that of many years continuance in which I thought that
it meant all; but of late years I have begun to fear that it means little.
At all events more is conveyed to my mind & far more definitely in the
affirmation that the true aim & object of a State & its implied definition
is—by the restraint of all—to enlarge the outward spheres of the truly
free, so as at the same time to increase the inward freedom of those,
whose outward spheres it has contracted.' Notebook No. 20, BM,
Add. MSS. 47517, ff. 42–41.

Corn Laws,[1] factory legislation, and Catholic emancipation. Coleridge's judgements are as inseparable from his fully imagined if not completely articulated system as is *la parole* from *la langue* in modern linguistic theory. While R. H. Fogle and J. A. Appleyard have recently demonstrated the inseparable connection between theory and practice in Coleridge's critical writings, no similar task has been performed for the political writings, although indeed it was the main thesis of my *Coleridge: Critic of Society* that the political theories were evolved in direct response to the challenge of contemporary issues and that his attitude to these issues was only fully intelligible in relation to the theory thus developed. For example, his 'sacred principle' that ' a person can never become a thing, nor be treated as such without wrong', a principle ultimately derived from Kant, underlies all his social criticism. It underlies his forthright answer to the political economists of his day:

> You talk about making this article cheaper by reducing its price in the market from 8*d* to 6*d*. But suppose, in so doing, you have rendered your country weaker against a foreign foe; suppose you have demoralized thousands of your fellow-countrymen, and have sown discontent between one class of society and another, your article is tolerably dear, I take it, after all.
>
> (*Table Talk,* 17 March 1833)

And the 'sacred principle' led him to intervene on behalf of 'the hopeless cause of our poor little White-Slaves, the children in our cotton Factories, against the unpitying cruel spirit of Trade, and the shallow heart-petrifying Self-conceit of our Political Economists' (CL, IV, 922) by writing pamphlets in support of Sir Robert Peel's Bill. In the second *Lay Sermon*, it led him to expostulate:

---

[1] For example, his hostility to the Corn Laws needs to be read in terms of a whole system of ideas made up from: 'land as a sacred trust', agriculture as 'a positive good' and not a mere adjunct to the national economy, the overbalance of the commercial interest, and opposition to the political economists, who 'would dig up the charcoal foundations of the temple of Ephesus to burn as fuel for a steam engine'. See entries in *Table Talk* for 17 March 1833, 3 May and 20 June 1834, and Harold Beeley's succinct account in *Coleridge: Studies by Several Hands,* ed. E. Blunden and E. L. Griggs, 166–7.

But persons are not things—but man does not find his level. Neither in body nor in soul does the man find his level. After a hard and calamitous season, during which the thousand wheels of some vast manufactory had remained silent as a frozen waterfall, be it that plenty has returned and that trade has once more become brisk and stirring: go, ask the overseer, and question the parish doctor, whether the workman's health and temperance with the staid and respectful manners best taught by the inward dignity of conscious self-support, have found their level again! Alas! I have more than once seen a group of children in Dorsetshire, during the heat of the dog-days, each with its little shoulders up to its ears, and its chest pinched inward, the very habit and fixtures, as it were, that had been impressed on their frames by the former ill-fed, ill-clothed, and unfuelled winters. But as with the body, so or still worse with the mind. Nor is the effect confined to the labouring classes, whom by an ominous but too appropriate change in our phraseology we are now accustomed to call the labouring poor.

In recording the plight of the Dorsetshire children and—in a later passage—the plight of the Highland widow who complains that even the very birds have left the once populous village, Coleridge combines the compassion of the novelist with the analytic power of the social scientist. Here he refutes the glib and comforting doctrines of the classical economists by reference to a rival theory of man, by reference to social facts, and by an appeal to elementary human compassion.

His analysis of the disastrous effects of an overbalance of the spirit of commerce on statesmen (Pitt, for example) and on the moral life of the country springs from, and is directly related to, his idea of the constitution, with its dynamic tension between the forces of permanence and progression. To state that Coleridge was opposed to the First Reform Bill tells us very little about his attitude to the theory and practice of representation. But almost any of the conversations on this subject recorded in *Table Talk* is a vital expression of the art of seeing a specific problem in the light of an idea or general principle, for example the entry for 21 November, 1830:

Is the House of Commons to be re-constructed on the principle of a representation of interests, or of a delegation of men? If on the former, we may, perhaps, see our way; if on the latter, you can never in reason, stop short of universal suffrage.

And he was opposed to universal suffrage because he thought it would bestow power without responsibility, since those with no property and therefore no stake in the country would have the vote. Another example is the entry on 20 March 1831:

> The phrases—higher, middle, and lower classes, with reference to this point of representation—are delusive; no such divisions as classes actually exist in society. There is an indissoluble blending and interfusion of persons from top to bottom.

After which he goes on to say that he cannot find 'a ray of principle' in the government's £10 householder distinction, a distinction that might seem to satisfy Coleridge's demand for a property qualification, but which did not since it appeared quite arbitrary and totally unrelated to his idea of 'the balance of the estates in the realm.' All Coleridge's political criticism needs to be read in the light of another remark recorded in *Table Talk* (11 May 1830): 'no man can rightly apprehend an abuse till he has first mastered the idea of the use of an institution'. By idea, of course, he means knowledge of its ultimate end.

What Coleridge's contemporaries and nineteenth-century successors found most interesting in his political writing is not necessarily what most interests the twentieth-century reader, although it is true that we still value him for many of the same reasons. Mill's attempt to create a synthesis from the rival systems of the two 'seminal minds' of the nineteenth century, Bentham and Coleridge, now appears heroic but misguided, particularly so since it ignored Coleridge's central insight that all political systems take their origin and derive their authenticity from a particular theory of the human mind. The attempt to graft Coleridge's philosophy of history and society onto Bentham's psychology of man was bound to fail, but it is failure of a notable and exemplary kind. There never was a Germano-Coleridgean school (though Leavis appears to endorse the phrase in his Introduction to *Mill's Essays on Bentham and Mill*); and Mill was thoroughly misguided in linking Coleridge's philosophy of history with that of the French cause-

and-effect school of Michelet[1]; but he was superbly right in suggesting that Coleridge was one of the first 'who enquired with any comprehensiveness or depth, into the laws of existence and growth of human society'. The occasional papers published by the Centre for Contemporary Cultural Studies at Birmingham University illustrate in a striking fashion the pervasive influence of Coleridge's pioneering approach, as it is mediated through Raymond Williams's *Culture and Society* and Richard Hoggart's writings.

Without in any way wishing to minimize the qualities that the nineteenth century valued in Coleridge (his social criticism, his constitutional theory, his vision of the Church's role in society), I would like to point to the four very modern aspects of Coleridge: his concern with culture, his clear recognition of the importance of the idea of 'consensus' in political affairs, his structural approach to all problems, a kind of 'organic structuralism'[2] that interestingly anticipates the approach of

[1] A point made very firmly by Robert Preyer in *Bentham, Coleridge and the Science of History*. Beiträge zur Englischen Philologie, 41. Heft, 1958.

[2] There is ample justification for using the term 'organic structuralism'. For example, Coleridge makes a clear distinction between an 'organic' and a 'mechanic' approach to structure in an imaginary dialogue recorded in a notebook entitled 'Marginalia intentionalia' in the Berg Collection, New York.

'A. You see clearly that Life is not a result of *structure* generally—or a watch would be alive. Do you think it then the result of that particular structure, which we call organization?

C. So far from it, that I have never been able to understand how it is possible for a man to be a materialist in that sense. For what is that which the organic super-adds to structure since herein (that is, in the matter being organized, not in its being *constructed*) does its relation to Life consist whatever that relation may be, whether cause or effect or re-agency, whether antecedent, consequent or simply co-existent.'

Coleridge was deeply involved in the contemporary medical debate on the relationship of structure to function in accounting for the origin of life. With Abernethy, he advanced organic, vitalist views in opposition to William Lawrence, who argued that function, and even mind itself, was the mechanic product of structure. See 'Coleridge's *Theory of Life*', Alice D. Snyder, *Coleridge on Logic and Learning*, New Haven, 1929, 16–23, and *Philosophical Lectures*, 353–9 and 457.

the anthropologist Lévi-Strauss; and, finally, his rare sensitivity to the significance of language both as an index to underlying structures of the human mind and as a reflector of unanalysed social assumptions.

Little need be said here about Coleridge's analysis of the health of a society in terms of its culture, or of the interesting distinction he draws in *Church and State* between 'civilization' and 'culture', the first seen as largely materialistic, the second involving 'the harmonious development of those qualities and faculties that characterize our humanity', since these aspects have been thoroughly explored by Raymond Williams in *Culture and Society*. But Coleridge's very modern insight into the importance of 'consensus' as the basis of social cohesion and government deserves brief attention. The story of Coleridge's encounter with Harriet Martineau helps to crystallise the difference between Coleridge's organic view of society and the prevailing atomic view of the age. 'You appear to consider that society is an aggregate of individuals!' exclaimed the poet. To which the grim Utilitarian blue-stocking replied: 'I certainly do.' Only by means of an organic view could Coleridge explain the cohesive forces in society, the State 'being a result from, and not a mere total of, the parts, and yet not so merging the constituent parts in the result, but that the individual exists integrally within it' (*Table Talk*, 18 December 1831). His recognition of the importance of shared language, customs, myths, and irrational desires, 'the immortal life of the nation, generation linked to generation by faith, freedom, heraldry and ancestral fame', enabled him to give a more profound and satisfying account of national unity than the Utilitarians, without following Herder into a mystique of Volk or Hegel into idolatrous worship of the nation state. It also enabled him to distinguish, as Wordsworth too distinguished in *The Convention of Cintra*, between an unreal cosmopolitanism (epitomized in the abstract ideals of the French Revolution) and the real possibilities of international understanding, based on consensus and the recognition of national difference.

Together with the importance of consensus, the vital role of the political imagination in Coleridge's thought has been investigated by David Calleo. 'The good society,' Calleo remarks, 'requires a perpetual exercise of creative political thought, of what might be called the political imagination. Coleridge is a conspicuous example of a creative political imagination at work on the needs of the age.' Nevertheless, in reading Calleo's *Coleridge and the Idea of the Modern State*, one needs to bear in mind the temptation that exists for recreating Coleridge in the guise of a privileged American academic of the extreme Right. Conor Cruse O'Brien in his Introduction to the Penguin *Reflections on the French Revolution*, has pointed to a similar process of distortion in the current American re-interpretation and championing of Burke.

Looking at the totality of Coleridge's work, we become aware of two characteristic movements of mind: one is the search for the organizing principle that will explain the inner coherence of a single system, the other is the quest for correspondences between different systems, or disciplines of knowledge. The first expresses itself in his organic theory, with its ideal of reconciling polar opposites, equally applicable to his biological theory of life, his idea of beauty, his distinction between imagination and fancy, and his idea of the constitution. And, as a subjective reflection of this objective law of organicism, there is his idea of method, which involves the 'principle of unity with progression', outlined in the 'Essays on the Principles of Method' in *The Friend*. The other movement of mind, the quest for correspondences, expresses itself in those ingenious paradigms that he constructed in his notebooks, letters and published prose works. Sometimes they serve as speculative instruments through which to achieve extraordinary unity between apparently separate intellectual disciplines, at other times merely as psychological compensations for a frustrated idealism. Both these main movements of mind express a fundamental structural approach to knowledge. It is illuminating to compare Coleridge's organic structuralism with the definition of structuralism that Claude Lévi-Strauss gave in his inaugural lecture on his appointment to the Chair of Social Anthropology, at the Collège de France, in 1960:

> That arrangement alone is structured which meets two conditions: that it be a system, ruled by an internal cohesiveness; and that this cohesiveness, inaccessible to observation in an isolated system, be revealed in the study of transformations, through which the similar properties in apparently different systems are brought to light.[1]

[1] Lévi-Strauss, *The Scope of Anthropology*, tr. S. O. & R. A. Paul, London, 1967, 31.

Granted that Coleridge's paradigms of different systems might not meet Lévi-Strauss's rigorous criteria for defining valid transformations; nevertheless, in this area as in so many other areas (existential thought, I-Thou theology, the workings of the sub-conscious, the relevance of dreams, child psychology) Coleridge anticipates what has proved most fruitful in twentieth-century thought. John Sterling confessed to J. C. Hare: 'to Coleridge . . . I owe *education*. He taught me . . . that all criticism, whether of literature, laws, or manners, is blind, without the power of discerning the organic unity of the subject.'[1] 'The great maxim of Legislation', Coleridge wrote in a marginal note in Baxter's *Reliquiae Baxterianae*, 'intellectual or Political is *Subordinate not exclude*. Nature in her ascent leaves nothing behind: but each step subordinates and glorifies Mass, Crystal, Organ, sensation, sentience, reflection.' (*Philosophical Lectures*, 447, n. 3)

The analysis of the language of politics has become a somewhat dry and respectable academic pastime in the twentieth century. But in Coleridge it is, together with the attention to different theories of mind, one of his main methods of laying bare the essential features of any approach to politics. Here the sensitive literary critic and the philosopher unite. The famous portrait of Pitt in the *Morning Post* best illustrates the approach at work. From the philosopher comes the distinction between the man of genius and the man of talent, a characteristic example of Coleridge's favourite desynonymizing process. The literary critic, philosopher, and psychologist combine to expose Pitt's lack of genius as a statesman:

> One character pervades his whole being. Words on words, finely arranged, and so dexterously consequent, that the whole bears the semblance of argument, and still keeps awake a sense of surprise; but when all is done, nothing rememberable has been said; no one philosophical remark, no one image, not even a pointed aphorism.   (EOT, II, 327–8)

Behind this lies not only the distinction between genius and talent, but also the distinction between mechanical order and creative method.

---

[1] John Sterling, *Essays and Tales*, 1848, I, xvi ('Sketch of the Author's Life').

The latter involves progression with continuous transformation. Pitt commands only mechanical order, so too do his auditors, a fact that determines 'that peculiar constitution of human affairs in their present State, which so eminently favours' his power.

In the fifth of the Philosophical Lectures Coleridge gave in 1819, he spoke of the 'visionary sophisms by which men might through the medium of words impose false momentary convictions on each other' (*Philosophical Lectures*, 191). One way of exposing these sophisms was through desynonymizing. An example occurs as early as the lecture *On the Present War* in 1795. There the poet claimed: 'In the Dictionary of aristocratic Prejudice, Illumination and Sedition are classed as synonimes, and Ignorance prescribed as the only infallible Preventive for contention', a trivial example, but an anticipation of Coleridge's mature approach to popular political sophisms. As Mill remarked of Bentham and Coleridge, Bentham asked of anything 'Is it true?', Coleridge 'What does it *mean*?'. Coleridge recognized that politicians betray their deepest assumptions through the language they use. Consequently, he seized eagerly on such phrases as 'the labouring poor' and 'hands' used of factory workers, and referred them back to the attitudes of mind that produced them. He was as antipathetic as Peacock towards the growth of the Mechanics' Institutes and the much vaunted 'March of Mind', seeing each as a characteristic product of that same mechanic philosophy that reduced men to the level of things, instruments, mere 'hands'. 'What are all these Mechanics' Institutes', he exclaimed, 'but so many confessions of the necessity & of the absence of a National Church.'[1] F. D. Maurice recalled Coleridge's distinction in his six lectures on *Learning and Working* in 1855, when he praised Dr Birkbeck, a champion of the Mechanics' Institutes, for treating craftsmen 'not as hands or as machines, but as men capable of being . . . educated'.

In rebutting Godwin's arguments on the universal availability of truth, Coleridge denied that everyone would eventually understand Newton's *Principia*. On the contrary, he believed that the most that could be hoped for would be that the results of a discovery would ultimately trickle down to become 'part of a general language, so that

[1] BM, Egerton MS 2801, f. 210.

men by the mere mechanism of language can think as a man can do sums, by a carpenter's rule'; and elsewhere he referred to the 'blessed machine of language', a curious phrase for someone wedded to organicism. But it expressed an important insight, one that he applied consistently to the language of politics. If one wished to change the structure of society one must purify the structure of language. And one must do this by analysing the intellectual attitudes it reflected and by exposing sophistry and political cant; linguistic and structural approaches unite in Coleridge as they do in what is most original in twentieth-century thought and they are enriched in Coleridge's political writings by an unrivalled understanding of personal and social psychology.

As a political critic, Coleridge's psychological insight served him better than the natural speculative cast of his mind. Speculation all too easily became an end in itself, a fatal flaw in the armoury of a critic of society. His profound understanding of individual and group psychology which is everywhere in evidence in his works has, more than any other single quality, guaranteed their survival and constitutes their chief claim to attention today. This rare insight into the human mind and patterns of social behaviour, the 'System of our Nature' as he called it in an unpublished sermon in 1799, enabled him to reject convincingly all political systems that either ignored 'the facts of the mind' or were built on a false psychology of man. It also enabled him to sketch the outline of a constitution which would satisfy the individual citizen's basic physical and spiritual needs. 'Fear, hope, and memory', he realized, 'are the three great agents, both in the binding of a people to a government, and in the rousing of them to a revolution.' The most important of these is hope. Since hope is an instinct of our nature and 'a natural instinct constitutes a right, as far as its gratification is compatible with the equal rights of others', the State must hold out some promise to the citizen of bettering his condition or those of his children. It must also do all within its powers to humanize and ennoble its citizens. Whatever tended to debase the nobility of human nature, whether it was slavery, the employment of young children in the cotton mills, or the acceptance on the part of the commercial classes of Malthusian economic doctrine, became an object of bitter attack. 'A Slave is a Person perverted into a Thing; Slavery, therefore, is not so properly a deviation from Justice, as an absolute subversion of all morality', he noted, and longed to release all those who had fallen into the clutches of the nightmare Life-in-Death. Psychological insight, too, led him to distinguish sharply between political and all other forms of consciousness and to prescribe a different code of morality for the relation of the citizen to the State from that for the individual and his own conscience. The 'subtle-souled psychologist' is much in evidence.

Unfortunately, it has been the practice for writers to repeat uncritically the judgements of Coleridge as a political thinker that are enshrined in histories of English literature and political textbooks. In these (as in the *Cambridge History of English Literature*) we find Coleridge invariably labelled as 'the heir to Burke', or, with a slight air of sophistication, as someone who 'was to develop the ideas of Burke with a new mystical content' (John Bowle, *Politics and Opinion*).[1] Mill's contention that Coleridge was 'an arrant driveller' in political economy has been repeated *ad nauseam* in spite of the evidence to the contrary (his analysis of the 'trade cycle' and the essays on the bullion controversy), and in spite of William Kennedy's study of his economic ideas in a monograph called *Humanist Versus Economist*. His political thought is often said to be 'ludicrously out of date' (C H F L), but it only appears so if we concentrate on externals at the expense of seminal ideas. Thus it is perfectly true that Coleridge's enthusiastic faith in the educational role of the Church of England was somewhat out of date even at the time, but this in no way affects the permanent value of the idea that education should foster the harmonious development of all the faculties, nor the idea that the state should provide funds for education and the arts. Moreover, his insight into the life of institutions and the forces

---

[1] 'But there is this difference between them [Burke and Coleridge], . . . that while in the statesman's mind the balance actually attained by the British Constitution dominated all his thinking, Coleridge regarded all actual Constitutions, including that of his own country, as temporary and imperfect embodiments of an "idea" that was slowly revealing itself on earth, if not as a city of God, at any rate as a society of seekers after Him. And the source of this vital difference was the despised metaphysical root of the poet's thought.' J. H. Muirhead, *Coleridge as Philosopher*, London, 1930, 194.

that make societies more than mere aggregates of individuals is far less anachronistic than the abstract formulations of Bentham and Mill. It is fitting therefore to conclude this account with a quotation from a writer, David Calleo, who is convinced of Coleridge's modern relevance.

> Coleridge's way of looking at the world made him exceptionally suited to develop an adequate theory of the modern constitutional State. His method—the doctrine of Reason and the Understanding—reconciled him to continuous change. It made him tolerant of diversity, yet concerned with unity. His psychology allowed him profound insight into the nonrational forces that reinforce consensus. Finally his doctrine of the Imagination led him to be sensitive to the need for imagination and leadership in politics and the essential role of education in creating an adequate governing class.[1]

In Coleridge we may perhaps find the modern 'Statesman's Manual'.

[1] *Coleridge and the Idea of the Modern State*, 20.

Selected Bibliography and
List of Abbreviations

For a checklist of Coleridge's canon in chronological order, see *New CBEL* III (1969) coll 215–20; in general, sub-canonical works are included in coll 220–6. See also §2 below. Place of publication is London unless otherwise indicated.

The list in §1 shows the edn used for reference in this volume (unless otherwise indicated), other available edns, location in Shedd's *Complete Works*, and the published or projected edn in the *Collected Coleridge*, (CC).

I. PRIMARY TEXTS AND LIST OF ABBREVIATIONS

Aids to Reflection Aids to Reflection in the formation of a manly character, on the several grounds of prudence, morality and religion, illustrated by select passages from our elder divines, especially from Archbishop Leighton. London 1825 | rptd 1831, 1836 | ed H. N. Coleridge 1839 | Bohn edn (with *Confessions of an Inquiring Spirit*) 1884 &c | Shedd I | to be CC 9, ed John Beer. The 1831 edn contains variants.

Anima Poetae Anima Poetae, from the unpublished note-books of Samuel Taylor Coleridge. Ed E. H. Coleridge, London 1895. Entries to about Dec 1807 superseded by *Notebooks* I and II.

Biog. Lit. Biographia Literaria: or biographical sketches of my literary life and opinions. Ed J. Shawcross, 2 vol Oxford 1907 &c. | 1st edn 2 vol 1817 | ed H. N. & Sara Coleridge, 2 vol 1847 | Bohn edn (with 2 *Lay Sermons*) 1898 &c; Everyman edn ed A. Symons 1906, ed G. Watson 1956 | Shedd III | to be CC 7, ed M. H. Abrams.

CC The Collected Works of Samuel Taylor Coleridge. General editor

Kathleen Coburn. 16 titles (about 22 vol) + index volume projected.
Published: C C1, *Lectures 1795: On Politics and Religion,* ed Lewis
Patton & Peter Mann, 1970; C C 2, *The Watchman,* ed Lewis Patton,
1970; C C 4, *The Friend,* ed Barbara E. Rooke, 2 vol 1969.

C L   Collected Letters of Samuel Taylor Coleridge. Ed Earl Leslie
Griggs, 6 vol Oxford 1956, 1959, 1971. Letters after Dec 1819 are
found in *Letters,* ed E. H. Coleridge (2 vol 1895), in U L, and elsewhere.

E O T   Essays on his own Times, forming a second series of *The Friend.*
Ed Sara Coleridge 3 vol London 1818 | Contents expanded in *The
Watchman,* ed Lewis Patton, 1970 (C C 2); Bristol Lectures 1795 on
Politics and Religion, ed Lewis Patton & Peter Mann, 1970 (C C 1);
other journalism to be C C 3, ed David V. Erdman.

Friend   The Friend. Ed Barbara E. Rooke, 2 vol London & New York
1969 (C C 4) | 1st version, 28 nos, Penrith 1809–10; re-issue with sup-
plementary matter 1812; new edn 3 vol 1818 | ed H. N. Coleridge
1837 | Bohn edn 1866 &c | Shedd II.

Inquiring Spirit   Inquiring Spirit: a new presentation of Coleridge from
his published and unpublished prose writings. Ed Kathleen Coburn,
London 1951; Minerva Books 1968 as *Inquiring Spirit: A Coleridge
Reader.*

Lay Sermon   'Blessed are ye that sow beside all waters.' A Lay Sermon
addressed to the higher and middle classes on the existing distresses
'and discontents. ('2nd Lay Sermon'.) London 1817 | ed H. N. Cole-
ridge (with *Church and State* and *Statesman's Manual*) 1852 | Bohn
edn (with *Statesman's Manual* and *Biographia Literaria*) 1865 | ed
(with omissions) R. J. White in *Political Tracts of Wordsworth,
Coleridge, and Shelley* Cambridge 1953 | Shedd VI | to be in C C 6,
ed R. J. White.

Literary Remains   The Literary Remains of Samuel Taylor Coleridge.
Ed H. N. Coleridge, 4 vol London 1836, 1838, 1839 | Shedd IV, V |
to be *seriatim* and extended, in C C 5, 11, 12, 16, various editors.

Lyrical Ballads   Lyrical Ballads, with a few other poems. [?Bristol&]
London 1798 (anonymous); 'by William Wordsworth', 2 vol
London 1800, 1802, 1805 | ed R. L. Brett & A. R. Jones, 1963 (1798–
1805 edn); ed W. J. B. Owen Oxford 1967 (1798 edn).

[Marginalia]   Principal published collections: *Literary Remains; Notes*

Theological, Political, and Miscellaneous, ed D. Coleridge, 1853; *Shakespeare Criticism; Miscellaneous Criticism; Coleridge on the Seventeenth Century,* ed R. F. Brinkley, 1955. Periodical publications: J. Aynard, 'Notes inédites de Coleridge', *Revue de littérature comparée* II, 1922; H. Nidecker, 'Notes marginales de Coleridge', *Revue de littérature comparée* VII–VIII, X–XIII, 1927–33; *Philosophical Lectures; Inquiring Spirit*; and see also *New CBEL* coll 220–6. Descriptions: [H. Zimmern], 'Coleridge marginalia [in the BM]', *Blackwood's* Jan 1882; J. L. Haney, *A Bibliography of Coleridge,* 1903 (Ch 10);— 'The Marginalia of Coleridge', *Schelling Anniversary Papers* ed J. L. Haney, New York 1923; — 'Coleridge the commentator', *Coleridge Studies,* 1934; George Whalley, 'The harvest on the ground', UTQ XXXVIII, 1969; — 'Coleridge books lost', *Book Collector* XVII, 1968. Collective edn to be CC 12, ed George Whalley.

Miscellaneous Criticism Coleridge's Miscellaneous Criticism. Ed T. M. Raysor, London 1936. (Includes revised version of 1818 literary lectures).

Notebooks The Notebooks of Samuel Taylor Coleridge. Ed Kathleen Coburn. Vol I, II (4 parts) [of 5 vol in 10 pts + index volume]. New York & London 1957, 1961.

Philosophical Lectures The Philosophical Lectures of Samuel Taylor Coleridge hitherto Unpublished. Ed Kathleen Coburn, London 1949 | to be CC 8, ed Thomas McFarland.

PW The complete Poetical Works of Samuel Taylor Coleridge. Ed E. H. Coleridge, 2 vol Oxford 1912 | 1st collective edn, *Sibylline Leaves* 1817; then *Poetical Works* 3 vol 1828, 1829, 1834 | ed J. D. Campbell 1893 | Everyman edn *Poems,* ed John Beer | Shedd VII | to be CC 16, ed George Whalley.

Sh. Crit. Coleridge's Shakespeare Criticism. Ed T. M. Raysor, 2 vol London 1960 (Everyman's Library) | 1st edn, 2 vol London 1930. Supersedes *Literary Remains* II and *Notes and Lectures upon Shakespeare,* ed Sara Coleridge, 1849 &c. The 1930 and 1960 edns of *Sh. Crit.* do not coincide in text or pagination.

Statesman's Manual The Statesman's Manual, or the Bible the best guide to political skill and foresight: a lay sermon addressed to the higher classes of society, with an appendix containing contents and

essays connected with the study of the inspired writings. ('1st Lay
Sermon'). London 1816 | ed H. N. Coleridge (with *Church and State*
and *Lay Sermon*) 1839 | ed (with omissions) R. J. White in *Political
Tracts*, Cambridge 1953 | Shedd I | to be in C C 6, ed R. J. White.

Table Talk Specimens of the Table Talk of the late Samuel Taylor
Coleridge. Ed H. N. Coleridge, 2 vol London 1835; revised 1836 |
ed T. Ashe in *Table Talk and Omniana* (including extracts from T.
Allsop *Recollections*) 1884, Oxford 1917 &c | Shedd VI | to be C C 14
ed Carl Woodring.

U L Unpublished Letters of Samuel Taylor Coleridge including certain
letters republished from original sources. Ed Earl Leslie Griggs, 2
vol London 1932. Progressively superseded by C L.

W L The Letters of William and Dorothy Wordsworth. Ed Ernest de
Selincourt, 6 vol Oxford 1935–9 | Vol I revised by Chester L.
Shaver 1967; Vol II revised by Mary Moorman 1969.

W P W The Poetical Works of William Wordsworth. Ed Ernest de
Selincourt and Helen Darbishire, 5 vol Oxford 1940–9 | Vol I–IV
revised by Helen Darbishire 1952–8. Not included in this edn: *The
Prelude, or growth of a poet's mind: an autobiographical poem*, ed E. de
Selincourt (texts of 1805 and 1850), Oxford 1926; revised by Helen
Darbishire 1957.

Journals of Dorothy Wordsworth. Ed Ernest de Selincourt. 2 vol.
Oxford 1939 | The Oxford Paperbacks edn, ed Mary Moorman, 1971
offers the best text for the Alfoxden and Grasmere Journals.

Abbreviations of Periodicals Cited

C Q *The Critical Quarterly*; E C *Essays in Criticism*; E L H *English
Literary History*; E S M E A *Essays and Studies by Members of the English
Association*; J H I *Journal of the History of Ideas*; M L N *Modern Language
Notes*; M P *Modern Philology*; N Q *Notes and Queries*; P M L A *Publica-
tions of the Modern Language Association of America;* P Q *Philological
Quarterly*; Q R *Quarterly Review*; R E L *Review of English Literature*;
R E S *Review of English Studies*; S P *Studies in Philology*; T L S *Times
Literary Supplement*; U T Q *University of Toronto Quarterly*.

2. BIBLIOGRAPHIES AND CONCORDANCE

J. L. Haney, *A Bibliography of Samuel Taylor Coleridge,* Philadelphia 1903 (priv ptd).

Richard Haven, *Coleridge 1793–1970: An Annotated Bibliography* Projected for 1972.

George Healey, *The Cornell Wordsworth Collection,* Ithaca 1957. Includes Coleridge items.

V. W. Kennedy, M. N. Barton, *Coleridge: A Selected Bibliography,* Baltimore 1935.

Sister Eugenia Logan, *A Concordance to the Poetry of S. T. Coleridge,* Saint-Mary-of-the-Woods Indiana 1940.

A. D. Snyder, 'Books borrowed by Coleridge from the library of the University of Göttingen', MP XXV 1928.

George Whalley, 'The Bristol Library Borrowings of Southey and Coleridge 1793–8', *The Library* 5th series IV 1949. Expands Paul Kaufman, 'The Reading of Southey and Coleridge: the record of their borrowings from the Bristol Library 1793–8', MP XXI, 1924.

Thomas J. Wise, *The Ashley Library: A Catalogue of Printed Books and Manuscripts,* 11 vol 1922–36 (priv ptd). Coleridge items chiefly in I, VIII, X.

— *A Bibliography of the Writings in Prose and Verse of S. T. Coleridge,* 1913 (priv ptd); supplement of *Coleridgeana* 1919 (priv ptd).

— *Two Lake Poets: A Catalogue of Printed Books, Manuscripts and Autograph Letters,* 1927 (priv ptd).

3. BIOGRAPHICAL STUDIES

W. J. Bate, *Coleridge,* New York 1969.

A. M. Buchan, 'The Influence of Wordsworth on Coleridge', UTQ XXXII, 1963.

J. D. Campbell, *Samuel Taylor Coleridge: A Narrative of the Events of his Life,* 1894; reptd 1970.

Clement Carlyon, *Early Years and Late Reflections,* 4 vol 1836–58.

E. K. Chambers, *Samuel Taylor Coleridge: A Biographical Study,* Oxford 1938.

Kathleen Coburn, 'Coleridge redivivus', *The Major Romantic Poets* ed C. D. Thorpe et al, Carbondale 1957.

— 'Poet into Public Servant', *Transactions of the Royal Society of Canada* LIV, 1960.

Coleridge the Talker: A series of Contemporary Descriptions and Comments, ed R. W. Armour & R. F. Howe, Ithaca 1940.

Coleridge: The Critical Heritage, ed J. R. de J. Jackson, 1970. Reviews 1794–1834.

Laurence Hanson, *The Life of Samuel Taylor Coleridge: The Early Years* [to June 1800], Vol I [all pbd] 1938.

Sara Hutchinson, *Letters of Sara Hutchinson 1800–1835,* ed Kathleen Coburn, 1954.

J. I. Lindsay, 'Coleridge and the University of Vermont', *Vermont Alumni Weekly* XV, 1936.

Sister Eugenia Logan, 'Coleridge's Scheme of Pantisocracy and American travel accounts', P M L A XLV, 1930.

J. R. MacGillivray, 'The Pantisocracy scheme and its immediate background', *Studies in English by Members of University College Toronto,* 1931.

H. M. Margoliouth, *Wordsworth and Coleridge 1795–1834,* 1953.

Sylvia Norman, 'The Two Selves of Coleridge', *University of Texas Quarterly* VII (1964).

T. M. Raysor, 'Coleridge and "Asra"', S P XXVI, 1929.

Henry Crabb Robinson, *On Books and their Writers,* ed E. J. Morley, 3 vol 1938.

George Whalley, *Coleridge and Sara Hutchinson and the Asra Poems,* 1955.

4. STUDIES OF POEMS

R. C. Bald, 'Coleridge and *The Ancient Mariner*: Addenda to *The Road to Xanadu*', *Nineteenth Century Studies* ed H. Davis et al, Ithaca 1940.

David Beres, 'A dream, a vision and a poem: a psychoanalytic study of the origins of the *Rime of the Ancient Mariner*', *International Journal of Psychoanalysis* XXXII, 1951.

E. E. Bostetter, *The Romantic Ventriloquists,* Seattle 1963.

John Beer, *Coleridge the Visionary,* 1959.

R. L. Brett, *Reason and Imagination: A Study of Form and Meaning in Four Poems,* Oxford 1960.

Irene Chayes, 'A Coleridgean reading of *The Ancient Mariner*', *Studies in Romanticism* IV, 1965.

Kathleen Coburn, 'Coleridge and Wordsworth on the supernatural', UTQ XXV, 1956.

—'Reflexions in a Coleridge mirror: some images in his poems', *From Sensibility to Romanticism: Essays presented to Frederick A. Pottle,* 1965.

Ernest de Selincourt, 'Dejection: an Ode', ESMEA XXII, 1927; also in his *Wordsworthian and Other Studies,* Oxford 1947.

R. Gerber, 'Keys to *Kubla Khan*', *English Studies* XLIV, 1963.

Eli Marcovitz, 'Bemoaning the lost dream: Coleridge's *Kubla Khan* and addiction', *International Journal of Psychoanalysis* XLV, 1964.

D. F. Mercer, 'The Symbolism of *Kubla Khan*', *Journal of Aesthetics* XII, 1953.

A. C. Purves, 'Formal Structure in *Kubla Khan*', *Studies in Romanticism* I, 1962.

I. A. Richards, *Coleridge's Minor Poems,* a lecture in honour of . . . Edmund L. Freeman, Montana State University, 8 Apr 1960.

G. M. Ridenour, 'Source and allusion in some poems of Coleridge', SP LX, 1963.

Elisabeth Schneider, *Coleridge, Opium and Kubla Khan,* Chicago 1953.

Max Schulz, *The Poetic Voices of Coleridge,* Detroit 1963.

Bernard Smith, 'Coleridge's *Ancient Mariner* and Cook's Second Voyage', *Journal of the Warburg and Courtauld Institutes* XIX, 1956.

Marshall Suther, *Visions of Xanadu,* New York 1965.

Twentieth Century Views of 'The Rime of the Ancient Mariner', ed James Boulger, Spectrum Books 1969.

Robert Penn Warren, 'A poem of pure imagination: *The Ancient Mariner', Kenyon Review* VIII, 1946; reprinted as introduction to his edition of *The Ancient Mariner,* New York 1946, and in his *Selected Essays,* 1958. For replies to this interpretation, see Elder Olson 'The Rime of the Ancient Mariner', MP XLV, 1948, reprinted in *Critics and Criticism* ed E. S. Crane, 1952; E. E. Stoll. 'Symbolism in

Coleridge', PMLA LXIII, 1948; Kathleen Coburn, UTQ XXV, as above.

George Watson, *Coleridge the Poet*, 1966.

George Whalley, 'Late autumn's amaranth: Coleridge's late poems', *Transactions of the Royal Society of Canada*, 4th ser, II, 1964.

S. C. Wilcox, 'The water imagery of the *Ancient Mariner*', *Personalist* XXXV, 1954.

Carl Woodring, 'Coleridge and the Khan', EC IX, 1959.

— *Politics in the Poetry of Coleridge*, Madison 1961.

5. STUDIES OF THEORY, PHILOSOPHY, AND IDEAS

M. H. Abrams, *The Mirror and the Lamp*. New York 1953 &c.

J. A. Appleyard, *Coleridge's Philosophy of Literature 1791–1819*, Cambridge Mass 1965.

Irving Babbitt, 'Coleridge and imagination', *Nineteenth Century*, Sept 1929.

M. M. Badawi, 'Coleridge's Formal Criticism of Shakespeare's Plays', EC X, 1959.

J. V. Baker, *The Sacred River: Coleridge's Theory of Imagination*, Baton Rouge 1958.

J. R. Barth, *Coleridge and Christian Doctrine*, Cambridge Mass 1969.

W. J. Bate, *From Classic To Romantic*, New York 1961.

R. L. Brett, 'Coleridge's theory of imagination', ESMEA, new series II, 1949.

— *Fancy and Imagination*, 1969.

Nicholas Brooke, 'Coleridge's "true and original realism"', *Durham University Journal* LIII, 1961.

Justus Buchler, *The Concept of Method*, 1961.

David P. Calleo, *Coleridge and the Idea of the Modern State*, New Haven 1966.

Kathleen Coburn, 'The Interpretation of man and nature', *Proceedings of the British Academy* XCIX, 1963.

Coleridge: A Collection of Critical Essays, ed Kathleen Coburn (Twentieth Century Views), Spectrum Books 1967.

Coleridge: Studies by Several Hands on the Hundredth Anniversary of his Death, ed E. Blunden & E. L. Griggs, 1934. Essays by H. Beeley, G. H. B. Coleridge, A. J. Eagleston, E. L. Griggs, J. L. Haney, G. M. Harper, J. H. Muirhead, A. D. Snyder, C. H. Wilkinson.

John Colmer, *Coleridge: Critic of Society*, Oxford 1959.

Paul Deschamps, *La Formation de la pensée de Coleridge 1771–1804*, Paris 1964.

D. M. Emmet, 'Coleridge on the growth of the mind', *Bulletin of the John Rylands Library* XXXIV, 1952.

D. V. Erdman, 'Coleridge in Lilliput: the quality of parliamentary reporting in 1800', *Speech Monographs* XXVII, 1960. For other articles by D. V. Erdman, see *New CBEL* III col 249.

M. H. Fisch, 'The Coleridges, Dr Prati and Vico', MP XLI, 1943. See also George Whalley, 'Coleridge and Vico', *Giambattista Vico: An International Symposium*, ed Giorgio Tagliacozzo, Baltimore 1969.

R. A. Foakes, *The Romantic Assertion*, 1958.

R. H. Fogle. *The Idea of Coleridge's Criticism*, Berkeley & Los Angeles 1962, For articles by R. H. Fogle, see *New CBEL* col 245.

David F. Foxon, 'The printing of *Lyrical Ballads*', *The Library* 5th series IX, 1954.

Albert Gérard, 'On the logic of romanticism', EC VII, 1957.

Richard Haven, *Patterns of Consciousness: An Essay on Coleridge*, [Amherst] 1969.

— 'Coleridge, Hartley and the Mystics', J H I XX, 1959.

G. Hough, 'Coleridge and the Victorians', *The English Mind: studies . . . presented to Basil Willey*, ed H. S. Davies & G. Watson, Cambridge 1964.

Humphry House, *Coleridge: The Clark Lectures, 1951–2*, 1953.

J. Isaacs, 'Coleridge's critical terminology', ESMEA XXI, 1936.

J. R. de J. Jackson, 'Coleridge on dramatic illusion and spectacle in the performance of Shakespeare's plays', MP LXII, 1964.

—— *Method and Imagination in Coleridge's Criticism*, 1969

D. G. James, *The Romantic Comedy*, Oxford 1948.

—— *Scepticism and Poetry*, 1937.

— 'The Thought of Coleridge', *The Major Romantic Poets*, ed C. D. Thorpe, C. Baker and B. Weaver, Carbondale 1964.

R. Kato, 'Coleridge as aesthetician', *Studies in English* XXXIX, 1962.

E. I. Klimenko, 'The language reform in the poetry of the English romanticists Wordsworth and Coleridge', *Trans. First Leningrad Pedagogical Institute of Foreign Languages* I, 1940.

F. R. Leavis, 'Coleridge in criticism', *Scrutiny* IX, 1941.

A. O. Lovejoy, 'Coleridge and Kant's two worlds', E L H VII, 1940; also in his *Essays in the History of Ideas,* Baltimore 1948.

J. L. Lowes, The *Road to Xanadu: A Study in the Ways of the Imagination,* Boston 1927, revised 1930, Vintage Books 1959, Sentry Books 1964 &c.

Thomas McFarland, *Coleridge and the Pantheist Tradition,* Oxford 1969.

Gordon McKenzie, *Organic Unity in Coleridge,* University of California Publications in English, 7, 1939.

Eileen Mackinlay, *The Shared Experience,* 1969.

J. S. Mill, *Mill on Bentham and Coleridge,* ed F. R. Leavis, 1950.

J. H. Muirhead, *Coleridge as Philosopher,* 1930.

G. N. G. Orsini, *Coleridge and German Idealism: A Study in the History of Philosophy,* Carbondale 1969.

H. W. Piper, *The Active Universe,* 1962.

Raymond Preston, 'Aristotle and the modern literary critic'. *Journal of Aesthetics and Criticism* XXI, 1962.

Stephen Prickett, *Coleridge and Wordsworth: the Poetry of Growth,* Cambridge 1970.

Review of English Literature No 7: 'Coleridge Number', ed A. N. Jeffares, 1966. Articles by E. Blunden, J. R. de J. Jackson, P. Kaufman, W. Schrickx, J. Shelton, G. Whalley, C. Woodring.

I. A. Richards, *Coleridge on Imagination,* 1934, revised 1950, Bloomington 1960, London 1962.

C. R. Sanders, *Coleridge and the Broad Church Movement,* Durham N C 1942. For articles by C. R. Sanders, see *New C B E L* coll 240–1.

William Schrickx, 'Coleridge and Friedrich Heinrich Jacobi', *Revue belge de philologie et d'histoire* XXXVI, 1958.

A. D. Snyder, 'Coleridge and Giordano Bruno', M L N XLII, 1927.

— *Coleridge on Logic and Learning,* New Haven 1929.

N. P. Stallknecht, *Strange Seas of Thought,* Durham N C 1945, Bloomington 1958.

C. D. Thorpe, 'Coleridge as aesthetician and critic', J H I V, 1941.

William Walsh, *Coleridge: The Work and the Relevance,* 1967.

— *The Use of Imagination: Educational Thought and the Literary Mind,* 1959.

René Wellek, 'Coleridge's philosophy and criticism', *The English Romantic Poets: A Review of Research,* ed T. M. Raysor, New York 1956.

— *Immanuel Kant in England,* 1931.

Lucyle Werkmeister, 'Coleridge and Godwin on the communication of truth', M P LV, 1958.

— 'Coleridge on science, philosophy, and poetry: their relation to religion', *Harvard Theological Review* LXII, 1958. For other articles by Lucyle Werkmeister, see *New CBEL* col 248.

George Whalley, 'Coleridge unlabyrinthed', U T Q XXXII, 1963.

— 'The Integrity of *Biographia Literaria*', E S M E A VI, 1953.

Basil Willey, *Nineteenth Century Studies: Coleridge to Matthew Arnold,* 1949.

L. A. Willoughby, 'Coleridge and his German contemporaries', *English Goethe Society Publications* X, 1934.

— 'English romantic criticism : on fancy and imagination', *Weltliteratur: Festgabe für Fritz Strich,* Berne 1952.

Elisabeth Winkelmann, *Coleridge und die Kantische Philosophie,* Leipzig 1933.

Wordsworth and Coleridge: Studies in Honor of George Maclean Harper, ed E. L. Griggs, Princeton 1939. Coleridge essays by G. H. B. Coleridge, E. L. Griggs, J. R. McElderry, E. J. Morley, C. D. Thorpe.

G. WHALLEY
December 1970

Index